The New Deal

SECOND EDITION

Edited By
ALONZO L. HAMBY

The New Deal

ANALYSIS & INTERPRETATION

Longman
New York & London

THE NEW DEAL
Analysis and Interpretation

LONGMAN INC.
19 West 44th Street, New York, N.Y. 10036
Associated companies, branches, and representatives throughout the
world.

Developmental Editor: Nicole Benevento
Editorial and Design Supervisor: Judith Hirsch
Cover Design: Dan Serrano
Manufacturing and Production Supervisor: Louis Gaber
Composition: Eastern Graphics
Printing and Binding: The Hunter Rose Company Ltd.

Manufactured in Canada

Library of Congress Cataloging in Publication Data

Hamby, Alonzo L   comp.
  The New Deal, analysis and interpretation.

  Bibliography: p.
  1. United States—Politics and government—1933-
1945—Addresses, essays, lectures. I. Title.
E806.H294   1979   320.973   80-14778
ISBN 0-582-28204-7

9 8 7 6 5 4 3 2 1

TO MY HISTORY TEACHERS

Southwest Missouri State College, 1956–1957
Southeast Missouri State College, 1957–1960
Columbia University, 1961–1962
The University of Missouri, 1962–1965

CONTENTS

PREFACE

The purpose of this volume is the same as that of its predecessor—to reproduce some of the best writing on the New Deal. In choosing selections for this edition, I have retained those essays that I consider still as important as they were ten years ago, have found substitutes for those that seem to have been superseded in one way or another, and have attempted to provide coverage for viewpoints not represented in the first edition. The result is a slightly larger book, but one that I hope will be even more useful as an introduction to its topic. My own contribution, an attempt to define some major issues, is purely personal and not meant to represent any academic consensus.

As before, I am indebted to many individuals who have assisted and encouraged me, both with this volume and in more general ways. Joyce helped in so many ways that I must thank her specifically. The others know they have my gratitude. I have dedicated this book to a group of people whom I shall always respect and admire.

A.L.H.

Athens, Ohio
February 1980

Introduction: Historians and the Challenge of the New Deal

ALONZO L. HAMBY

The New Deal was the greatest epoch in the history of American reform. In the six years that it existed as an effective political force, 1933–1938, it produced (and was produced by) one of the most important political leaders in American history, instituted dramatic changes in American social and political patterns, and established the basis for further episodes of change through Lyndon Johnson's Great Society. Not surprisingly, the New Deal has brought forth some of the best and most significant historical writing of the post–World War II era.

To a remarkable extent, the analyses and interpretations in this book share common values. In American society as a whole, social and political opinion ranges over a wide spectrum from the far Right to the far Left with the center of gravity located somewhere in the middle. In the American intellectual community the span is much narrower, running from moderate liberalism to various forms of socialist radicalism. Most historians have written of the New Deal with obvious sympathy and approval, establishing a liberal consensus that still dominates New Deal historiography. Criticism of that consensus has almost always come from the Left, usually taking the form of an attack on the New Deal for its modest accomplishments and its commitment to the capitalist system.

American conservatism long made it easy for liberal-oriented historians to discount right-wing critiques of the New Deal. Until recently, conservatives responded to Franklin D. Roosevelt and the New Deal with irrational declarations of outrage that persuaded only those already committed to the politics of yesterday. The only significant conservative scholarly history of the New Deal, Edgar Eugene Robinson's *The Roosevelt Leadership* (1955), has had little impact on historical thought. If anything, its tone represents a step backward from the relatively dispassionate contemporary criticism by Robert A. Taft reprinted in this volume, itself one of Taft's most temperate statements

1

on the subject. To a large extent, conservatives must blame themselves for the narrowness of the dialogue on the New Deal.

A historian seeking to understand the New Deal must attempt to discover its intellectual foundations. One method of doing so is to examine its relationship to early twentieth-century reform. To many, this relationship is direct and immediate: the Great Depression simply returned to power a progressive movement disrupted by World War I and the decade of conservatism that had followed. According to this view, the New Deal drew the support of and was staffed by many old progressives, including President Roosevelt himself. Its use of national power to raise farm income was an idea that went at least as far back as the Populists, received some initial implementation from the farm credit acts of the Wilson administration, and was further advanced during the 1920's by the fight for the McNary-Haugen bill. The debate that developed between economic planners and antitrusters during the 1930's was reminiscent of the old argument between the New Nationalism and the New Freedom. The Social Security Act grew out of welfare legislation passed by the states, Wisconsin especially, during the progressive era, and FDR's conservation programs were simply a continuation of Theodore Roosevelt's efforts. The increasingly militant attacks on big business and privilege were part of the traditional rhetoric of American reform.

Some historians, however, have presented an increasingly influential argument: the idea that the New Deal broke significantly with the old progressive tradition. To these authors, early twentieth-century progressivism was a middle-class reaction against both big business and organized labor. If the progressives sponsored some rudimentary welfare legislation, they did so out of a paternal, Victorian humanitarianism. They saw themselves as opponents of special privilege and sought to establish a government that would be subservient to neither the plutocratic power of the very wealthy nor the equally menacing threat of an organized proletariat; they wanted a state that would act as an impartial arbiter among competing groups, and in Theodore Roosevelt's apt phrase, give everyone, including the unorganized middle class, a Square Deal. The progressives thus saw only a limited role for government. The New Deal was different on all these counts. The depression was its first concern, and unlike progressivism it frankly attempted to manage the business cycle. The New Deal's strongest and most durable support came from labor and the lower classes, and it made the state a frank partisan of these classes. Its labor and welfare legislation, Richard Hofstadter has argued, was the product of a "social democratic" outlook, not Victorian paternalism. Its appeal to class feeling, its flexibility, its downright opportunism shocked and alienated many old progressives.

The argument between these two schools of thought cannot really be resolved. Neither the progressives nor the New Dealers were as homogeneous as many of their interpreters seem to assume. There appears to have been an important progressive tradition upon which the New Deal drew; but not all those reformers whom historians have called "progressives" subscribed to it. It is very difficult to determine if the advanced progressivism that paved the way for the New Deal represented the mainstream of early twentieth-century reform. It is certain that with a little selectivity one can find many examples to support either side of the argument. The debate over change and continuity in twentieth-century reform has been valuable and thought-provoking; it should continue but with more precise categories and better definitions of key terms.

An equally important, but separate, problem is to determine the extent of change that the New Deal actually made in American life, and it is unfortunate that those who discuss the change-and-continuity question have tended to blur the distinction. When one moves from the question of intellectual outlook and objectives to the fact of real accomplishment, it seems undeniable that the New Deal effected an important transformation in American society.

If previous reformers had worked for government action to raise farm prices and bring agricultural purchasing power toward parity, only the New Deal achieved their objective. It did so, moreover, with new methods—crop destruction and acreage allotments—which old agrarian reformers accepted with reluctance. Its programs brought a large degree of organization and prosperity to an agricultural community that, caught in the chaos of perfect competition, had been in a state of depression for almost a decade and a half.

The New Deal brought even greater changes to many American workers. It prohibited child labor, established national wage and hours legislation, and, most important, guaranteed the right of collective bargaining. Efforts to unionize unskilled workers generally had been unsuccessful since the days of the Knights of Labor. Since the end of World War I, even the trade unions had experienced difficulty, and the stolid, conservative American Federation of Labor had found its membership steadily decreasing. After an abortive beginning during the NRA period (1933–1935), the New Deal promoted the greatest and most successful organizing compaign in the history of American labor. The AFL recovered and began a period of growth. A new labor federation, the Congress of Industrial Organizations, established unions in the mass-production industries and openly entered politics to become an important element in the New Deal coalition. By the time the New Deal ended, organized labor occupied a more important and powerful position in American society than ever before, a development consolidated and institutionalized by World War II.

On the other hand, the New Deal brought few lasting changes to the business community. For two years, the National Recovery Administration attempted to bring a high degree of centralized economic coordination to American industry, but in practice it gave sanction to a loose cartelism. After the Supreme Court ruled the NRA unconstitutional, New Deal policy moved in general to a rhetorically militant antitrust program, which in the end accomplished little. The New Deal seemed, as Ellis Hawley brilliantly argues, to be caught in a dilemma that has plagued modern American reform. It accepted and for a time attempted to promote the benefits of organization and centralization; yet it also yearned for the opportunity and openness of the competitive, atomistic society. Consequently, it did little to alter the structure of American business, though it did impose some much needed regulation on the financial community.

Yet by enhancing the positions of agriculture and, especially, labor, the New Deal did manage to reduce in relative terms the prestige and authority of big business. It had created a system of "countervailing powers." And if it could not bring the nation out of the depression, it did succeed in putting a large variety of economic stabilizers into the economy. These stabilizers—ranging from deposit insurance and stock market regulation to minimum wages, agricultural price supports, and social security—have been instrumental in preventing a new depression.

The New Deal did more than bring these important changes to American society; it brought hope to a free world that had nearly lost faith in itself. Fascism was a steadily expanding force throughout the 1930's, and it seemed for a time that only communism had the strength to oppose it. One of the most important accomplishments of the New Deal, as Arthur Schlesinger, Jr., has written, was its success in convincing so many Americans and Europeans that democratic reform represented a viable alternative to totalitarianism.

Despite all these achievements, the New Deal experienced important failures. Foremost among them was the failure to lift the nation entirely out of the depression; by mid-1939 unemployment was still at the intolerable level of 10 million, a rate of more than 16 percent. It is true that the New Deal offered more to the unemployed than did its opponents on the Right; in fact, much of its political support was based on the benefits that its employment and mortgage relief programs distributed. Ultimately, however, the New Deal's failure to solve the problem of unemployment contributed heavily to its political defeat. If it ended the crisis of 1932–1933, its lack of success in dealing with the recession of 1937–1938 emboldened its opponents and greatly facilitated the formation of a conservative coalition in Congress. Its halfway measures, even if they lifted the nation above the low point of the depression, were an important factor in its undoing. Prosperity and full employment would come only with World War II.

Moreover, the benefits of countervailing power did not extend to all deprived Americans. When one considers that the New Deal could not end mass unemployment, it is hardly surprising that it also was unable to come to grips with the problem of hard-core poverty. Few of its programs were designed specifically for those who had been jobless or impoverished during the prosperous 1920's. A notable exception was the Farm Security Administration, which attempted in a variety of ways to assist sharecroppers, tenant farmers, and migrant laborers. The FSA's objectives were noble, and the agency brought the problem of rural poverty to national attention. But the FSA existed on the fringes of the New Deal; its funds were limited, and its life was short and difficult. The New Deal gave great assistance to those who had lived on the margins of poverty; it lifted many blue-collar workers and small commercial farmers into the middle class. But it offered much less to those who lived in a state of deep and permanent poverty. Perhaps it would have been impossible to direct an attack on hard-core poverty as long as the depression and mass unemployment continued; certainly, the New Deal was unable to do so. It gave the least to those who needed the most.

The New Deal perceived the problems of America's blacks only dimly. As with the unemployed and the poor, it could offer more than the conservatives. Such New Dealers as Harold Ickes and Eleanor Roosevelt displayed genuine sympathy for black aspirations, and the establishment of an informal "black Cabinet" along with a few key appointments constituted token recognition. But there was never a New Deal civil rights program; Roosevelt's priorities lay elsewhere, and he was unwilling to give support to even such elementary measures as antilynching bills. With the threat of impending war and massive black demonstrations, the President established a Fair Employment Practices Commission, but he refused to end discrimination in the armed forces. Of course, the failure to understand the plight of black people was a national failure, and, given the overwhelming economic problems of the 1930's, it is difficult to question Roosevelt's sense of priorities. Nevertheless, on this problem, so crucial to present-day America, the New Deal was largely another period of postponement.

To some historians, many of them identified with the new political radicalism of the 1960's, these failures have overshadowed even the accomplishments of the New Deal; certainly, they raise the question of why the New Deal could not have accomplished more. One answer may lie in the leadership of Franklin D. Roosevelt and the intellectual style of the New Deal.

Arthur Schlesinger, Jr., has eloquently depicted Roosevelt's receptivity to new ideas and the New Deal's eagerness to experiment as a triumph of the pragmatic mood. Its rejection of dogma, he believes, was the central element in its success. But others, most notably James

MacGregor Burns, argue that flexibility and opportunism should not be confused with pragmatism. Following the contemporary criticism of the great American pragmatist, John Dewey, these historians assert that the half-planned, compromised, and inconsistent improvisations of the New Deal were indicative simply of a lack of coherence and direction; their prime example, of course, is Roosevelt's failure to grasp Keynesian economic theory and make the wholehearted commitment it required. In addition, they believe that Roosevelt failed as a party leader. Lacking the imagination to effect the political realignment the nation required, he was unable to rebuild the Democratic party and make it a genuinely liberal force. As these critics see it, FDR failed to give America the truly great leadership that the times demanded and may actually have done long-range harm to the cause of reform.

Yet it is impossible to place sole responsibility for the unfinished nature of the New Deal on Roosevelt. After 1938, reform was blocked in Congress by a conservative coalition whose pivotal element was composed of Democrats. Some flaws in Roosevelt's leadership may have encouraged the formation of this informal but powerful coalition; however, its existence was possible only because of the loosely structured and undisciplined character of the American party system, and because of the rigid separation of powers in the American Constitution. An American President acting as party leader has little disciplinary power; his party members in Congress are not constitutionally responsible to him, and the patronage at his disposal is limited. He may appeal to public opinion, but in order to bring results, his appeals must bring a response from the specific constituencies of unfriendly congressmen. The formation of the conservative coalition became possible only when a large number of Democratic congressmen, unfavorably disposed toward the New Deal, realized that their constituencies differed sufficiently from President Roosevelt's national constituency to tolerate an antiadministration voting record. Unable to control the constituencies of these congressmen, Roosevelt could not wield effective power as a party leader. He could and did continue to dominate the Democratic "presidential party," the coalition that controlled the Democratic nominating conventions and provided the margin of victory in presidential elections. However, he could not control the Democratic "congressional party"; after 1938, he could hope to achieve legislation only through the weak and largely ineffective method of persuasion.

Many liberals, then and since, felt that the conservative coalition was an undemocratic and illegitimate conspiracy. Actually, it was a natural development of the American political system; one need only read James Madison's contributions to *The Federalist* to understand that the Constitution was designed to protect different interests by giving each a veto on important legislation. On the whole, the Founding Fathers sought to contain government, not promote change. It was remarkable that the New Deal was able to break through these carefully devised constitutional barriers for so long.

By 1939, however, Congress was so hopelessly deadlocked that it was balking at even the inadequate relief appropriations Roosevelt was requesting. The massive government spending suggested by John Maynard Keynes and his followers was now impossible. The business community, alienated and demoralized, was unwilling to initiate stimulative capital spending in a bleak economic environment. As long as peacetime conditions continued, the nation could look forward only to a permanent depression. Had not World War II intervened with its huge defense expenditures and resultant prosperity, historians might today be writing of the New Deal as a well-intentioned failure. One may even wonder whether representative government could have endured had the depression persisted indefinitely. Although they may be inclined to hail the New Deal's achievements, scholars are also obligated to acknowledge its shortfalls.

Despite all the explorations of the historians, the New Deal remains an inviting topic. There will always be opportunities for monographic coverage of personalities or programs, but the future of New Deal historiography seems to be primarily in the realm of broad interpretation and the development of new perspectives. Perhaps the most obvious need is for an acceptable conservative interpretation based on rational analysis and temperate criticism rather than red-faced name-calling. The emergence in recent years of a "neoconservative" body of thought may presage such an accomplishment. A disparate group of intellectuals who lack the emotional involvement of the old Right, accept the essentials of the post–New Deal state while criticizing its soft spots, and seek to apply conservative principles to today's realities, the neoconservatives stand a good chance of producing a scholar capable of broadening the historical debate.

Other directions are at least as promising. We need more study of the effects of the New Deal on American social and political institutions. One of the most obvious possibilities is the trail blazed by James Patterson in his work on the institution of federalism. In recent years several historians have followed him; however, none has produced a general synthesis that supersedes his imaginative but suggestive work. Another possibility might involve an examination of the effect of the depression and the New Deal on traditional American values and attitudes, especially about such matters as work and unemployment, self-reliance and welfare; most of the writing on this topic has been sketchy and impressionistic. Another approach would be to recognize that the depression was a worldwide phenomenon and to analyze the New Deal in comparative perspective. Here, John A. Garraty has made a brave beginning, which other historians must follow. There are, one need hardly say, many other ways of attacking the subject profitably; New Deal historiography has reached a point of maturity that requires a breadth of vision transcending narrow, easily prescribed research plans.

None of this should be taken to denigrate the work of the past generation of historians. They have given us splendid overall accounts of the New Deal, rewarding biographical interpretations of Roosevelt, useful analyses of the political dynamics of the 1930's, and provocative examinations of the New Deal's place in the broader history of American reform. They have produced monographic works that cover substantially all of the New Deal's programs, interpret many of its leading personalities, and discuss state and local politics. Rarely, if ever, have scholars so thoroughly dissected a historical period so quickly after its close. It is this remarkable achievement that permits us to envision new horizons of historical understanding.

I | The Conflict of Ideas in Overview

1 A Liberal Viewpoint: The New Deal in Historical Perspective

FRANK FREIDEL

Frank Freidel, a professor of history at Harvard University, is one of the major biographers of Franklin D. Roosevelt; the four volumes he has published thus far carry the story of Roosevelt's life through the first year of his Presidency. The essay below, written some twenty years ago, remains Freidel's major statement on the nature of the New Deal; in addition, it is a nearly ideal representation of the favorable liberal interpretation still dominant within the historical community. Freidel, however, does more than give us a point of view; he provides a convenient, if necessarily sketchy, overview of his subject, and his interpretations represent the mature opinion of one of the closest and most eminent students of the Roosevelt era.

Stressing what he believes to be the essential moderation of Roosevelt and the New Deal, Freidel attempts to show that both the man and the movement had strong connections with the progressive era. He also argues that despite important continuities in Roosevelt's attitude, there was, beginning in 1935, a definite shift in the style and policies of the New Deal, a change so significant that one may speak of a "first New Deal" characterized by relatively conservative consensus politics and a "second New Deal" based on class politics. The reader should attempt to find the evidence for each interpretation; one should remember also that both are controversial and by no means have won unanimous acceptance among historians.

* * *

From *The New Deal in Historical Perspective* by Frank Freidel (2d ed.; Washington, D.C.: American Historical Association Service Center for Teachers of History, 1965), pp. 1–20. Copyright © 1959 by the American Historical Association. Reprinted by permission of the publisher and the author.

In less than a generation, the New Deal has passed into both popular legend and serious history. The exigencies of American politics long demanded that its partisans and opponents paint a picture of it either in the most glamorous whites or sinister blacks. Long after the New Deal was over, politicians of both major parties tried at each election to reap a harvest of votes from its issues.

Gradually a new generation of voters has risen which does not remember the New Deal and takes for granted the changes that it wrought. Gradually too, politicians have had to recognize that the nation faces new, quite different problems since the Second World War, and that campaigning on the New Deal has become as outmoded as did the "bloody shirt" issue as decades passed after the Civil War. At the same time, most of the important manuscript collections relating to the New Deal have been opened to scholars so rapidly that careful historical research has been possible decades sooner than was true for earlier periods of United States history. (The Franklin D. Roosevelt papers and the Abraham Lincoln papers became available for research at about the same time, just after the Second World War.)

It has been the task of the historians not only to analyze heretofore hidden aspects of the New Deal on the basis of the manuscripts, but also to remind readers of what was once commonplace and is now widely forgotten. A new generation has no firsthand experience of the depths of despair into which the depression had thrust the nation, and the excitement and eagerness with which people greeted the new program. Critics not only have denied that anything constructive could have come from the New Deal but they have even succeeded in creating the impression in the prosperous years since 1945 that the depression really did not amount to much. How bad it was is worth remembering, since this is a means of gauging the enormous pressure for change.

Estimates of the number of unemployed ranged up to 13 million out of a labor force of 52 million, which would mean that one wage-earner of four was without means of support for himself or his family. Yet of these 13 million unemployed, only about a quarter were receiving any kind of assistance. States and municipalities were running out of relief funds; private agencies were long since at the end of their resources. And those who were receiving aid often obtained only a pittance. The Toledo commissary could allow for relief only 2.14 cents per person per meal, and the Red Cross in southern Illinois in 1931 was able to provide families with only 75 cents a week for food. It was in this crisis that one of the most flamboyant members of the Hoover administration suggested a means of providing sustenance for the unemployed: restaurants should dump left-overs and plate scrapings into special sanitary cans to be given to worthy unemployed people willing to work for the food. It was a superfluous suggestion, for in 1932 an observer in Chicago reported:

Around the truck which was unloading garbage and other refuse were about thirty-five men, women, and children. As soon as the truck pulled away from the pile, all of them started digging with sticks, some with their hands, grabbing bits of food and vegetables.

The employed in some instances were not a great deal better off. In December 1932 wages in a wide range of industries from textiles to iron and steel averaged from a low of 20 cents to a high of only 30 cents an hour. A quarter of the women working in Chicago were receiving less than 10 cents an hour. In farming areas, conditions were equally grim. In bitter weather on the Great Plains, travelers occasionally encountered a light blue haze that smelled like roasting coffee. The "old corn" held over from the crop of a year earlier would sell for only $1.40 per ton, while coal cost $4 per ton, so many farmers burned corn to keep warm. When Aubrey Williams went into farm cellars in the Dakotas in the early spring of 1933 farm wives showed him shelves and shelves of jars for fruits and vegetables—but they were all empty. Even farmers who could avoid hunger had trouble meeting payments on their mortgages. As a result a fourth of all farmers in the United States lost their farms during these years.

Despairing people in these pre–New Deal years feared President Herbert Hoover had forgotten them or did not recognize the seriousness of their plight. As a matter of fact he had, more than any other depression president in American history, taken steps to try to bring recovery. But he had functioned largely through giving aid at the top to prevent the further collapse of banks and industries, and the concentric rings of further collapses and unemployment which would then ensue. Also he had continued to pin his faith upon voluntary action. He felt that too great federal intervention would undermine the self-reliance, destroy the "rugged individualism" of the American people, and that it would create federal centralization, thus paving the way for socialism.

President Hoover was consistent in his thinking, and he was humane. But it would have been hard to explain to people like those grubbing on the Chicago garbage heap, why, when the Reconstruction Finance Corporation was loaning $90 million to a single Chicago bank, the President would veto a bill to provide federal relief for the unemployed, asserting, "never before has so dangerous a suggestion been seriously made in this country." It was not until June 1932 that he approved a measure permitting the RFC to loan $300 million for relief purposes.

It seems shocking in retrospect that such conditions should have existed in this country, and that any president of either major party should so long have refused to approve federal funds to alleviate them. It adds to the shock when one notes that many public figures of the period were well to the right of the President—for instance, Secretary of the Treasury Andrew Mellon—and that almost no one who was likely to be in a position to act, including Governor Roosevelt of New York, was ready at that time to go very far to the left of Hoover.

Roosevelt, who was perhaps the most advanced of the forty-eight governors in developing a program to meet the depression, had shown little faith in public works spending. When he had established the first state relief agency in the United States in the fall of 1931, he had tried to finance it through higher taxes, and only later, reluctantly, abandoned the pay-as-you-go basis. He was, and he always remained, a staunch believer in a balanced budget. He was never more sincere than when, during the campaign of 1932, he accused the Hoover administration of having run up a deficit of three and three-quarter billions of dollars in the previous two years. This, he charged, was "the most reckless and extravagant past that I have been able to discover in the statistical record of any peacetime Government anywhere, any time."

Governor Roosevelt's own cautious record did not exempt him from attack. In April 1932, seeking the presidential nomination, he proclaimed himself the champion of the "forgotten man," and talked vaguely about raising the purchasing power of the masses, in part through directing Reconstruction Finance Corporation loans their way. This little was sufficient to lead many political leaders and publicists, including his Democratic rival, Al Smith, to accuse Roosevelt of being a demagogue, ready to set class against class.

Smith and most other public figures, including Roosevelt, favored public works programs. A few men like Senators Robert F. Wagner of New York and Robert M. La Follette of Wisconsin visualized really large-scale spending on public construction, but most leaders also wanted to accompany the spending with very high taxes which would have been deflationary and thus have defeated the program. None of the important political leaders, and none of the economists who had access to them, seemed as yet to visualize the decisive intervention of the government into the economy of the sort that is considered commonplace today. The term "built-in stabilizers" had yet to be coined.

The fact was that Roosevelt and most of his contemporaries, who like him were products of the Progressive Era, were basically conservative men who unquestioningly believed in the American free enterprise system. On the whole, they were suspicious of strong government, and would indulge in it only as a last resort to try to save the system. This was their limitation in trying to bring about economic recovery. On the other hand, part of their Progressive legacy was also a humanitarian belief in social justice. This belief would lead them to espouse reforms to improve the lot of the common man, even though those reforms might also take them in the direction of additional government regulation. Roosevelt as governor had repeatedly demonstrated this incon-

sistency in his public statements and recommendations. He had ardently endorsed states rights and small government in a truly Jeffersonian
way. Then in quite contrary fashion (but still in keeping with Jeffersonian spirit applied to twentieth-century society) he had pointed out one
or another area, such as old age security, in which he believed the
government must intervene to protect the individual.

At this time, what distinguished Governor Roosevelt from his fellows
were two remarkable characteristics. The first was his brilliant political
skill, which won to him an overwhelming proportion of the Democratic
politicians and the general public. The second was his willingness to
experiment, to try one or another improvisation to stop the slow economic drift downward toward ruin. During the campaign of 1932, many
a man who had observed Roosevelt felt as did Harry Hopkins that he
would make a better president than Hoover, "chiefly because he is not
afraid of a new idea."

Roosevelt's sublime self-confidence and his willingness to try new
expedients stood him in good stead when he took over the presidency.
On that grim March day in 1933 when he took his oath of office, the
American economic system was half-paralyzed. Many of the banks were
closed; the remainder he quickly shut down through presidential proclamation. Industrial production was down to 56 percent of the 1923–25
level. Yet somehow, Roosevelt's self-confidence was infectious. People
were ready to believe, to follow, when he said in words that were not
particularly new, "The only thing we have to fear is fear itself." He
offered "leadership of frankness and vigor," and almost the whole of the
American public and press—even papers like the Chicago *Tribune* which
soon became bitter critics—for the moment accepted that leadership
with enthusiasm.

For a short period of time, about one hundred days, Roosevelt had
behind him such overwhelming public support that he was able to push
through Congress a wide array of legislation which in total established
the New Deal. It came in helter-skelter fashion and seemed to go in all
directions, even at times directions that conflicted with each other.
There was mildly corrective legislation to get the banks open again, a
slashing of government costs to balance the budget, legalization of 3.2
beer, establishment of the Civilian Conservation Corps, of the Tennessee Valley Authority, and of a wide variety of other agencies in the
areas of relief, reform, and, above all in those first months, of recovery.

What pattern emerged in all of this legislation? How sharply did it
break with earlier American political traditions? The answer was that it
represented Roosevelt's efforts to be president to all the American
people, to present something to every group in need. And it was based
squarely on American objectives and experience in the Progressive Era
and during the First World War. It went beyond the Hoover program
in that while the word "voluntary" remained in many of the laws, they

now had behind them the force of the government or at least strong economic incentives.

It has been forgotten how basically conservative Roosevelt's attitudes remained during the early period of the New Deal. He had closed the banks, but reopened them with relatively little change. Indeed, the emergency banking measure had been drafted by Hoover's Treasury officials. What banking reform there was came later. His slashing of the regular government costs was something he had promised during his campaign, and in which he sincerely believed and continued to believe. He kept the regular budget of the government low until the late thirties. While he spent billions through the parallel emergency budget, he did that reluctantly, and only because he felt it was necessary to keep people from starving. He was proud that he was keeping the credit of the government good, and never ceased to look forward to the day when he could balance the budget. For the first several years of the New Deal he consulted frequently with Wall Streeters and other economic conservatives. His first Director of the Budget, Lewis Douglas, parted ways with him, but late in 1934 was exhorting: "I hope, and hope most fervently, that you will evidence a real determination to bring the budget into actual balance, for upon this, I think, hangs not only your place in history but conceivably the immediate fate of western civilization" (Douglas to FDR, November 28, 1934).

Remarks like this struck home with Roosevelt. Douglas's successors as Director of the Budget held much the same views, and Henry Morgenthau, Jr., who became Secretary of the Treasury at the beginning of 1934, never failed to prod Roosevelt to slash governmental expenditures.

We should add parenthetically that Roosevelt always keenly resented the untrue newspaper stories that his parents had been unwilling to entrust him with money. As a matter of fact he was personally so thrifty when he was in the White House that he used to send away for bargain mail-order shirts, and when he wished summer suits, switched from an expensive New York tailor to a cheaper one in Washington. This he did despite the warning of the New York tailor that he might thus lose his standing as one of the nation's best-dressed men.

Financial caution in governmental affairs rather typifies Roosevelt's economic thinking throughout the entire New Deal. He was ready to go much further than Hoover in construction of public works, but he preferred the kind which would pay for themselves, and did not think there were many possibilities for them in the country. His estimate before he became president was only $1 billion worth. In 1934, he once proposed that the government buy the buildings of foundered banks throughout the nation and use them for post-offices rather than to construct new buildings. This is how far he was from visualizing huge public works expenditures as a means of boosting the country out of the depression. His course in this area was the middle road. He wished to bring about recovery without upsetting the budget any further than absolutely necessary. He did not launch the nation on a program of deliberate deficit financing.

When Roosevelt explained his program in a fireside chat at the end of July 1933, he declared:

"It may seem inconsistent for a government to cut down its regular expenses and at the same time to borrow and to spend billions for an emergency. But it is not inconsistent because a large portion of the emergency money has been paid out in the form of sound loans . . . ; and to cover the rest . . . we have imposed taxes. . . .

"So you will see that we have kept our credit good. We have built a granite foundation in a period of confusion."

It followed from this that aside from limited public works expenditures, Roosevelt wanted a recovery program which would not be a drain on governmental finances. Neither the Agricultural Adjustment Administration nor the National Recovery Administration were. He had promised in the major farm speech of his 1932 campaign that his plan for agricultural relief would be self-financing; this was achieved through the processing tax on certain farm products. The NRA involved no governmental expenditures except for administration.

Both of these programs reflected not the progressivism of the first years of the century, but the means through which Progressives had regulated production during the First World War. This had meant regulation which would as far as possible protect both producers and consumers, both employers and employees. Here the parallel was direct. The rest of Roosevelt's program did not parallel the Progressives' wartime experience, for during the war, in terms of production regulation had meant output of what was needed to win the war. Now the problem in the thirties was one of reducing output in most areas rather than raising it, and of getting prices back up rather than trying to hold them down.

Certainly the nation badly needed this sort of a program in 1933. The products of the fields and mines and of highly competitive consumers' goods industries like textiles were being sold so cheaply that producers and their employees alike were close to starvation. The overproduction was also wasteful of natural resources. In an oilfield near Houston, one grocer advertised when 3.2 beer first became legal that he would exchange one bottle of beer for one barrel of oil. They were worth about the same. In other heavy industries like automobiles or farm machinery, production had been cut drastically while prices remained high. One need was to bring prices throughout industry and agriculture into a more equitable relationship with each other, and with the debt structure.

The NRA scheme in theory would help do this. Its antecedents were in the regulatory War Industries Board of the First World War, and indeed it was run by some of the same men. The War Industries Board had functioned through industrial committees; in the twenties these committees had evolved into self-regulatory trade associations. Unfortunately, as Roosevelt had found when he headed the association created to discipline one of the largest and most chaotic of industries, the American Construction Council, self-regulation without the force of law behind it, had a tendency to break down. When the depression had hit, some businessmen themselves had advocated the NRA scheme, but Hoover would have none of it. Roosevelt was receptive.

The theory was that committees in a few major fields like steel, textiles, bituminous coal, and the like, would draw up codes of fair practice for the industry. These would not only stabilize the price structure, but also protect the wages and working conditions of labor. Even consumers would benefit, presumably through receiving more wages or profits, and thus enjoying larger purchasing power with which to buy goods at somewhat higher prices.

In practice, the NRA program went awry. Too many committees drew up too many codes embodying many sorts of unenforceable provisions. There was a code even for the mopstick industry. What was more important, some manufacturers rushed to turn out quantities of goods at the old wage and raw material level before the code went into effect, hoping then to sell these goods at the new higher prices. Consequently during the summer of 1933 there was a short NRA boom when industrial production jumped to 101 percent of the 1923–25 level, and wholesale prices rose from an index figure of 60.2 in March to 71.2 by October. The crop reduction program of the AAA led to a corresponding rise in agricultural prices.

Had consumers at the same time enjoyed a correspondingly higher purchasing power, the recovery scheme might well have worked. Some of its designers had visualized pouring the additional dollars into consumers' pockets through a heavy public works spending program. Indeed the bill which created the NRA also set up a Public Works Administration with $3.3 billion to spend. This money could have been poured here and there into the economy where it was most needed to "prime the pump." But Roosevelt and his most influential advisers did not want to give such an enormous spending power to the administrator of the NRA, nor had they really accepted the deficit spending school of thought. Hence while some of the money being spent by the New Deal went for immediate relief of one form or another, it went to people so close to starvation that they were forced to spend what they received on bare necessities. This was of little aid in priming the pump. The public works fund, which could have served that purpose, went to that sturdy old Progressive, "Honest Harold" Ickes. He slowly went about the process of allocating it in such a way that the government and the public would get a return of one hundred cents (or preferably more) on every dollar spent. Raymond Moley has suggested that if only the cautious Ickes had headed the NRA and the impetuous [Hugh] Johnson the Public Works Administration the scheme might have worked.

Without a huge transfusion of dollars into the economy, the industrial and agricultural recovery programs sagged in the fall of 1933. Roosevelt turned to currency manipulation to try to get prices up. He explained to a critical Congressman, "I have always favored sound money, and do now, but it is 'too darn sound' when it takes so much of farm products to buy a dollar." Roosevelt also accepted a makeshift work relief program, the Civil Works Administration, to carry the destitute through the winter.

Already the New Deal honeymoon was over, and in 1934 and 1935 a sharp political struggle between Roosevelt and the right began to form. To conservatives, Roosevelt was shattering the constitution with his economic legislation. Al Smith was attacking the devaluated currency as "baloney dollars," and was writing articles with such titles as "Is the Constitution Still There?" and "Does the Star-Spangled Banner Still Wave?" Former President Hoover published his powerful jeremiad, *The Challenge to Liberty*.

Many businessmen complained against the NRA restrictions, the favoritism allegedly being shown to organized labor, and the higher taxes. Although some of them had advocated the NRA, the significant fact was that the thinking of most businessmen seems to have remained about what it had been in the 1920's. They were eager for aid from the government, as long as it involved no obligations on their part or restrictions against them. They wanted a government which could protect their domestic markets with a high tariff wall, and at the same time seek out foreign markets for them, a court system which could discipline organized labor with injunctions, and a tax structure which (as under Secretary of the Treasury Mellon) would take no enormous bite of large profits, and yet retain disciplinary levies on the lower-middle income groups. All these policies they could understand and condone. The New Deal, which would confer other benefits upon them, but require corresponding obligations, they could not.

This hostile thinking which began to develop among the business community was sincere. Businessmen genuinely believed that under the New Deal program too large a share of their income had to go to organized labor, and too much to the government. They freely predicted federal bankruptcy as the deficit began to mount. If they had capital to commit, they refused to expend it on new plants and facilities (except for some introduction of labor-saving machinery). They were too unsure of the future, they complained, because they could not tell what that man in the White House might propose next. Business needed a "breathing spell," Roy Howard wrote Roosevelt, and the President promised one. Nevertheless, the legislative requests continued unabated.

All this, important though it is in delineating the ideology of businessmen, is not the whole story. The fact is that during the long bleak years after October 1929 they had slipped into a depression way of thinking. They regarded American industry as being over-built; they looked upon the American market as being permanently contracted. By 1937 when industrial production and stock dividends were up to within 10 percent of the 1929 peak, capital expenditures continued to drag along the depression floor. Industrialists did not engage in the large-scale spending for expansion which has been a significant factor in the boom since 1945. As late as 1940 to 1941, many of them were loathe to take the large defense orders which required construction of new plants. Unquestionably the pessimism of businessmen during the thirties, whether or not linked to their hatred of Roosevelt and fear of the New Deal, was as significant a factor in perpetuating the depression, as their optimism since the war has been in perpetuating the boom.

The paradox is that some of the New Deal measures against which the businessmen fought helped introduce into the economy some of the stabilizers which today help give businessmen confidence in the continuation of prosperity. These came despite, not because of, the businessmen. Roosevelt long continued to try to co-operate with the leaders of industry and banking. Their anger toward him, and frequently expressed statements that he had betrayed his class, at times bewildered and even upset him. For the most part he laughed them off. He hung in his bedroom a favorite cartoon. It showed a little girl at the door of a fine suburban home, apparently tattling to her mother. "Johnny wrote a dirty word on the sidewalk." And the word, of course, was "Roosevelt."

To some of his old friends who complained to him, he would reply with patience and humor. Forever he was trying to point out to them the human side of the problem of the depression. Perhaps the best illustration is a witty interchange with a famous doctor for whom he had deep affection. The doctor wired him in March 1935:

"Pediatricians have long been perplexed by difficulty of weaning infant from breast or bottle to teaspoon or cup. The shift often establishes permanent neurosis in subsequent adult. According to report in evening paper twenty-two million citizen infants now hang on federal breasts. Can you wean them doctor and prevent national neurosis?"

Roosevelt promptly replied:

"As a young interne you doubtless realize that the interesting transitional process, which you describe in your telegram, presupposes that the bottle, teaspoon, or cup is not empty. Such vehicles of feeding, if empty produce flatulence and the patient dies from a lack of nutrition. "The next question on your examination paper is, therefore, the following:

"Assuming that the transitional period has arrived, where is the Doctor to get the food from to put in the new container?"

As time went on, and the attacks became virulent from some quarters, at times even passing the bounds of decency, Roosevelt struck back vigorously. During his campaign in 1936 he excoriated the "economic royalists." When he wound up the campaign in Madison Square Garden, he declared:

"We had to struggle with the old enemies of peace—business and financial monopoly, speculation, reckless banking, class antagonism, sectionalism, war profiteering. They had begun to consider the Government of the United States as a mere appendage to their own affairs. And we know now that Government by organized money is just as dangerous as Government by organized mob.

"Never before in all our history have these forces been so united against one candidate as they stand today. They are unanimous in their hate for me—and I welcome their hatred."

To these sharp words Roosevelt had come from his position early in the New Deal as the impartial arbiter of American economic forces. He had come to them less because of what he considered as betrayal from the right than through pressure from the left. How had this pressure applied between 1934 and the campaign of 1936?

Back in 1934, while the economic temperature chart of the near frozen depression victim had fluctuated up and down, still dangerously below normal, the dispossessed millions began to look at the New Deal with despair or even disillusion. Those workers going on strike to obtain the twenty-five or thirty-five cents an hour minimum wage or the collective bargaining privileges promised by the NRA began to wisecrack that NRA stood for the National Run-Around. Some of them and of the unemployed millions in northern cities still dependent upon meager relief handouts, began to listen to the stirring radio addresses of Father Charles Coughlin. Old people began to pay five cents a week dues to Dr. Francis Townsend's clubs, which promised them fantastically large benefits. Throughout the South (and even in parts of the North) the dispossessed small farmers listened with enthusiasm to the exhortations of the Louisiana Kingfish, Huey Long, that he would share the wealth to make every man a king.

Many Democratic politicians were surprisingly oblivious to these rumblings and mutterings. Much of the private conversation of men like Vice President John Nance Garner sounded like the public demands of the Liberty Leaguers: cut relief and balance the budget. Garner, who spent the 1934 campaign hunting and fishing in Texas, predicted the usual mid-term loss of a few congressional seats back to the Republicans. Instead the Democrats picked up a startling number of new seats in both houses of Congress. The dispossessed had continued to vote with the Democratic party—but perhaps because there was no alternative but the Republicans who offered only retrenchment. Charles Beard commented that the 1934 election was "thunder on the left."

President Roosevelt, who was brilliantly sensitive to political forces, sensed fully the threat from the left. At the beginning of that crisis year 1935 he proposed in his annual message to Congress the enactment of a program to reinforce "the security of the men, women, and children of the nation" in their livelihood, to protect them against the major hazards and vicissitudes of life, and to enable them to obtain decent homes. In this increased emphasis upon security and reform, Professor Basil Rauch sees the beginnings of a second New Deal.

Certainly the pattern as it emerged in the next year was a brilliant one. Roosevelt neutralized Huey Long with the "soak the rich" tax, the "holding company death sentence," and with various measures directly of benefit to the poorer farmers of the South. Before an assassin's bullet felled Long, his political strength was already undercut. Similarly Roosevelt undermined the Townsend movement by pressing passage of the Social Security Act, which provided at least small benefits for the aged, at the same time that a congressional investigation disclosed how men around Townsend were fattening themselves on the nickels of millions of the aged. As for Father Coughlin, the Treasury announced that money from his coffers had gone into silver speculation at a time he had been loudly advocating that the government buy more silver at higher prices. More important, Coughlin had less appeal to employed workers after the new National Labor Relations Act raised a benign federal umbrella over collective bargaining. For the unemployed, a huge and substantial work relief program, the Works Progress Administration, came into existence.

Partly all this involved incisive political counterthrusts; partly it was a program Roosevelt had favored anyway. In any event, combined with Roosevelt's direct and effective appeal in radio fireside chats, it caused the dispossessed to look to him rather than to demagogues as their champion. Millions of them or their relations received some direct aid from the New Deal, whether a small crop payment or a WPA check. Millions more received wage boosts for which they were more grateful to Roosevelt than to their employers. Others through New Deal mortgage legislation had held onto their farms or homes. All these people, benefiting directly or indirectly, looked to Roosevelt as the source of their improved economic condition, and they were ready to vote accordingly. Roosevelt, who had been nominated in 1932 as the candidate of the South and the West, the champion of the farmer and the middle-class "forgotten man," after 1936 became increasingly the leader of the urban masses and the beneficiary of the growing power of organized labor.

What happened seems sharper and clearer in retrospect than it did at the time. Secretary Ickes, recording repeatedly in his diary during the early months of 1935 that the President was losing his grip, was echoing what many New Dealers and part of the public felt. They did not see a sharp shift into a second New Deal, and that is understandable. Roosevelt ever since he had become president had been talking about reform and from time to time recommending reform measures to Congress. He seems to have thought at the outset in two categories, about immediate or short-range emergency recovery measures to bring about a quick economic upswing, and also in terms of long-range reform legislation to make a recurrence of the depression less likely. Some of these reform measures, like TVA, had been ready for immediate enactment; others, like a revision of banking legislation and the social security legislation, he had planned from the beginning but were several years in the making. Frances Perkins has vividly described in her memoirs the lengthly task she and her associates undertook of drafting and selling to Congress and the public what became the Social Security Act of 1935.

Then Roosevelt had to face the additional factor that the emergency legislation had not succeeded in bringing rapid recovery. He had to think in terms of more permanent legislation with which to aim toward the same objectives. That meant he ceased trying to save money with a temporary program of cheaper direct relief, and switched instead to work relief (in which he had always believed) to try to stop some of the moral and physical erosion of those unfortunates who had been without employment for years.

In part the Supreme Court forced the recasting of some of his legislation. It gave a mercy killing in effect to the rickety, unwieldy NRA code structure when it handed down the Schechter or "sick chicken" decision of May 1935. On the whole the NRA had been unworkable, but it had achieved some outstanding results—in abolishing child labor, in bringing some order in the chaotic bituminous coal industry, and the like. Roosevelt was furious with the court, since the decision threatened to undermine all New Deal economic regulation. He charged that the justices were taking a horse and buggy view of the economic powers of the government. There followed six months later the court invalidation of the Triple-A processing tax, which for the moment threw out of gear the agricultural program.

The answer to these and similar Supreme Court decisions was Roosevelt's bold onslaught against the court after he had been reelected in the great landslide of 1936. He had carried every state but Maine and Vermont; he considered himself as having a great mandate from the people to continue his program. Nor had he any reason to doubt his ability to push a court reform program through Congress, since the already bulging New Deal majorities had become still bigger. He was wrong; he failed. His failure came as much as anything through a great tactical error. He disguised his program as one to bring about a speedier handling of cases, when he should have presented it frankly as a means of ending the court obstruction of the New Deal. This obstruction was real. Many corporations openly flaunted the National Labor Relations Act, for example, they were so confident that the Supreme Court would invalidate it.

However laudable the end, to many a well-educated member of the middle class who had supported Roosevelt even through the campaign of 1936, Roosevelt's resort to subterfuge smacked of the devious ways of dictators. In 1937, Americans were all too aware of the way in which Hitler and Mussolini had gained power. It was not that any thinking man expected Roosevelt to follow their example, but rather that many objected to any threat, real or potential, to the constitutional system including the separation of powers. After Roosevelt, they argued, the potential dictator might appear. It may be too that times had improved sufficiently since March 1933 so that constitutional considerations could again overweigh economic exigencies. In any event, Roosevelt lost his battle—and won his war.

While the struggle was rocking the nation, the justices began exercising the judicial self-restraint which one of their number, Harlan F. Stone, had urged upon them the previous year. They surprised the nation by upholding the constitutionality of the National Labor Relations Act and the Social Security Act. In large part this eliminated the necessity for the New Dealers to make any change in the personnel of the court, and thus helped contribute to Roosevelt's defeat in Congress. Further, the fight had helped bring into existence a conservative coalition in Congress which from this time on gave Roosevelt a rough ride. Many old-line Democratic congressmen now dared proclaim in public what they had previously whispered in private. All this added up to a spectacular setback for Roosevelt—so spectacular that it is easy to overlook the enormous and permanent changes that had come about.

In the next few years the Supreme Court in effect rewrote a large part of constitutional law. The federal and state governments were now able to engage in extensive economic regulation with little or no court restraint upon them. The limits upon regulation must be set for the most part by the legislative branch of the government, not the judiciary. Not only were the National Labor Relations Act and Social Security constitutional, but a bulging portfolio of other legislation.

These laws were not as spectacular as the measures of the Hundred Days, but in the bulk they were far more significant, for they brought about lasting changes in the economic role of the federal government. There was the continued subsidy to agriculture in order to maintain crop control—based upon soil conservation rather than a processing tax. There were all the agricultural relief measures which came to be centralized in the Farm Security Administration. Although that agency has disappeared, most of its functions have continued in one way or another. There was a beginning of slum clearance and public housing, and a continuation of TVA, held constitutional even before the court fight. There was a stiffening of securities regulation. There was a continuation of much that Roosevelt had considered beneficial in the NRA through a group of new laws usually referred to as the "little NRA." These perpetuated the coal and liquor codes, helped regulate oil production, tried to prevent wholesale price discriminations and legalized the establishment of "fair trade" prices by manufacturers. Most important of all, the Fair Labor Standards Act [of 1938] set a national minimum of wages and maximum hours of work, and prohibited the shipping in interstate commerce of goods made by child labor. These are lasting contributions of the New Deal, either substantial laws in themselves or the seeds for later legislation.

What, then, is to be said of the recession and the anti-monopoly program? A Keynesian point of view is that public works spending, the other New Deal spending programs, and the payment of the bonus to veterans of the First World War (over Roosevelt's veto, incidentally), all these together had poured so much money into the economy that they brought about a substantial degree of recovery, except in employment, by the spring of 1937. At this point Roosevelt tried to balance the budget, especially by cutting public works and work relief expenditures. The result was a sharp recession. Roosevelt was forced to resort to renewed pump-priming, and in a few months the recession was over.

Even this recession experience did not convert Roosevelt to Keynesianism. Keynes once called upon Roosevelt at the White House and apparently tried to dazzle him with complex mathematical talk. Each was disappointed in the other. In 1939, after the recession when a protégé of Mrs. Roosevelt's proposed additional welfare spending, Roosevelt replied by listing worthwhile projects in which the government could usefully spend an additional $5 billion a year. Then he pointed out that the deficit was already $3 billion, which could not go on forever. How, he inquired, could an $8 billion deficit be financed?

As for economists, many of them saw the answer in the enormous spending power which would be unleashed if the government poured out billions in time of depression. To most of them the lesson from the recession was that the only way to right the economy in time of upset was through spending.

As for businessmen, they could see in the recession only the logical outcome of Roosevelt's iniquitous tinkering with the economy. They had been especially angered by the protection the Wagner act had given to collective bargaining with the resulting militant expansion of organized labor. Roosevelt reciprocated the businessmen's feelings and blamed the recession upon their failure to co-operate. To a considerable degree he went along with a powerful handful of Progressive Republicans and Western Democrats in the Senate, like William E. Borah of Idaho and Joseph O'Mahoney of Wyoming, in attacking corporate monopoly as the villain. There are some indications, however, that the anti-monopoly program that he launched in the Department of Justice through the urbane Thurman Arnold was intended less to bust the trusts than to forestall too drastic legislation in the Congress. Roosevelt gave his strong backing to Arnold's anti-trust division only for the first year or two, and Arnold functioned for the most part through consent decrees. These in many instances allowed industries to function much as they had in the NRA days. The new program was in some respects more like a negative NRA than the antithesis of the NRA.

Thus from the beginning of the New Deal to the end, Roosevelt functioned with a fair degree of consistency. He heartily favored humanitarian welfare legislation and government policing of the economy, so long as these did not dangerously unbalance the budget. He preferred government co-operation with business to warfare with it.

Many of the New Dealers went far beyond Roosevelt in their views, and sometimes saw in his reluctance to support them, betrayal rather than a greater degree of conservatism. They had valid grievances some of the time when Roosevelt stuck to a middle course and seemed to them to be compromising away everything for which they thought he stood, in order to hold his motley political coalitions together. It is a serious moral question whether he compromised more than necessary, and whether at times he compromised his principles. It has been charged that his second four years in the White House represented a failure in political leadership.

In terms of gaining immediate political objectives, like the fiasco of the court fight, and the abortive "purge" in the 1938 primaries, this is undoubtedly true. In terms of the long-range New Deal program, I think the reverse is the case. These were years of piece-meal unspectacular consolidation of the earlier spectacular changes. It was many years before historians could say with certainty that these changes were permanent. By 1948 various public opinion samplings indicated that an overwhelming majority of those queried, even though Republican in voting habits, favored such things as social security and the TVA. The election of a Republican president in 1952 did not signify a popular repudiation of these programs. In the years after 1952 they were accepted, and in some instances even expanded, by the Republican administration. The only serious debate over them concerned degree, in which the Republicans were more cautious than the Democrats. The New Deal changes have even come for the most part to be accepted by the business community, although the United States Chamber of Commerce now issues manifestoes against federal aid to education with all the fervor it once directed against Roosevelt's proposals. The fact is that the business community in part bases its plans for the future upon some things that began as New Deal reforms. It takes for granted such factors as the "built-in stabilizers" in the social security system—something, incidentally, that Roosevelt pointed out at the time the legislation went into effect.

In January 1939 Roosevelt, concerned about the threat of world war, called a halt to his domestic reform program. What he said then, concerning the world crisis of 1939, is remarkably applicable to the United States more than two decades later:

"We have now passed the period of internal conflict in the launching of our program of social reform. Our full energies may now be released to invigorate the processes of recovery in order to preserve our reforms, and to give every man and woman who wants to work a real job at a living wage.

"But time is of paramount importance. The deadline of danger from within and from without is not within our control. The hour-glass may be in the hands of other nations. Our own hour-glass tells us that we are off on a race to make democracy work, so that we may be efficient in peace and therefore secure in national defense."

2 A Conservative Critique: The New Deal and the Republican Program

ROBERT A. TAFT

Robert A. Taft (1889–1953), the most prominent son of former President William Howard Taft, established himself as the political and intellectual leader of Republican conservatism almost immediately after winning election to the U.S. Senate in 1938. In this radio address, an effort largely free of partisan hyperbole, he soberly criticizes the New Deal and presents an alternative formula for combating the depression.

The New Deal, he argues, had demonstrably failed to restore prosperity, and the reasons for this failure could be found in its hostility toward private enterprise. The Roosevelt administration had refused to manage the government according to sound business principles; instead it had debased the currency and had engaged in a deficit spending so reckless that the nation was approaching the verge of bankruptcy. It had overregulated business and, on occasion, had even brought the government into direct competition with private capitalism. The results were the demoralization of the business community, the discouragement of individual enterprise, and the prolongation of the depression.

Taft's conservative alternative conceded the necessity of government assistance for the unemployed and underemployed, but the core of his own program was the encouragement of capitalist enterprise, which alone could restore prosperity. It was this argument that placed Taft squarely in an American tradition of business-oriented conservatism stretching back to Alexander Hamilton.

* * *

Robert A. Taft, Radio Address, March 18, 1939. From the *Congressional Record,* 76th Cong., 1st sess. (Appendix), pp. 1355–1357.

The Republican Party today is still the minority party, but the general impression in Washington and throughout the country is that the New Deal tide is rapidly receding and that the people are again looking to the Republican Party for leadership. It is most important that the Republicans, even though they are still in the opposition, formulate their program on which to appeal to the people for a change of administration. . . .

We find an overwhelmingly difficult problem before us. After six years of New Deal rule, after every kind of experiment, and the addition of $20 billion to the national debt, the fundamental problems are still unsolved. More than 10 million people are unemployed in the United States today, about 3 million of them receiving a bare subsistence from WPA. Twenty million people are looking to the Government for food. Millions more are receiving inadequate wages and fall in that underprivileged class for whom the New Dealers have shed tears in every speech, and to whom they have repeatedly promised prosperity and security. And yet there are more people underprivileged today, more people who have barely enough to live on, or not enough to live on, than there have been at any time except at the very bottom of the depression.

The national income in 1938 was not much more than $60 billion. If we go back ten years, we find a national income of $80 billion and 10 million fewer people among whom to divide it. The average income per individual is 30 percent less than it was in 1928. Of course, times are hard.

There can be no absolute proof that this condition has been created or prolonged by the policies of the present administration, but we have come out of every past depression more quickly, to a higher standard of income, and to greater employment, without measures of the New Deal character. Certainly there is no doubt that the New Deal policies have utterly failed in their objectives.

There can be only one main purpose in any intelligent program today—that is to improve the condition of the millions of unemployed and the other millions who are below a reasonable standard of life. If that problem cannot be solved, our whole republican form of government must admit itself a failure. When we see the conditions which exist in some of our cities, and I have seen them in Ohio as you have seen them in New York, we very quickly lose our pride in the statistics which show a higher average standard of living in the United States than elsewhere. When you see the conditions which social workers see every day you cannot be surprised that they are eager to adopt any measure which seems to furnish direct assistance to the bitter conditions their charges face, no matter what the other consequences of those measures.

It is a problem which challenges the Yankee ingenuity of the American people, and, of course, we Republicans claim a little more of that Yankee ingenuity, particularly from Maine and Vermont, than is possessed by the Democrats. The New Deal must have credit for trying every possible remedy which anyone suggested, sound or unsound, and through experimentation they have eliminated a considerable number of their favorite panaceas; at least they have eliminated them in the minds of all reasonable men, even if they themselves are unwilling to abandon them.

The New Deal is such a conglomeration of all kinds of measures that it is interesting for a moment to try to analyze just what it really is. Its objectives undoubtedly were to help the Nation, and particularly the lower-income groups, but from the beginning it has been motivated apparently by a complete distrust of our entire economic and business system, extending almost to every individual businessman. The assumption was that because a great depression occurred all of the former principles accepted as the cause for American leadership in the world should be discarded, and this in spite of the fact that the depression was world-wide and affected many other nations where an entirely different business system existed. There has been no real interest in trying to restore private industry, and the assumption has been that the Government could do everything better than it was done before.

This critical attitude extended to the most accepted fiscal principles, such as the belief (which has inspired every past President, Republican and Democrat) that there is a moral obligation to hold Government expenses down to revenues and conduct the United States Government on the same sound business principles which are necessary to avoid bankruptcy in private industry and ultimate repudiation by Government.

The President even abandoned the sound currency ideas which have always guided the United States, devalued the dollar under the almost childish Warren* theory that this would increase domestic prices, and flirted with the idea of an inflation of the currency. There is no doubt that the New Dealers have a deep-seated distrust of our entire system of individual initiative, free competition, and reward for hard work, ingenuity, and daring which have made America what it is.

They have relied on three types of Government activity. The first type consists of direct relief, in different forms, to the lower-income groups. Beginning with assistance to the States, which were building up a very satisfactory method of handling relief, a combination of direct and work relief under public-spirited citizen boards cooperating with private agencies, the New Deal suddenly decided that no one could do the job as well as they could, and, as a condition of the financial assis-

---

*George F. Warren, an eminent Cornell University economist.—Ed.

tance which was necessary, insisted on complete administrative control. Finding this too much of a job, they returned the unemployables to the States and undertook to provide work relief for all employables. That job has never been completely done, and the expense is so tremendous that it probably never will be. The attempt to administer from Washington a great work-relief program throughout the entire United States has resulted in inefficiency, politics, and a vast expense which threatens a complete bankruptcy of the Federal Government. Other relief measures are the CCC, the NYA, the Farm Security Administration, and other minor agencies.

The second type of New Deal activity includes the Government regulatory measures, which attempt to raise the income of this group or that group by controlling prices, wages, hours, and practices throughout the United States. Such were the NRA and the AAA. Such are the laws regulating agriculture today, the Guffey Coal Act, the wage-hour law. This type of law has completely failed in its purpose. Farm prices are as low today as they were five and a half years ago, before the agricultural control measures began. The administration of the Guffey Coal Act for two years has done no more than impose expense on the industry. The wage-hour law threatens to drive hundreds of people out of small business, and may do more harm than good. Attempts to fix prices have been frequent in history throughout the world. Without questioning the wisdom of the purposes sought, experience has shown, as in the case of the Brazil coffee control and the East Indian rubber control, that such attempts are doomed to failure. Our own experience does not contradict that conclusion.

Furthermore, this type of law is one of the most discouraging to private enterprise. No man can tell when the Government may step into his business and nullify all of the effort and energy and ingenuity he may have shown in developing that business. He is hounded by inspectors, excessive regulation, reports, and red tape. Many have gone out of business and many have stayed out of business because they could not feel certain that with all this Government regulation they might not be utterly wasting their time and their money.

The other type of New Deal experiment is direct Government business activity in fields where the Government thinks that private enterprise has fallen down on its job. Of this character are the TVA, the Rural Electrification Administration, the lending agencies extending Government credit to home owners and farm owners, the building of canals and other self-liquidating public works. Unquestionably some of this activity is justified, though usually the reason that private capital has failed to enter the field is because the enterprise is unprofitable in spite of the glowing prospectus of some Government departments.

But there are some unprofitable things which a government should start, and governments always have done something of this kind. It is a question of degree. It is very doubtful in my mind whether the TVA ever was justified in view of the development of public utilities in the Tennessee Valley, but now we have it and have to operate it to the best advantage. Private capital could not undertake the building of canals, but neither should the Government unless they are economically sound and justified by the tolls which can be collected.

The lending of funds to stimulate the building industry under the FHA seems to me justified as an emergency matter. And so also the Federal farm-loan banks fill a need which for one reason or another private capital could not reach. In this lending field, however, the Government, as far as possible, should create a set-up which can be taken over by private lending agencies under Government supervision, and in general, there should be no further extension of Government activity and competition unless it is absolutely necessary.

I have pointed out that the New Deal seemed to be inspired with a hostility to the entire preexisting American economic system. The result is that these three types of measures which I have described have not been administered with any special care to preserve the best features of private industry and encourage it to bring about recovery. The relief measures have been inefficient and expensive. They have resulted in a tremendous burden of taxation, which bears down on the man who is trying to make his own living. There has been no effort to preserve conditions under which a man, striving for a private job and doing his job well, shall be encouraged and preferred to the man on WPA. The other two types of measures, Government regulation and Government competition, have directly discouraged private activity of every kind. More men have gone out of business in the last five years than have gone into business because of the complete uncertainty whether they can survive a constant Government interference.

Now we are told that everything has changed and the administration is going to treat business like human beings. The very adoption of a so-called policy of appeasement admits that American businessmen and men who would like to go into business have been badgered and discouraged to an extent which requires an absolute reversal of Government policy. Secretary Hopkins made a speech in Des Moines and Secretary Morgenthau is having mottoes hung in the offices of the Treasury Department with the legend "Does it help recovery?"

But, as the old saying goes, "Fine words butter no parsnips." The appeasement policy is like the famous "breathing spell for business," only a smoke screen to conceal the real policies of the administration. It cannot be sincere. Whenever any question of action arises, the President is just as determined in his previous policies as he ever has been before.

Within the last few days Secretary Morgenthau and Secretary
Wallace* have argued for a continuation of the President's power to de-
value the dollar, although a stable currency is one of the greatest neces-
sities for mental reassurance to American business. The President himself has indicated that he wishes a continuation of his power to issue $3
billion in greenbacks, a power which he says is a convenient club in his
closet. A club against whom? Against Congress? Against the economic
royalists, in case the President chooses to blame them for depressed
prices? Nothing would be more calamitous to business revival than the
sudden decision of the President to issue billions of paper greenbacks
with no property whatever behind them. How easy for the President to
give up these monetary powers which hang over the business world like
the sword of Damocles.

Businessmen are agreed that the amendment of the National Labor
Relations Act would do much to reassure manufacturers, and stimulate
additional investment in plants. The American Federation of Labor
has demanded an immediate hearing on its amendments. Yet up to this
time the President and the CIO have successfully prevented the setting
of any date even for hearings on the amendments already introduced
before the Committee on Education and Labor in the Senate.

If taxes cannot be reduced, at least an increase can be prevented.
The payroll tax is today the most burdensome tax on business, and
incidentally a bonus to get rid of labor and install machinery and increase unemployment. The tax is already five percent of the payroll,
and goes up to six percent the 1st of January. This increase is wholly
unnecessary except to build up an imaginary reserve to astronomical
figures, and provide the New Deal with cash to pay deficits. Senator
Vandenberg has introduced an amendment to suspend the going into
effect of this increase, but the administration is definitely opposed.

The SEC still takes the attitude that businessmen are presumptively
crooks. Only this week a committee suggesting minor modifications in
the securities law, the merit of which I do not know, was met by a blast
from Mr. Douglas,† characterizing their plan as a "phoney," and im-
plying that their only interest was to line their own pockets at the
expense of the investors. The SEC is still pressing for a bill giving it
additional regulatory powers over the drafting of trust indentures and
the private business negotiations involved in such indentures. The
appeasement policy is completely insincere. The present administration has no confidence in the efficacy of private business activity. While

---

*Secretary of the Treasury Henry Morgenthau and Secretary of Agriculture Henry A.
Wallace.—Ed.
†William O. Douglas, Chairman of the Securities and Exchange Commission, later a
Supreme Court Justice.—Ed.

their policy continues, it is impossible to achieve any real progress toward the elimination of unemployment.

What then should be the Republican program? It must combine a policy of encouragement to private industry, which can put millions of men to work, with sincere and effective administration of relief measures to assist directly the lower-income groups. It must recognize the absolute necessity of relief measures in this country for many years to come. Before the great depression it was reasonable to hope that our economic system had reached a point where Government help was unnecessary except in cases of misfortune. It was reasonable to hope that a man who worked diligently during his active life could provide a home and an income for his old age. But the depression of 1929–32 showed us that our system had not reached that point. Even if we eliminated unemployment, the fact remains that many people must work at poor jobs, the product of which is of so little value that the rest of the population will not pay them an adequate living. And so we must assist the lower-income groups by direct relief, by work relief, by old-age pensions, by unemployment insurance, and by some form of housing subsidy.

But the administration of this relief must be carried on with the greatest care that it may not destroy our entire American system and put the whole population on relief. It must be carried on with economy, because the cost of supporting those who do not work is undoubtedly borne by those who are working. The return from capital will never support but a small proportion of the population. The greatest part of the cost of relief can only come from the income of those who are actually working, and if we impose too heavy a burden on that income there will no longer be any incentive to work, and certainly no incentive to put other men to work.

I think we must recognize, after all, that relief will never do more than provide a bare living and will never be a satisfactory substitute for real work in private industry. Old-age pensions can never be so high as to be a satisfactory substitute for a house and a reasonable income, saved by the effort of the family which has worked successfully. We see today that we have reached the limit of popular approval of further expenditures for WPA, and if we were raising by taxation our entire budget we would find the popular opposition even stronger. And it is right that it should be so, because the burden of supporting those who do not work cannot be allowed to grow to a point at which it will discourage all initiative and all effort on the part of the other two-thirds of the population.

For the same reason the relief agencies must be administered so that those on relief are not better off than the people who are working. A man who has saved and built his home should certainly be better off than the man who has the good fortune to live in a subsidized apartment house built by the Government.

In short, in administering relief, we must recognize that it is only a palliative, only a stopgap, and that it is not an end in itself, as many of our New Deal friends seem to think.

In the second place, we must take every possible measure to cure the unemployment problem. It can only be cured by more jobs in private industry. We must, therefore, take every possible measure to encourage people to put their time and money again into the development of private industry. We must see that there is an incentive and a reward for initiative, hard work, and persistence. The problem is partly psychological and partly practical. The people must feel again that the making of a deserved profit is not a crime, but a merit. They must feel again that the Government is interested in the prosperity of the businessman. They must feel again that the Government does not regard every businessman as a potential crook.

But there must be more than mental reassurance. There must be an abandonment as far as possible of Government fixing of prices, wages, and business practices. Americans must be assured that they will not be met by Government competition in their field of business activity. They must feel that Government activity will be confined to keeping their markets open, free, and competitive, so that they will have an equal chance with their little neighbor or their big neighbor. They must feel that Government expenses will be held down as far as possible, so that the tax burdens may not deprive them of the fruits of their most successful efforts. They would like to know that the currency is stable, the Government's fiscal policy sound, and all danger of inflation of the currency removed.

If we can restore business activity to the conditions which existed in 1928 we would have a national income of $90 billion, nearly 50 percent more than we have today. If it could be done then, why can't it be done now? If there were any such increase in income in this country millions of men would be employed, not only in manufacture, but in transportation, in distribution, in agriculture, and in mining. Certainly the greater part of those unemployed today would reach the goal of real jobs. Taxes can be reduced. We can reduce the payroll tax today and still take care of all present requirements. We can cut down the cost of every Government department and eliminate a reasonable number or make them self-supporting. The return of relief to local administration, with a liberal Federal grant, will still cost the Federal Government much less than the present WPA expenditure, amounting to more than $20 billion this year. I do not underestimate the difficulty of doing it, and it is almost impossible for Congress to do it against the opposition of an extravagant Executive, whose party still controls both branches of Congress and is opposed to cutting down the present expanded functions of the Federal Government. Its cost can certainly be reduced to $7 billion, twice what it was in the days of Hoover, and a reasonable increase of prosperity would provide the taxes to balance the Budget.

But prosperity can only be brought about by increased production. This country was built up by millions of men, starting new enterprises, putting their time and money into some machine shop, or store, or farm, or any one of a thousand commercial activities. Perhaps they could employ two men, then ten men, then hundreds, and in the case of the great industries, finally thousands or hundred of thousands. Employment increased steadily for 150 years, not by arbitrary building up of consumers' purchasing power, but by encouraging production and putting men to work. The theory that relief payments stimulate production is disproved by our own experience.

We hear a good deal today about the necessity of lending more money to little business and railroads and other enterprises; but it isn't loans that are needed by any business enterprise I know of. If they are entitled to borrow, they can borrow today from the banks. What they need is more capital, more people willing to put their money into building up new enterprises and developing new products; more people willing to abandon the low fixed return from Government bonds for the chance of a material profit from business enterprise.

This was the way America was built up, and the only way to resume it is to assure people again that Government will not interfere with their normal and reasonable efforts to make a living, and raise themselves and their families to a condition a little better than that of their neighbors; that Government will not take away from them the profit which they may make; that reasonable success will receive the recognition it deserves, at least from their friends and neighbors.

If we can stop spending money now, if we can stop the tremendous expansion of Government activity, regulation, and taxation, it is not too late to resume the progress which made this country the envy of the world; but if we continue for six years more the course which we have pursued, he is a bold man who will say that we can then restore prosperity under a democratic form of government.

3 A Radical Critique: The Myth of the New Deal

RONALD RADOSH

During the 1930's and 1940's, the strongest and most visible criticism of the New Deal came from the political Right. In the 1950's, the Eisenhower administration assimilated the essentials of the New Deal into the mainstream of American conservatism. Since then, debate about the New Deal has been largely academic, and most criticism of it has come from the Left. In this article, Ronald Radosh, a prominent socialist historian, attempts to overturn what he considers a liberal mythology that flourished during and immediately after the age of Roosevelt.

Radosh's critique of the New Deal is twofold. First, like other radical intellectuals, he deplores what he perceives as the meager accomplishment of the New Deal—primarily its failure to deal decisively with those issues that obsessed radicals of the 1960's and '70's, poverty, racism, and war. Second, he argues that the limits of the New Deal were effectively set by the corporate business elite. Drawing heavily on sociologist G. William Domhoff's *The Higher Circles,* he asserts that the shrewdest and most important leaders of American business, not anti-business liberal reformers, made the key contributions to the formulation of the New Deal. The hostility of the larger business community notwithstanding, the New Deal became a reform movement designed to preserve and strengthen the corporate enterprise system, a major chapter in the history of what radical social analysts call "corporate liberalism."

Radosh's critics would respond that he undervalues the accomplishments of the New Deal; that he overemphasizes the influence of the "corporate liberal" business leaders upon the Roosevelt administration; that he too easily dismisses the opposition of most businessmen, large and small, to the New Deal; and that he does not understand the motives of Roosevelt and most New Dealers. The reader must decide whether Radosh's socialist commitment has flawed his diagnosis or whether he has more accurately gauged the forces that went into the New Deal than did the liberal historians who preceded him.

* * *

Great Depression, labor unrest, massive unemployment, growing consciousness among the working classes, bitter hostility toward the multi-million-dollar corporations, failure of the reigning Republican administration to quiet the brewing explosion—and then the New Deal. The social revolution, which many expected and others feared, failed to materialize. Why? Was it because the New Deal, in its own special way, was indeed a third American Revolution?

From the perspective of the 1970's, with the stark realization that the United States had failed to deal with the race question, or to eradicate poverty, or even to begin to deal with the urban crisis, or to handle the general malaise and cultural poverty, or to adapt itself to the growing realization that revolutions abroad would have to be accepted and dealt with on their own terms, all of these events of the past ten years seemingly provided living evidence that a revolution had not occurred.

The new generation of New Left historians have asserted cogently that the New Deal instituted changes that only buttressed the corporate-capitalist order; that the vaunted Welfare State reforms hardly addressed themselves to the existing social needs of the 1930's, not to speak of working to end poverty, racism, and war. Historians Howard Zinn and Barton J. Bernstein have already written critical essays seeking to evaluate the New Deal from a radical perspective, and this essay shall not seek to repeat the critique advanced therein. The essence of their critical view has been best expressed by Bernstein:

> The liberal reforms of the New Deal did not transform the American system; they conserved and protected American corporate capitalism, occasionally by absorbing parts of threatening programs. There was no significant redistribution of power in American society, only limited recognition of other organized groups. . . . The New Deal failed to solve the problem of depression, it failed to raise the impoverished, it failed to redistribute income, it failed to extend equality and generally countenanced racial discrimination and segregation.

Once having presented this argument, however, the radical critic has in effect merely chastised the New Deal for what it failed to achieve. This does not work to answer the counterargument that Franklin D. Roosevelt and the New Dealers wanted more, but were stopped short because of the power of the congressional conservative bloc and other impenetrable obstacles.

It is undeniable that to many of the over-forty generation, Franklin D. Roosevelt was and remains the unassailable hero—the man who used all the powers at his command to ease the plight of the dispossessed, and who introduced dramatic reforms that would soon be accepted by the most staunch Old Guard Republican. That generation remembers the animosity with which many in the business community greeted Roosevelt, and the way in which Roosevelt condemned the forces of organized wealth that were out to destroy him. They did not have the tools of historical perspective to evaluate FDR's actual performance, or to understand what historian Paul Conkin has noted: that the New Deal policies actually functioned in a probusiness manner.

What Conkin was suggesting is that the anger of some businessmen was misdirected; another example of how members of the governing class can be so shortsighted that they will oppose their own best long-range interests. The confusion of the businessmen had its mirror image in the high regard in which so many members of the underclass held FDR and the New Deal. Roosevelt was able, for a while, to build and maintain the famous New Deal coalition that swept him into office in 1936. White workers from the North, blacks from the urban ghettos, and farmers from the Midwest all responded to the New Deal and claimed it as their own. Explaining this success as a result of the "powers of rhetoric," as did Bernstein, evades the real question. How could rhetoric alone convince so many that their lives had changed, if indeed, life was the same as it had always been? Perhaps reality did change just enough so that the failure of the New Deal to make substantive structural changes remained hidden.

Before we can begin to deal with these questions, it may be wise to start by citing the answer presented to the New Left historians by the dean of American corporate liberalism, Arthur M. Schlesinger, Jr., author in 1948 of the theory of a crucial "vital center" in American politics. Schlesinger has carefully presented his generation's answer to the New Left, and has defended the traditional view that the New Deal was a major watershed in American history.

A young radical told him, Schlesinger wrote, that all FDR did was

"abort the revolution by incremental gestures." At the same time, he dangerously cultivated a mood for charismatic mass policies, dangerously strengthened the Presidency, dangerously concentrated power in the national government. In foreign affairs, he was an imperialist who went to war against Germany and Japan because they were invading markets required by American capitalism.

Claiming that Roosevelt "will survive this assault from the left as he has survived the earlier assault from the right," Schlesinger ended with his own brief estimate of FDR's policies and times. Roosevelt

> led our nation through a crisis of confidence by convincing the American people that they had unsuspected reserves of decency, steadfastness and concern. He defeated the grand ideologists of his age by showing how experiment could overcome dogma, in peace and in war.

Schlesinger's writings help us to understand how those who only mildly benefited from the New Deal praised it, defended it, and allowed their experience during the 1930's to shape their social and political attitudes for more than a decade. Undoubtedly, many Americans have the same analysis of Social Security as does Schlesinger.

> No government bureau ever directly touched the lives of so many millions of Americans—the old, the jobless, the sick, the needy, the blind, the mothers, the children—with so little confusion or complaint. . . . For all the defects of the Act, it still meant a tremendous break with the inhibitions of the past. The federal government was at last charged with the obligation to provide its citizens a measure of protection from the hazards and vicissitudes of life. . . . With the Social Security Act, the constitutional dedication of federal power to the general welfare began a new phase of national history.

The assumptions behind Schlesinger's evaluation of Social Security are those he revealed years earlier. Writing in his classic *The Age of Jackson,* Schlesinger noted that "Liberalism in America has been ordinarily the movement of the part of the other sections of society to restrain the power of the business community." This statement assumes that a popular movement, opposed by business, continually arises in America to challenge the one-sided power of large corporate business. But new historical research by a generation of revisionists has all but wiped out this assumption. William Appleman Williams, Gabriel Kolko, James Weinstein, and Murray N. Rothbard have argued that liberalism has actually been the ideology of dominant business groups, and that they have in reality favored state intervention to supervise corporate activity. Liberalism changed from the individualism of laissez-faire to the social control of twentieth-century corporate liberalism. Unrestrained ruthless competition from the age of primitive capital accumulation became an anachronism, and the new social and political regulatory measures emanating from the Progressive Era were not so much victories for the people over the interests, as examples of movement for state intervention to supervise corporate activity on behalf of the large corporate interests themselves.

Just as all historians used to look at the accomplishments of the Progressive Era as antibusiness, equating state regulation with regulation over business, and with the assumption that corporate business opposed the new regulatory acts, so do many historians of the New Deal view the achievements of FDR's first two terms as a continuation of the Progressive tradition. The New Deal thus becomes the culmination of a "progressive" process that began with the age of Jackson. Once again, it is assumed that the "money changers" whom Roosevelt supposedly drove out of the temple were the New Deal's major opposition, and that government programs were per se progressive and part of a new phase of our history.

This analysis was stated most strongly by Carl N. Degler, when he referred to the New Deal as the "Third American Revolution." Seeing in the various New Deal measures "a new conception of the good society," Degler claimed pathbreaking significance once the "nation at large accepted the government as a permanent influence in the economy." Is such an influence sufficient to describe the New Deal as revolutionary?

To Degler it was. Like Schlesinger, historian Degler saw the Social Security Act as revolutionary because "it brought government into the lives of people as nothing had since the draft and the income tax." Yet another proof of revolutionary effect, even more important, was the "alteration in the position and power of labor." Noting that the decline in union growth had come to an end, and that the new spurt in unionism was that of the industrial unionism of the CIO, Degler argued that it was Robert F. Wagner's National Labor Relations Act that "threw the enormous prestige and power of the government behind the drive for organizing workers." The "placing of the government on the side of unionization," Degler wrote, "was of central importance in the success of many an organizational drive of the CIO, notably those against Ford and Little Steel."

In summation, the Wagner Act was depicted as revolutionary because, prior to the Act, no federal law prevented employers from discharging workers for exercising their rights or from refusing to bargain with a labor union, whereas after the Act was passed, workers had new rights against their employers. The result, according to Degler, was a truly pluralistic structure to American society. "Big Labor now took its place beside Big Business and Big Government to complete a triumvirate of economic power." The Wagner Act particularly revealed that

the government served notice that it would actively participate in securing the unionization of the American workers; the state was no longer to be an impartial policeman merely keeping order; it now declared for the side of labor.

Although the New Deal used traditional rhetoric, Degler asserted, "in actuality it was a revolutionary response to a revolutionary situation."

This estimate was upheld by even such a critical historian as William E. Leuchtenburg. Although he modified Degler's analysis a degree, by noting that the Wagner Act was partially motivated by a desire to "contain 'unbalanced and radical' labor groups," Leuchtenburg agreed that the New Deal was a "radically new departure." But to Leuchtenburg, the New Deal had major shortcomings. It failed to demonstrate "that it could achieve prosperity in peacetime," perhaps its greatest failure. The fact that the unemployed disappeared only with war production meant to Leuchtenburg that the New Deal was only "a halfway revolution; it swelled the ranks of the bourgeoisie but left many Americans—sharecroppers, slum dwellers, most Negroes—outside of the new equilibrium." But, argued Leuchtenburg, it was a revolution anyway. Here, we might raise the question of what type of "revolution" is it that fails to deal with the most basic problems produced by the old order, especially when an end to unemployment was the key task confronting the first New Deal, and while there were still by Leuchtenburg's count 6 million unemployed "as late as 1941."

The myth of a New Deal revolution, or a new departure, or a basic watershed, call it what you will, dies hard. New Left critics have correctly emphasized the New Deal's failures to destroy some part of the myth. But their critique, valuable as it has been, has failed to take up a more essential question. How does one confront the truth that the New Deal obviously did move in new directions, in some ways quite dramatically, and still keep the old order intact? And how is it that, although the old order remained basically untouched and even preserved, Roosevelt and the New Dealers were able to win the everlasting gratitude of the dispossessed and the white working class?

Rather than discuss all of the policies of the New Deal, we can begin to cope with this question by a more thorough look at a few key areas, particularly the National Recovery Administration (NRA), the birth of the Congress of Industrial Organizations (CIO) and the origins of the Wagner or National Labor Relations Act, and the passage of the Social Security Act. These three areas have been pointed to as evidence for the pathbreaking if not revolutionary character of the New Deal. Close attention to them should therefore prove most helpful in arriving at a more historically accurate assessment of what the New Deal wrought.

Most historians have discussed the Social Security Act in terms of what it offered American citizens for the first time, not in terms of how and why it was passed. Fortunately, sociologist G. William Domhoff has enabled us to take a new look at what lay behind some of the major New Deal reforms. Domhoff, following the lead supplied by the New Left revisionist historians, put his emphasis on the sponsorship of major reforms by leading moderate big businessmen and liberal-minded lawyers from large corporate enterprises.

What is important is that liberal historians have traditionally equated the NAM and small-business opposition to social reform legislation *as* business-community opposition. They have depicted an all-out fight between the forces of big business versus the people; the former opposing and the latter supporting reform. In his book Schlesinger wrote as follows:

> While the friends of social security were arguing out the details of the program, other Americans were regarding the whole idea with consternation, if not with horror. Organized business had long warned against such pernicious notions. "Unemployment insurance cannot be placed on a sound financial basis," said the National Industrial Conference Board; it will facilitate "ultimate socialist control of life and industry," said the National Association of Manufacturers. . . . One after another, business leaders appeared before House and Senate Committees to invest such dismal prophecies with what remained of their authority.
> Republicans in the House faithfully reflected the business position.

Of significance are Schlesinger's last words, "the business position." This telling phrase reveals the ideological mask on reality that helps to hide the manner in which the corporate state maintains its hegemony over the country. Schlesinger not only overstated big-business opposition; he did not account for the *support* given Social Security by moderate yet powerful representatives of the large-corporation community. Particularly important is the backing given the Act by the Business Advisory Council, which formed a committee on Social Security headed by Gerard Swope, president of General Electric, Walter Teagle of Standard Oil, Morris Leeds of the AALL* and Robert Elbert. These men were major corporate leaders, or as Domhoff put it, "some of the most powerful bankers and industrialists in the country."

Despite the support given the Act by these key corporate figures, the original bill was to be watered down by the Congress. This was because many congressmen and senators reflected their local constituencies, which included local antilabor and small-town mentality NAM business-types. Congress, in other words, did not have the political sophistication of the corporate liberals. Once the bill got to Congress, the setting of minimum state standards in old-age assistance was discarded. as was the concept that states had to select administering personnel on

---

*American Association for Labor Legislation.—Ed.

a merit basis. Workers were to contribute half of the old-age pension funds, while employers paid unemployment compensation. But the large corporations would still be able to pass the costs of their contribution to the consumer. Finally, the rich were not to be taxed to help pay for the program.

As Domhoff showed, the Social Security Act was the measured response of the moderate members of the power elite to the discontent of the thirties. These moderates took their program, based on models introduced by various corporate policy-making bodies during the previous twenty years, to the Congress. Congress, however, listened more to the NAM-type businessmen. The result was a legislative compromise between the original moderate and conservative position on the Act. Radicals among labor who wanted a comprehensive social-insurance program remained unsatisfied. It was their pressure, however, that induced the moderates to present their plan to Congress. The demands of the poor and the working class provided the steam that finally brought the modified Act to fruition.

The result, as Domhoff wrote:

> from the point of view of the power elite was a restabilization of the system. It put a floor under consumer demand, raised people's expectations for the future and directed political energies back into conventional channels. The difference between what could be and what is remained very, very large for the poor, the sick, and the aged. The wealth distribution did not change, decision-making power remained in the hands of upper-class leaders, and the basic principles that encased the conflict were set forth by moderate members of the power elite.

Social Security may have been a symbolic measure of the new Welfare State. But, to the corporate liberals in the governing class, it served as the type of legislation that eased tension, created stability, and prevented or broke any movements for radical structural change. Hence, it served an essentially conservative purpose because it helped maintain the existing system of production and distribution.

The pattern of corporate support to New Deal programs is even more vivid when we consider the first great program initiated by the New Deal to produce recovery, the National Recovery Administration. NRA arose from a background of collectivist plans such as the one proposed in 1931 by Gerard Swope, president of General Electric. Presented to a conference of the National Electrical Manufacturers Association, the plan, as Murray N. Rothbard has described it, "amounted to a call for compulsory cartelization of American business—an imitation of fascism and an anticipation of the NRA."

Swope argued that antitrust laws had to be suspended, so that producers in a given industry could meet and agree on a certain amount of production. All companies engaged in manufacturing and commercial enterprises could form one trade association supervised by a federal commission that would outline trade practices, as well as proper business ethics. Federal legislation had to be passed that would suspend the Sherman Antitrust Law and permit manufacturers to combine for the purpose of making agreements. Swope also revealed that he favored establishment of a "national economic council" that would enable trade associations to interact and permit coordination between different industries. Companies within one industry would join together in their own trade association to coordinate production, consumption, and unemployment benefits. Each association would then elect delegates to a national body that would meet together "and choose from amongst themselves, or from outside, a national economic council."

Trade associations were the "natural organizations to study the economic elements of each industry." Each would hold itself responsible for coordination of production and consumption to stabilize industry. They would

> then be the foundation stones upon which to erect the superstructure of the national economic council. This might be created by bringing together officers, or duly elected representatives of these various associations

to choose a council that would study the needs of industry as a whole. The men would come up through industry itself and would be able to work to solve their problems. "If you do that for each of the various industries," Swope commented, "and then have a similar body from the banking group, from the transportation, labor," and other bodies, delegates from each would meet "to form this national economic council."

Swope hoped for a national economic council. In essence it would function through an elite group, the leaders of the different functional economic groups. Although they would make major decisions and all groups were to be represented, decision-making would remain within the hands of the elite who ruled for the society at large. Swope was seeking an end to the imbalance caused by blunt contests for power between the various groups, each jockeying for more for itself from the state's administrators. He wanted to substitute corporate cooperation and mold previously warring constituencies into one corporate body. He sought, in plain language, an American corporate state. As such, his views paralleled the developments in Italy. In that fascist country, trade associations were called corporations, and given power to regulate all operations. The corporation was to be ruled by a representative group of employers and workers. The difference was that, in Italy, three members had to belong to the Fascist Party, and the major presiding officer was to be appointed by the Prime Minister.

During the 1930's, many liberals viewed fascist economic theory as a

promising alternative to what they considered the twin evils of an unre-
constructed laissez-faire capitalism and a rampant increase of socialism.
To such liberals, John P. Diggins has explained, fascism

> appeared to be a continuous creative effort that found its affirmation in
> the subordination of end to means. In its attempt to strike a balance
> between the dogmas of capitalism and socialism, moreover, Fascism
> avoided doctrinal myopia. Rejecting the fetishes of both the Left and
> Right, it presented an admirable alternative to an ironclad ideology on the
> one hand and a tenaciously shallow sentimentalism on the other.

To liberals, fascism appeared to be a system of planning that trans-
cended classes and led to an equilibrium of contending social forces.
Thus it was "essentially the theoretical appeals of corporatism that
interested" the liberals.

It is no accident that the early New Deal was characterized by the
introduction of planning techniques that had antecedents in trade associations developed within industry during the Hoover years. Bernard
Baruch's War Industries Board and the Hoover trade associations
reached fruition with FDR's NRA. Men who had been involved with
wartime planning were brought back to government service.

Roosevelt undertook to repeat and build upon the experiences of the
past administrations. But in building upon the past epoch, he was
building upon a probusiness program. The War Industries Board,
Leuchtenburg has aptly pointed out,

> had, after all, been run chiefly by business executives. If they learned
> anything from the war, it was not the virtues of collectivism but the poten-
> tialities of trade associations, the usefulness of the state in economic war-
> fare with the traders of other nations, and the good-housekeeping prac-
> tices of eliminating duplication and waste. The immediate consequence of
> the war was not a New Jerusalem of the planners but the Whiggery of
> Herbert Hoover as Secretary of Commerce. While the war mobilization
> did establish meaningful precedents for New Deal reforms, it was hardly
> the "war socialism" some theorists thought it to be. Perhaps the outstand-
> ing characteristic of the war organization of industry was that it showed
> how to achieve massive government intervention without making any
> permanent alteration in the power of the corporations.

This significant insight holds as well for the reforms of the New Deal.
As Leuchtenburg went on to state, the New Dealers also rejected class
struggle, as well as "mass action and socialist planning, and assumed a
community of interest of the managers of business corporations and
the directors of government agencies." They feared not discredited
conservatives, but the "antiplutocratic movements," or we might put it,
the forces of the radical left. Hence the New Deal cartelization efforts,
which culminated in NRA.

One of NRA's major architects was Donald Richberg, who had been chosen for his position because of his prolabor background. But again, Richberg's commitment to labor lay within the framework of the corporate state. As a young Chicago lawyer, Richberg had written both the Railway Labor Act of 1926 and later the Norris-LaGuardia Act of 1932. He was chosen to help frame the NRA, Schlesinger pointed out, because Hugh Johnson wanted Richberg because "he assumed that Richberg had the confidence of labor and liberals." No other early appointment of FDR's, Schlesinger concluded, gave "more satisfaction to labor and liberals than that of Richberg."

As a prolabor formulator of the NRA, Richberg revealed his private vision of a new corporate state, but one in which industrial unions would have to become the prerequisite for an American corporatism. "If industrial workers were adequately organized," he explained, "it would be entirely practical to create industrial councils composed of representatives of managers, investors and workers and then to create a national council composed of similar representatives of all essential industries." In this council, "all producing and consuming interests would be so represented that one group could hardly obtain sanction for a policy clearly contrary to the general welfare." Richberg was critical of craft-union leaders. He wished they had "seized" labor's great "opportunity to organize the unemployed," and simply ignore "the hampering tradition of craft unionism" by organizing men and women "denied their inherent right to work." Labor should have demanded that "their government should no longer be controlled by rulers of commerce and finance who have utterly failed to meet their obligations." If such a movement had been built, if labor had created one "mighty arm and voice" of the "unemployed millions," Congress would have listened to the dispossessed.

Richberg also forecast the conservative role that industrial unions would play. "Let me warn those who desire to preserve the existing order," he cautioned, "but intend to do nothing to reform it, that if this depression continues much longer the unemployed will be organized and action of a revolutionary character will be demanded." To avoid that, people had to be put back to work and mass purchasing power had to be increased. The solution was to mobilize the nation "through the immediate creation of a national planning council, composed of representatives of major economic interests who recognize the necessity of a planned economy." The need: to avoid radicalism. The means: a formal American corporate state, or the NRA.

The NRA, which became law on June 16, 1933, was the agency meant to evolve into a corporate state. The NRA, John T. Flynn perceptively noted in 1934, was based on the need of businessmen to have the government control prices, production, and trade practices. "Industry wanted not freedom from regulation," he wrote, "but the right to enjoy regulation." Modification of antitrust laws was desired "so that employers might unite to fabricate and enforce regimentation of industry through trade associations." The NRA also developed plans for shorter working hours and payment of minimum wages; but Flynn noted that it was "pure fiction" that such legislation was forced on big business against its will. Actually, the corporations wanted the opportunity to force the NRA on the "unwilling 10 percent" of smaller operators who competed unfairly by cutting costs through wage reductions. The NRA, Flynn remarked, represented almost "entirely the influence and ideal of big businessmen."

The NRA reformers, unlike our contemporary liberal historians, understood that their program was meant to be a conservative prop to the existing order. They also realized the dire need to include social reform as an essential component of the corporate state. They understood that many liberals and even political radicals would overlook the conservative origin and effect of the NRA if reform, especially public works, was offered as part of a package deal. Hence Title I of the NRA promoted the organization of industry to achieve cooperative action among trade associations, and it included the codes of fair competition and exemption of industry from prosecution under the antitrust laws. Title II set up a Public Works Association with a federal appropriation of $3 billion. It should be understandable why Henry I. Harriman, president of the United States Chamber of Commerce, argued that there was "ample justification for a reasonable public works program" in conjunction with a corporate plan that would free industry from antitrust restrictions. If there was any doubt that the large corporations would support a program that would result in wage increases along with a fair return on dividends, Harriman assured reluctant congressmen that the "big ones will rush to it."

But the problem was to win the allegiance not of the big ones, but of the "liberals." The means to this end was the technique of public works. Of all the New Deal reforms, public works seemed to most people to have the aura of "socialism" or at least of an attack on private interests. To the hungry and unemployed, it symbolized a direct concern by the government for their plight. That public works, as Murray N. Rothbard has shown, was introduced effectively by the Hoover administration was unrecognized. That the New Deal's public works was of a limited nature and did not interfere with private business prerogatives went unnoticed. In the area in which public-works development was most needed, housing, the New Deal program was hardly successful and in many ways a total failure. All this was ignored. The name "public works" and the PWA itself produced a sympathetic response from the populace, the "liberal" political groups, and the organized political left.

The commitment to support reform if the liberals and radicals would cease criticism of the NRA was understood by Donald Richberg. In a private draft prepared for the committee that drew up the NRA legislation, Richberg suggested that "it would be at least a tactical error not to begin the bill with a public works program," with the provision for trade agreements following as further stimulation to industrial stabilization.

It is true, as Leuchtenburg wrote, that NRA gave jobs to 2 million workers, stopped renewal of a deflationary spiral and established a national pattern of maximum hours and minimum wages, thus wiping out child labor and the hated sweatshops. But as he added, the NRA did not speed recovery,

> and probably actually hindered it by its support of restriction-minded businessmen moved into a decisive position of authority. By delegating power over price and production to trade associations, the NRA created a series of private economic governments. . . . The large corporations which dominated the code authorities used their powers to stifle competition, cut back production, and reap profits from price-rising rather than business expansion.

In the words of William Appleman Williams, our leading radical historian:

> the New Deal saved the system. It did not change it. Later developments and characteristics of American society which suggest an opposite conclusion are no more than the full extension and maturation of much earlier ideas and policies that were brought together in what a high New Dealer called a shotgun approach to dealing with the depression.

Unlike Williams, most of our contemporary historians do not seem to realize that institution of "a new set of plans" is conservative, not to speak of not being radical or revolutionary. But what happens when an area emerges where the "old methods" are entirely done away with? Can one rightly call such an area of innovation revolutionary? As Degler has argued, this is indeed the case with organized labor, and the passage of the Wagner or National Labor Relations Act. More than any other piece of New Deal legislation, the policy toward labor seemed to suggest a new revolutionary stance toward the worker on the part of government.

In reality, the role played by the Wagner Act was the same as that of the NRA and the other conservative New Deal programs. It was the Wagner Act that allowed the administration to obtain the final integration of organized labor into the existing political economy of corporation capitalism. Unions, which had a sudden revival under the NRA, even before the Wagner Act period, were industrial in nature—the United Mine Workers and the Amalgamated Clothing Workers showing exceptional growth. Craft unions grew only 13 percent between 1933 and 1935, as against 132 percent by the AF of L's four industrial unions and 125 percent for their semi-industrial unions. The NRA provided the original impetus to organization. Between July and August 1933, the AF of L issued 340 new charters to affiliated local trade and federal labor unions, and Green estimated that in two months AF of L membership increased by about 1.5 million members.

With the NRA, the federal government took over the traditional organizing function that had previously been an exclusive union domain. The old AF of L craft unions had refused to initiate a widespread program of unionization in unorganized basic industries. But now the New Deal was seeking a labor movement that would gain working-class support and provide the necessary structural parallel to industry that would allow integration of the labor force into the new system. The New Deal, contemporary reporter Benjamin Stolberg observed, "needed organized labor to save big business." While the NRA was a "price fixing mechanism to enable big industry to regain the control of scarcity," it needed big labor to police "the 'social planning' of stabilizing prices in an economic system" that was "partly irresponsibly competitive and partly dictatorially monopolistic." Thus the NRA turned the labor movement "into a semipublic unionism whose organization was part of a government program."

The government became heavily involved, through the early NRA efforts, in the traditional function of union organization. The government did not tell the workers what form of union to organize, but only the industrial unions had any success. Moreover, it was the more politically radical unions that led the integration of labor into the corporate structure. "In short," Stolberg explained,

> the socialist unions, whose militancy had been kept alive these last few years by an inner left wing opposition, fitted very easily into the drift towards state capitalism, which characterizes the New Deal.

Not all members of the corporate elite opposed labor's new gains. But unlike the Social Security Act, which obtained an overwhelming corporate consensus for its support, many members of the governing class were not friendly to union organization. A split developed between the moderate sophisticated corporate leaders and the old-line antilabor diehards.

The leading figure among the moderates was Gerard Swope, president of General Electric. As chieftain of one of the key multimillion-dollar corporations, Swope was quite an important figure in the corporate community. Herbert Hoover had stood fast against introduction of his plan, viewing it as a stepping stone toward a business fascism. But during FDR's administration, Swope began to get results.

As early as 1926, Swope had sought to convince AF of L president William Green to form a nationwide union of electrical workers organized on an industrial basis. He felt that having an industrial union might mean "the difference between an organization with which we could work on a businesslike basis and one that would be a source of endless difficulties."

William Green, because he had to maintain his commitment to the craft unions comprising the AF of L, rejected Swope's pleas. Swope preferred industrial organization for one simple reason: he saw his industry "intolerably handicapped if the bulk of our employees were organized into different and often competing craft unions." They could deal easily with one bargaining agent, but not with more than one dozen. When the CIO was eventually built and the left-led United Electrical Workers began to organize General Electric, Swope rejoiced. He informed one of his vice-presidents that "if you can't get along with these fellows and settle matters, there's something wrong with you." The UEW was praised by Swope as "well led, the discipline good."

Because Swope recognized the necessity of integrating the working class into the existing corporate system, he helped develop the mechanism that would be written into the Wagner Act. It was Swope who proposed creation of a National Labor Relations Board to supervise labor relations, as well as the method of holding secret-ballot elections in factories to judge which group was the accurate representative of organized labor. It was this device that insured victory to the industrial unions in their factory contests with both craft and company unions. Swope argued that a majority vote had to be binding on all workers, and he opposed the intransigence of employers who believed workers should have no voice in picking their own representatives.

Swope understood what many contemporary historians do not. Industrial unionism was not inherently radical, and its recognition by government was not revolutionary. Rather, industrial unions functioned in the era of corporate capitalism to exert discipline on the work force so that labor productivity would be improved and cooperative relations with employers would emerge. The existence of such an industrial unionism benefited the long-range interests of the corporations. It was precisely for this reason that so many employers ignored section 7-a of the NRA, and continued to build their own company unions. They simply preferred to deal with their own unions organized industrially rather than with "legitimate" trade unions organized on a craft basis.

The New Dealers devised, in this case, a means to integrate big labor into the corporate state. But only unions that were industrially organized, and which paralleled in their structure the organization of industry itself, could play the appropriate role. A successful corporate state required a safe industrial-union movement to work. It also re-

quired a union leadership that shared the desire to operate the economy from the top in formal conferences with the leaders of the other
functional economic groups, particularly the corporate leaders. The
CIO unions, led by Sidney Hillman of the Amalgamated Clothing
Workers, provided such a union leadership.

It was for this reason that the moderates in the governing class
pushed for passage of the Wagner Act. As Domhoff noted, the anti-
union diehards did have leverage for one major reason.

> From the point of view of the employers, it had to be an all or nobody
> proposition, for any holdouts would supposedly have the competitive
> advantage brought about by lower wage costs. Thus, the diehards held
> great power over the majority, making it ultimately necessary to legislate
> against them. Perhaps there is something to the claim that most employers
> would go along with union recognition if all their compatriots would. But
> not every employer would go along, which set the stage for the battle over
> the Wagner Act, a battle which precipitated a serious split in the power
> elite.

As Domhoff showed, the moderate members of the power elite
played shrewd politics. After a vast amount of strikes occurred, they
refused to heed the many calls for sending in troops. The result was
that the diehards were forced into negotiation and compromise.
Roosevelt even accused the NAM forces of trying to precipitate a general strike. But in refusing to stand with the antilabor groups, Roosevelt was not the master broker, a man who favored "a balance between
business and labor"; rather, he was an

> integral member of the upper class and its power elite. However, he was a
> member of that part of the power elite that had chosen a more moderate
> course in attempting to deal with the relationship of labor and capital. . . .
> While he did not encourage unionism, his record during the thirties makes
> very clear, he was nonetheless unwilling to smash it in the way the NAM
> had hoped to do since 1902.

Referring back to Roosevelt's prolabor ideology formed during World
War I, when he was a member of the Executive Board of the National
Civic Federation, Domhoff noted that when the "time came for choosing, he and the moderate members of the power elite chose bargaining
rather than repression."

Even if a majority of businessmen opposed the Wagner Act, the
moderate group within the elite was able to use political power to its
own advantage. Once the Supreme Court voted in favor of the Act, the
NLRB, an administrative body, became the final arbitrator of all labor
disputes. This was, as Domhoff wrote, the "favorite solution of the

moderate members of the power elite, the 'nonpolitical' administrative body or regulatory agency."

Even before the Court decision favorable to the Act, FDR had moved to conciliate diehards among the elite. Working through Thomas Lamont, Roosevelt made overtures toward United States Steel. Lamont brought FDR and U.S. Steel president Myron Taylor together, and a contract with the Steelworkers was signed on March 3, 1937, one month before the Court decision. Only Little Steel held out on its anti-union course. Roosevelt similarly worked with Bill Knudsen, head of General Motors, and with Walter P. Chrysler, who backed him in the 1936 election. According to Perkins, FDR was able to gain help from Averell Harriman and Carl Grey of the Union Pacific Railroad, Daniel Willard of the Baltimore & Ohio, Walter Teagle of Standard Oil, Thomas Lamont of J. P. Morgan, Myron Taylor of U.S. Steel, Gerard Swope of General Electric, and textile manufacturer Robert Amory. "It may be surprising to some people," Perkins wrote:

> to realize that men looked upon as the conservative branch of the Roosevelt Administration were cooperative in bringing about a new, more modern, and more reasonable attitude on the part of employers toward collective bargaining agreements.

But the final goal for which these conservative industrialists worked was the creation of an American corporate state. This was made clear in the 1960's by Leon Keyserling, who had been legislative assistant to Robert F. Wagner during the 1930's and who helped the group that formulated the Wagner Act's principles. In 1960, economist Keyserling called for a "new national agency to embody top level discussions among those who hoped that such a body would move the country away from fruitless wrangles between competing groups." He hoped that a new agency would bring the "organized powers in our enterprise system," unions and trade associations, into a "relationship of participation and concert with the efforts of government." He then noted that this was the goal fought for by Wagner during the 1930's.

This detailed examination of the roots of the Wagner Act, as well as the NRA and the Social Security Act, should help us to assess the meaning of the New Deal. We now should be able to answer some of the questions raised earlier. First, it is clear that nonelite groups—the unemployed, workers, farmers—were the beneficiaries of many of the new social reforms. Social Security did produce benefits despite its limitations, NRA did eliminate sweatshops, and organized labor was able to strengthen its position in society. Reform, after all, would be a meaningless word if it did not have any partial effect. That is, indeed, the very meaning of reform.

But reform is not revolution. Revolution means a substantive fundamental change in the existing social structure, a massive dislocation and revamping of the existing system of production and distribution. Schlesinger's "New Left" student, if he is quoted correctly, has emphasized the wrong issue. The New Deal reforms were not mere "incremental gestures." They were solidly based, carefully worked out pieces of legislation. They were of such a character that they would be able to create a long-lasting mythology about the existence of a pluralistic American democracy, in which big labor supposedly exerts its countering influence to the domination that otherwise would be undertaken by big industry.

One cannot explain the success of the New Deal by pointing to its rhetoric. The populace responded to FDR's radical rhetoric only because it mirrored their own deeply held illusions. They could not comprehend how the reforms that changed their lives only worked to bolster the existing political economy, and they did not realize that many sponsors of the reforms came from the corporation community themselves. The integration of seemingly disparate elements into the system was successful. Labor did get its share and it did benefit from the development of a permanent war economy and the military-industrial complex. Many of those who lived through and benefited from the New Deal most likely view its accomplishments in much the same way as Schlesinger or Carl Degler. One can never be sure whether they reflect the explanations offered by the "vital center" historians, or whether these historians merely reflect the false consciousness of their own epoch.

The New Deal policies, as that conservative Chicago lawyer so aptly put it, were only a change in the way of doing things. They were a means of working out new arrangements to bolster the existing order. That so many businessmen were shortsighted and rejected acting in terms of the system's long-term interests does not change that truth. One cannot judge the meaning of an era's policies by pointing to the opposition these policies generated. The NAM and small-business types, with their own conservative mentality, responded to the epoch in terms of the consciousness of a previous era. The moderates in the governing class had to put up a stubborn, prolonged fight until the law would be able to reflect the realities of the new epoch of corporation capitalism.

That many on the political left viewed the New Deal as "progressive" or "neosocialist" is also no clue to the meaning of New Deal policies. Like the small businessmen, the left was a victim of its own particular myths, and its support of FDR cannot tell us anything about New Deal policies either. It may reveal the essential liberalism of the 1930's left, but this is another story. The failure of contemporaries properly to evaluate the epoch in which they live is traditional. One can never, as

Karl Marx warned, evaluate an era by concentrating on the consciousness of an era's major protagonists. The New Deal was conservative. Its special form of conservatism was the development of reforms that modernized corporate capitalism and brought corporate law to reflect the system's changed nature. To many, these New Deal reforms seemingly proved that the system had changed its basic essentials. As we move into the era of a fully matured corporate capitalism, whose contradictions are just beginning to emerge, it has become easier to see what the New Deal accomplished. Only in an epoch where consciousness begins to soar beyond the capitalist marketplace can a critique of the major reform era that marketplace had to offer emerge. This is such an epoch. Understanding how the New Deal worked will enable us to resist policies based on further extensions of the Welfare State, and to commit ourselves instead to the collective effort to forge a socialist community in America.

II | The Political Economy of the New Deal

4 The New Deal and Agriculture

RICHARD S. KIRKENDALL

Richard S. Kirkendall, a professor of history at Indiana University and executive secretary of the Organization of American Historians, is among the most thoughtful and prominent students of the New Deal for agriculture. In this broad survey, he establishes that the New Dealers were united in their determination to raise the standard of living for farmers, to employ collectivist techniques in doing so, and to preserve the capitalist system. Yet he also discerns conflicts between those concerned primarily with the interests of middle-class commercial farmers and those who envisioned the agricultural program as a vehicle for such social reforms as rational land-use planning and the amelioration of rural poverty.

In the end, he believes, the New Deal accomplishment in agriculture was important but well short of the goals of the social reformers. The commercial farmer emerged from the 1930's with more security than he had possessed before but with less independence. No longer part of an atomistic, classically competitive economic system, he now relied on government aid and organization and on his own political interest groups. The New Deal had fit agriculture into a larger pattern of "a collectivist or organizational type of capitalism" that it did much to create. Its social reform objectives, however, did not enjoy strong political support and went largely unrealized. Consequently, the major New Deal achievement for rural America was the resuscitation of the agrarian middle class.

* * *

The New Deal for agriculture illustrated the Roosevelt administration's commitment to capitalism and its determination both to preserve and to change the system. Farming was extremely depressed in 1933, and New Dealers worked, with some success, to raise farm prices and restore profits to the farm business. They tried to do even more: to fit the farmer into a collectivist type of capitalism. Again, their efforts succeeded. The federal government became more important in American agriculture, seeking among its objectives to regulate farm production, and farm organizations grew in membership and importance. The individual farmer came out of the 1930's less independent than he had been before the New Deal. Some New Dealers also hoped to serve more than the business interests of the commercial farmer. Although their efforts were partially successful, they encountered major obstacles that limited their accomplishments. Farm politics during the 1930's was dominated by men interested, first of all, in higher farm prices.

American capitalism had been moving in a collectivist direction for more than half a century before 1933. Large organizations, both public and private, had been taking shape and gaining power in the economic system. Businessmen had moved first, breaking with individualism and forming giant organizations before the end of the nineteenth century. Antitrust laws had been passed in hopes of restoring the old system, but they had failed. Somewhat more successful efforts had been made in pre–New Deal days to bring government and various economic groups into harmony with the collectivist trends. Government regulatory agencies, such as the Interstate Commerce Commission and the Federal Trade Commission, had been established; and a labor movement, with the American Federation of Labor as its largest component, had developed.

Although farmers often battled against the drive away from individualism, they too were caught up in the trend. Long before the 1930's, they had joined organizations such as the Grange and the National Farmers' Union. In 1920, the American Farm Bureau Federation was formed, and it quickly became the largest farm organization, with a membership of more than 300,000 farm families throughout the 1920's, most of them in the Middle West. The federation devoted a large portion of its time to the formation of other organizations—cooperatives—for the marketing of agricultural commodities.

The Farm Bureau made no effort to organize all of the people who lived on the land. It was interested only in the rural businessman, the farmer who produced and sold a substantial crop. And the "farm problem," as the organization defined it, was the most obvious problem faced by this type of farmer: low farm prices. The organization's aim was to make the farm business profitable once again.

Farming was not a highly profitable business during the 1920's. During World War I, farmers had enjoyed prosperity and had increased their acreage and their production, raised their standard of living, and gone into debt; but the price break of 1920 had dropped farm income from nearly $17 billion in 1919 to less than $9 billion in 1921. Throughout the 1920's, farm income never reached $12 billion; and in 1929, the purchasing power of farm goods was only 91 percent of the prewar level. The price problem was a consequence of an increase in production, due largely to a greater use of fertilizer and machinery, and a drop in demand both at home and abroad.

During the 1920's, the Farm Bureau devoted much of its energy to efforts to get help for the farmer from the federal government, and the organization championed a plan—the McNary-Haugen plan—that was designed to bring the farmer into harmony with practices of the urban business world. In fact, an urban businessman, George Peek, was chiefly responsible for the development of the plan. The president of the Moline Plow Company, a company that was severely damaged by the farm depression, Peek had turned to farm relief to solve his economic problems. "You can't sell a plow to a busted customer," he explained. The basic problem of the rural businessman, as Peek saw it, was that he bought in a protected market and sold in a highly competitive one. Rather than propose the destruction of the protective tariff system, he advocated a plan to get the tariff to do for the farmer what it did for the industrialist. The government, Peek suggested, should help farmers relate supply to domestic demand as industrialists did. According to the plan, the farmer would sell in the American market the amount of his production that could be sold at a price that would give him the purchasing power he had had before the war; and then a government corporation, financed by the participating farmers, would purchase the surplus at the American price and "dump" it abroad at the world price. Helped by the tariff, industrialists had long behaved in a similar fashion, charging one price at home and another abroad, and Peek encouraged the farmer to conform to the practices of the urban business world.

Peek's plan did not gain an opportunity to demonstrate that it could raise farm prices and, by doing so, help other parts of the economy. Congress passed the McNary-Haugen bill in 1927 and again in 1928, but President Coolidge successfully vetoed the measure both times.

By 1933, the farm business was one of the most seriously depressed parts of the American economic system. Few farmers, large or small, were prosperous. When the general depression hit, it had reduced demand for farm products below the unsatisfactory levels of the 1920's, and farm income fell to $5 billion. The price of cotton, which had averaged 12.4 cents per pound from 1909 to 1914 was only 5.5 cents in February 1933; the price of wheat had dropped from 88.4 to 32.3 cents per bushel; but the farmer's tax burden had doubled since 1914. His debts remained high, and the prices of goods he needed to buy had not dropped nearly as far as farm prices. While agricultural prices fell 63 percent from 1929 to 1933, industrial prices slipped only 15 percent. Industrialists could control production more effectively, so that agricultural production declined only 6 percent while industrial production dropped 42 percent. Thus, by February 1933, farm commodities could purchase only half as much as they could before the war.

Under the impact of the depression, the Farm Bureau suffered a sharp drop in membership. It had had more than 320,000 members in 1930, but it had fallen below 165,000 by 1933. As membership dropped, the organization resumed its battle for the McNary-Haugen plan.

Suffering was intense in rural America, and some farmers expressed their frustration and resentment in loud and at times violent protests. Many corn-hog farmers in the Middle West, who had known prosperity but were now faced with falling income and threatened with the loss of property, joined the Farmers' Holiday Association and participated in "the most aggressive agrarian upheaval of the twentieth century" and "a final great attempt by the family farmer to save himself from absorption and annihilation." The association organized a farm strike that began in August and ran into November 1932, and the participants, though usually peaceful, did employ violence on several occasions in their efforts to keep farm products off the market. The FHA and Wisconsin dairy farmers, who staged a strike in February 1933, threatened new strikes in the spring if the new administration failed the farmer. In addition, there were many protest marches and meetings during the fall and winter of 1932–33, including one in Washington in December by the Farmers' National Relief Conference that demanded immediate action to halt debt payments, evictions, and property seizures; raise prices; distribute food to the needy; and cut the profits of middlemen. Furthermore, farmers took direct action, including "penny" and "Sears-Roebuck" sales to halt the great wave of foreclosures and sales for tax delinquency that was turning landowners into tenants or farm laborers or placing them on relief rolls. Neighbors would appear at forced sales, intimidate those who wished to make serious offers, buy the property at very low prices, such as $1.18 for a farm, and return it to the owner. Mobs also moved against judges, police officers, and lawyers; troops were called into action against farmers; insurance companies suspended foreclosure suits; and farm states passed moratorium laws.

For devotees of "law and order," the situation seemed filled with dangerous possibilities. The Communist party participated in the protest movement, and farm leaders warned of "a revolution in the countryside in less than 12 months" and suggested that the "mental attitude of the farmer is strained to the breaking point." According to a careful student of the "agricultural crisis," revolution was "not outside the realm of possibility," and "the immediate prospect was for a more widespread, and possibly increasingly violent, reaction."

The New Deal's response to the crisis testified to the administration's commitment to capitalism and to its determination to promote further evolution along collectivist lines. The New Dealers discarded the view that farming is a highly individualistic enterprise and insisted that it must be dealt with on a collective basis. They also ignored romantic notions of the farmer as a self-sufficient yeoman, defined him as a businessman, rejected proposals of farm groups of an earlier day designed to destroy the power and change the practices of big business, and broke with the traditional emphasis upon the expansion of agricultural production. Instead, New Dealers urged farmers to imitate the production control methods of the most successful businessmen and brought the power of government to the aid of the farmer so that he could behave like the urban businessman who benefited from the corporate form of organization. The federal government became much more important in decisions about agricultural production, devising production plans designed to coordinate the work of the nation's farmers and establish a profitable balance between supply and demand.

The production control scheme was developed by social scientists, not by farm organization leaders or politicians. The largest contribution came from M. L. Wilson, an agricultural economist from Montana State College who had firsthand knowledge of the critically depressed conditions of Montana's wheat farmers and was permitted by his college to work for agricultural legislation. Wilson was helped by other economists, including William J. Spillman, John D. Black, Howard Tolley, and Mordecai Ezekiel. The result was the Voluntary Domestic Allotment Plan.

To Wilson and his associates, the leading alternatives to the allotment plan, though valuable for their recognition of the importance of farm purchasing power and their endorsement of action by the federal government to raise farm prices, had fatal flaws. One alternative was the McNary-Haugen plan. It seemed certain to encourage the farmer to increase production and thus worsen his situation. Cuts in production seemed necessary. Production now, according to the advocates of the allotment plan, should be limited to the effective demands of the domestic and foreign markets, and no efforts should be made to dump surpluses abroad because dumping would force other countries to push their tariff walls even higher.

Another alternative was the effort of the Hoover administration to encourage farmers to reduce output. Those efforts emphasized persuasion, rejected stronger methods of control, and assumed that the chief role of government in agricultural production was to supply advice so that farmers could devise sound production plans as industrial corporations did. Wilson proposed that the government should do more than talk to farmers: it should employ its taxing and spending powers to promote reductions in output. His plan involved a tax on farm commodities to be paid by the processors when they handled these products and to be used to finance a system of payments to farmers who agreed to adjust production. Each farmer would be free to refuse to participate, but would be encouraged to do so not merely by the promise of higher prices in the market but by payments to him from the government.

Although the leading farm organizations in 1932 preferred other farm relief schemes, production control became the major New Deal program for the farmers before the end of 1933. In achieving this result, Wilson received essential support from Franklin Roosevelt. Another economist with access to the candidate, Rexford Guy Tugwell, introduced Roosevelt to Wilson and his scheme, and the campaigner provided a somewhat vague endorsement of the plan in his major speech on agriculture. He committed himself sufficiently to promote willingness among some of the farm leaders to accept production control as at least one way to attack the farm problem. Roosevelt's support had limits, however. He was reluctant to press any one plan too hard for he hoped to have the support of all farm groups.

He did select an advocate of the allotment plan as secretary of agriculture; he rejected Peek and other opponents of the plan and chose Henry A. Wallace of Iowa, an agricultural journalist, scientist, and businessman who had often advised farmers to reduce their production. Wallace had concluded before 1932 that McNary-Haugen would hurt farmers and had helped Wilson promote interest in his plan. And he selected two other advocates of the plan, Ezekiel and Tugwell, as his top lieutenants. Ezekiel, who had worked for the department and the Farm Board for a decade, became the secretary's economic adviser, and Tugwell became assistant secretary.

In spite of these favorable developments, the advocates of the allotment plan did not achieve a complete victory during the "Hundred Days." The Agricultural Adjustment Act that was passed in May 1933 included major Wilsonian features: production control, voluntary participation encouraged by rental or benefit payments, self-financing through processing taxes, and a role for farmers in administration. But the law also included two programs with which Peek was most closely associated. One would sell surplus commodities in foreign markets, and the other would allow processors and distributors of farm products to reach agreements concerning the prices they would pay to farmers.

Advocates of production control, including Wilson, now moved into important positions in the new Agricultural Adjustment Administration, but Peek was appointed to the top spot. The appointment meant that the battle over farm policy would now rage inside government. Although Peek was forced to accept cuts in production, he did so reluctantly, resisted pressures to make this the main feature of the program, emphasized marketing agreements as the means of raising farm prices, and continued to seek ways to sell the surplus. Wallace, however, believed that marketing agreements divorced from production control could make only small increases in farm purchasing power. In the fall of 1933, he publicly criticized Peek's agreements; Peek challenged Wallace's authority to control the AAA; and Wallace and Tugwell vetoed Peek's plan to dump butter in Europe and pressed the president for a decision that would indicate clearly where authority lay. Forced at last to make a choice between representatives of different farm policies, Roosevelt moved Peek into a new post as special adviser to the president on foreign trade.

Wallace had crushed Peek's attempt to make the AAA an independent agency, free from control by the secretary and subordinate only to the president; and now he placed it under the direction of Chester Davis, who believed in production control. Although Davis had been Peek's top lieutenant in the McNary-Haugen fight, he had concluded that the growth of economic nationalism had invalidated that plan and that the United States must reduce its cropland. Now, under his vigorous leadership, which lasted until 1936, production control emerged clearly as the major program to raise farm prices.

Production control illustrated the New Deal's commitment to collective capitalism, and defenses of the program often emphasized its similarities to the practices of large corporations. This line was developed elaborately in 1934 by one of Wallace's advisers, Gardiner Means, a Columbia University economist who had collaborated with Adolf A. Berle on *The Modern Corporation and Private Property*, published in 1932. Means' studies of industrial prices revealed the ways in which giant corporations used their power to control production in order to uphold prices and disclosed the weaknesses of the farmer in such an economic system. The more individualistic farmer could not exercise the same control over production and thus "administer" prices. For him, in contrast to the corporation, price rather than production was the flexible factor. Furthermore, the farmer suffered from the industrialists' ability to restrict production because it led to higher industrial prices and reduced the demand for agricultural products. Factories working at less than full capacity needed fewer agricultural products, and unemployed workers had little purchasing power.

Means' work was highly regarded and frequently drawn upon by members of the Department of Agriculture, including Wallace, Tugwell, Ezekiel, and Wilson. They argued that developments in the distribution of power within the economy had placed the farmer in a disadvantageous position, and thus he needed help from the government so as to be able to imitate industrial practices. The AAA helped farmers achieve the results that industrialists achieved through corporate organization. If the industrialist could adjust production to demand, was it wrong to use government power to help farmers do the same? Had not the industrialist, by cutting back on his production and thereby reducing the demand for farm products, forced the farmer to reduce output?

The argument implied that the New Deal farm program was not a radical program. Farmers were merely behaving like urban businessmen. Farmers were not trying to destroy the production control practices of the corporate giants. Instead, the rural businessmen were accepting and seeking to employ an established feature of collective capitalism.

At the same time that the farm program promoted the further development of an organized type of capitalism, the program protected the system by undercutting agrarian protest. Farm protest had erupted once again in the fall of 1933 because relief had come more slowly than farmers expected, and the administration had then supplemented production control with crop loans, relief purchases, and moderate monetary inflation. As benefits began to reach the farm and prospects brightened, they sapped the strength of the protest movement. Few farmers had had revolutionary aspirations; they had protested in hopes of improvements in the farm business. The New Deal had made some and had thereby robbed the radicals of support.

Given the character of New Deal farm programs, it is not surprising that some business leaders were strong supporters of them. Among the most important were Henry I. Harriman, the president of the United States Chamber of Commerce from 1932 to 1935, R. R. Rogers, an official of the Prudential Life Insurance Company, and Robert E. Wood, the president of Sears, Roebuck and Company. These men were influenced by both economic and political considerations. They were troubled by the economic breakdown and convinced that farmers must have greater purchasing power in order to pay their debts and buy industrial products, and they were alarmed by the possibility that farmers would repudiate their debts and join radical movements. A successful farm program would promote general economic recovery and check radical action. It would protect the capitalistic system and promote its recovery. Such men helped Wilson gain support for his ideas in 1932 and applauded New Deal farm programs as they developed.

American business in the 1930's was not a solid power bloc, however, and some businessmen opposed the production control program. The processors and distributors of farm products were especially active foes. They had large sums invested in facilities designed to handle farm products, depended upon large sales, and would be harmed by cuts in farm production. Furthermore, they disliked the processing tax. Some of them advocated plans for the expansion of sales and suggested that the government should allow farm prices to drop and either work to reduce barriers to international trade or dump products abroad; and they tried to promote a sense of identity between their interests and those of wage-earners and urban consumers by arguing that the tax would promote unemployment in the processing plants and increase the cost of living. Some processors also favored marketing agreements that would exempt them from the antitrust laws, enable them to work out agreements to pay higher prices to the farmer, and allow them to enlarge their profits by charging consumers higher prices. Policy, these businessmen suggested, should be shaped by men who had "spent their lives in the accumulation of expert knowledge of the handling, processing and marketing of the country's grain crops—those engaged in the highly specialized business of grain marketing, and who know most about it," not by "pedagogues . . . who are without practical experience in handling grain, nor are possessed of any comprehension of the divergence from theory involved in the actual transaction of business of this kind."

These critics also challenged the constitutionality of the farm program, charging that it taxed processors (and ultimately consumers) in order to pay producers. The food industries led a legal battle in 1935, seeking injunctions against the collection of the processing taxes. Then, on January 6, 1936, the Supreme Court in *United States* v. *Butler* declared that the processing tax and the production controls violated the Constitution. The case grew out of hostility toward the AAA in the textile industry and the refusal of the receivers of the Hoosac Mills to pay the tax.

The New Deal for agriculture served important interests that were plagued with serious problems in depressed America. Commercial farmers were suffering and needed help, and small as well as large commercial farmers benefited from the farm programs.

Some of the New Dealers concerned with agriculture hoped to produce more than higher prices and higher profits for the commercial farmers. The farm organizations were interested chiefly in raising farm prices, but economists such as Wilson and Tugwell were interested, most of all, in establishing a permanent program of agricultural planning. They were not fully satisfied with the production control program for it simply took part of each farm out of production and did not guarantee that the best use would be made of farmland. Wilson assumed, however, that the farm relief scheme could lead to something better. By calling upon farmers to reduce their acreage, the scheme offered a way to stimulate discussion and planning and thus could open the way for long-range programs in which he had greater confidence. Tugwell hoped that the emergency efforts would evolve into a system of complete control that would restrict commercial agriculture to "the most efficient farmers operating the best of our lands," convert the other lands to other uses, and move the other farmers into other occupations.

After Davis became administrator of the AAA, he established a Division of Program Planning. Headed by Howard Tolley, who had left the University of California to join the AAA, it became the main planning agency in a department that for the first time had authority to plan a national agricultural program and to put the plan into effect. The assignment gave the economist a chance to move the existing program beyond mere reduction in production and to substitute the idea of adjustment.

Plans for reorganizing agriculture so that it could supply all Americans with a proper diet provided a significant illustration of the division's thinking. The Bureau of Home Economics had prepared recommendations for four diets at different levels of nutritive content and cost; and Tolley organized a study that converted the diets into their implications for agricultural production and concluded that, when prosperity and better knowledge of nutrition enabled Americans to consume the diet recommended as best, the United States would need more, not less, land in farms and would need to increase output of some crops and to reduce production of others.

The diet studies represented the planners' emphasis on "planned" or "balanced abundance." This concept implied that the long-run solution to the "farm problem" depended heavily on efficient and expanded industrial production, low industrial prices, full employment, migration to the cities, and high wages. Ezekiel was the department's leading promoter of this theory of the farmer's dependence on the cities, and Wallace both encouraged the economist's work and was influenced by it. It helped him move away from "agricultural fundamentalism," a belief "that agriculture is *par excellence* the fundamental industry, and that farmers are, in a peculiar sense and degree, of basic importance in society."

As head of the Planning Division in 1934 and 1935, Tolley frequently criticized the AAA, arguing, as did Wilson and Tugwell, that it was not producing the most desirable changes. Many features troubled him. The AAA paid little attention to regional and individual differences and did not allow the colleges and farmers to contribute as much as they could to planning. The farm program seemed likely to become rigid and to freeze existing patterns of farming rather than promote conservation and shift the production of crops into the regions in which they could be grown most successfully. The AAA treated each commodity separately, whereas the planners hoped for a regional approach that would recognize that the adjustments needed varied from region to region. Tolley also hoped to use the payments in a positive rather than a negative way. He wanted to pay farmers to improve farm management and to conserve the soil, rather than merely to reduce output.

Tolley's greatest fear was that the farm program would serve only the interests of established commercial farmers. He watched them organize and press their demands, and he warned against the "frequent tendency" of pressure groups "to think in terms of group monopoly rather than public welfare." He had confidence that "thorough education along economic and social lines" could prevent such a development. This education would teach farmers that a nation must import if it wished to export, and that the public interest required soil conservation and low-cost farming. Commercial farmers would also learn that tenants and laborers who were considered undesirable aliens in the industry they served could not be expected to function as "good citizens" within that industry and that the success of the farm program depended heavily upon increased purchasing power among city laboring people.

In line with these ideas, Tolley's division, working closely with Wilson, who was now assistant secretary of agriculture, developed four new projects in 1935. A regional adjustment project brought department and college officials together to study what adjustments in production were needed. The officials concluded that the production of cash crops should be reduced, the output of soil-conserving crops should be increased, and the adoption of soil conservation methods throughout the country would bring production in line with existing markets. A county planning project organized farmers into nearly 2,500 county planning committees in the hope of educating farmers and giving them a chance to shape the adjustment programs. These projects were supplemented by two educational programs, a discussion group program for farmers and "schools of philosophy" for extension workers, which were designed to broaden the outlook of people involved in planning and administering farm programs.

In spite of these encouraging developments, Tolley grew unhappy with the attitudes of officials in his department and returned to his post at the University of California in September 1935. It seemed to him that the AAA had become complacent. Many of its administrators seemed interested only in reducing production, making payments to farmers, and increasing their income. Satisfied with the program, these administrators did not welcome his proposals for change. Furthermore, his superiors, Davis and Wallace, were unwilling to apply pressure, and raised doubts about the political implications of Tolley's proposals and the wisdom of trying to move at the moment.

The Supreme Court, however, accomplished what Tolley could not. It forced the officials to make changes in their program and gave the social scientists a new opportunity to push their ideas successfully. After the decision in January 1936, Davis called Tolley back to Washington to help in the emergency, and the economist found that the justices had revived the old willingness to experiment among those administering the AAA and benefiting from it. Thus, he was able to achieve things he had been trying to achieve. He became the "driving personality" behind the development of the new legislation. Even the farm leaders, who had responded to the Court's action with determination to get new price-raising legislation, listened to the social scientist and endorsed his recommendations. The specific ideas about method came chiefly from the work of the Planning Division, and that work enabled the administration to move rapidly to a new type of program.

Congress quickly passed a new farm law that seemed capable of both conserving the soil and controlling production without running into trouble with the Court. The law established a scheme whereby payments obtained from general revenue were made to farmers who shifted acreage from soil-depleting to soil-conserving crops and employed soil-building practices. Because the soil-depleting crops happened also to be the surplus crops, including wheat and cotton, and the soil-conserving ones, such as grasses and legumes, were not surplus commercial commodities, production seemed certain to be shifted away from surplus crops and brought into line with domestic needs and anticipated exports. Tolley, who replaced Davis as administrator, was convinced that the new program would bring more benefits to the farmer and the nation than its predecessor had.

The new legislation enabled the AAA to participate more actively in the large-scale attack upon land problems that was under way by 1936 and to associate itself more closely with the increasingly popular efforts to conserve the soil. The great drought of the mid-thirties did much to stimulate interest and action. "The states and the nation are now unleashing the greatest broadside attack on land-use problems of our history," Tugwell announced enthusiastically. "If this task is completed, our national heritage will be secure," he prophesied. "If not, we shall go the way of Mesopotamia, Egypt, and China, and part with our collective birthright for a mess of individualistic potage."

The Soil Conservation Service was another agency involved in this work. It had been established in 1935 as part of the Department of Agriculture and was headed by Hugh Bennett, a veteran crusader for conservation. Also in 1935, a model statute was drafted that was designed to enlarge the work of the SCS and enable farmers to work together in the battle against erosion. The proposed statute authorized the establishment of soil conservation districts to carry on erosion control work, help farmers control erosion on their lands, and enforce needed conservation practices on lands of uncooperative farmers. A district was to be established after a majority of the farmers living there endorsed it in a referendum, and the district was to be controlled by them. In 1937, Roosevelt sent letters to all governors urging passage of the legislation; and in the next four years, nearly all states passed soil conservation laws and 548 districts were established.

Also in the mid-thirties, Tugwell developed other programs designed to serve more than the interests of commercial farmers. His efforts followed a dramatic "purge" in the AAA that revealed the difficulties involved in efforts to serve other interests. By 1930, over 45 percent of the nation's farms were operated by tenants; and most of them, especially the sharecroppers in the South, seemed to be caught in a system of permanent poverty. And the AAA did not rescue them. Although nearly three-fourths of the cotton farms were operated by tenants, they were not represented in the development and administration of the cotton program, and it harmed rather than helped many of them. Many received only a small share or no share at all of the benefit payment from the government because the landlords kept all or most of it, and many tenants were demoted from sharecropper, the lowest form of tenancy, to day laborer or evicted from the land as the cuts in production were made.

One group in the AAA developed a strong interest in the cotton tenants. Closely allied with Tugwell, the group was headed by Jerome Frank, an eastern lawyer and legal philosopher serving as head of the agency's Legal Division. Urban rather than rural in background, he and his associates looked upon the AAA as an opportunity for reform.

Early in 1935, the reformers made a bold move. The Southern Tenant Farmers' Union, a new, biracial group developed by Socialists and other critics of the southern way of life and the cotton program, was organizing tenants in the Mississippi delta, and some planters responded by evicting tenants who had joined the union and recruiting substitutes. The official interpretation of the contract between the government and the landowners in the program suggested that they were obligated to keep their normal number of tenants but were not required to keep the same people that had been on their land before 1933. In December 1934, the union took one of the landlords into court to test his right to make such changes. Informed of the episode and of the way in which the contract was being interpreted, the Legal Division issued a reinterpretation that required landlords to keep the same people, not just the same number. The ruling could help both the union and the tenants.

This was an attempt to use the farm program to provide greater security for these low-income people. The lawyers justified their efforts as needed to realize the basic purpose of the legislation. They argued that the goal was the economic welfare of all rural groups, not just the landowners, and that the alternative interpretation of the contract did not provide adequate protection for the tenants.

To Davis, the entire farm program seemed to be threatened by the ruling. It struck him as a dishonest distortion of the meaning of the contract and but another in a long series of impractical acts by the lawyers that had harmed the AAA, preventing it from operating efficiently and effectively and risking the hostility of the leading groups in farm politics. He believed that his agency existed to bring higher prices to commercial farmers, not to reform the southern social system, and he resented the view that the farm program was "entirely worthless so long as it did not result in a social revolution in the South." The AAA's task was economic recovery, a task that seemed to him to be of fundamental importance and one that had to be completed before progress along other lines could take place. He feared attempts to mix social reform with the recovery program. In addition, he had doubts about the ability of the federal government to develop a new social order in the South. Influenced by these beliefs, Davis decided that he must either dismiss the reformers or resign.

Fortunately for Davis, Wallace shared his views of political realities. The secretary had been working for more than a decade to develop a program capable of raising farm prices and had close ties with commercial farmers and their organizations and representatives. He had been growing concerned about the political difficulties the lawyers were generating, and now he believed that they had "allowed their social preconceptions to lead them into something which was not only indefensible from a practical agricultural point of view but also bad law." He denied that the farm legislation gave the department the power "to change the undesirable social system in the South," and, familiar with the "habits and customs" of southern farm leaders and congressmen, he feared that if he followed "the extreme city group there would be such a break with the men on the hill that the agricultural program might be destroyed."

Thus, on February 5, 1935, Davis "purged" Frank and several others from the AAA. The top officials were reluctant to challenge power arrangements in farm politics and were heavily influenced by concern about their relations with the leading farm groups and their allies. A week after the purge, Wallace ruled that the cotton contract did not bind landowners to keep the same tenants. Thereafter, landowners remained dominant in the AAA and received most of the benefits; and the administration, in spite of widespread criticism, remained reluctant to press for change and hopeful that many tenants and farm workers would find better opportunities in the cities.

After the purge, the Roosevelt administration, pressed by criticism from the Tenant Farmers' Union and others and troubled by conditions in the cotton country, did develop a larger and more active interest in the rural poor, but that development took place outside the AAA, as almost all department officials believed it must. In April 1935, Roosevelt established the Resettlement Administration, headed by

Tugwell, one of the boldest of the New Dealers and now a vocal critic of the AAA. The new agency combined and added to the small efforts on behalf of the rural poor that had developed during 1933 and 1934. The RA tried to improve land-use practices and help those who suffered seriously from past mistakes in the use of the land, such as destitute groups living in once-thriving but now exhausted lumbering, mining, and oil regions, sharecroppers in the South, and farmers on poor land in the drought area of the Middle West and in the Appalachians. Although Tugwell personally favored resettlement of the rural poor, his agency placed heavier emphasis on rehabilitation of them in the places they occupied.

The RA's programs assumed that rural poverty demanded an attack upon its causes, not just relief. The situations had taken many years to develop, and only long-run programs could correct them. Nor could solutions come entirely from indirect action, such as the expansion of urban employment. Rural poverty had to be dealt with directly through specially devised programs. And these programs needed to be devised because all Americans, not just the rural poor, suffered from poverty in agriculture, for it meant inadequate purchasing power, destruction of land, disease, and costly social services.

Most important, the planned attack needed to be made because worthy human beings suffered directly from rural poverty. The programs rested on democratic rather than business assumptions, looking upon all men, not just those who had demonstrated abilities in business, as worthy of help from government. Involved was a concept of man that stressed environment rather than innate qualities.

This democratic concept of man did not mean that all of the rural poor should be treated in the same way. Not all of them could be made into commercially successful farmers, for some knew only self-sufficient or plantation agriculture and some had physical or mental deficiencies. Nevertheless, the government should take action. It could help them form cooperatives or obtain more secure tenure arrangements, or it could provide relief. And nearly all of the poor should be provided with the guidance needed to raise their status. All but a few had capacity for improvement, and all were worthy of help.

Resettlement Administration officials agreed that rural America should be approached as something more than simply the home of rural businessmen and that government should do more than increase their profits. The program, in other words, challenged the dominant orientation of farm policies. Not surprisingly, therefore, Tugwell and the Resettlement Administration came under heavy attack and were forced to tackle vast problems with small sums of money.

His experiences in the RA and other frustrations helped to persuade Tugwell to resign after the 1936 election, but programs for the rural poor did not stop with his departure from Washington. In 1937, a

President's Special Committee on Farm Tenancy made a comprehensive analysis of the problems associated with low-income farm groups and a set of proposals relating to them; the Bankhead-Jones Farm Security Act was passed, with provisions on rural rehabilitation and the retirement of submarginal lands and an emphasis on loans to tenants to enable them to buy farms; and a new agency, the Farm Security Administration, was established as a substitute for the RA.

Reflecting the influence of agrarian traditions, the efficient family farm became the main goal of FSA activities. The rehabilitation program, the largest FSA activity, dealt chiefly with poor farmers—owners as well as tenants—who needed loans, grants, guidance, and other forms of help to maintain and improve their farm operations; and the tenant purchase program, the second-largest activity, helped tenants and laborers acquire and develop farms of their own.

The FSA became a significant participant in farm politics, especially in the South, challenging the "*status quo* in American agriculture" and putting pressure on others "to match the FSA in its fight against rural poverty and ignorance, and in its efforts to convert the ideals of democracy into democratic reality." Yet, its concrete accomplishments were small relative to the size of rural poverty. While the rehabilitation program grew for several years, Congress provided only small support for efforts to increase the number of family farmers. In its early years, the FSA was able to provide loans for fewer than 5 percent of the applicants and only 2 percent of the nation's tenants. The number of tenants in the South declined from 1.8 million in 1935 to 1.4 million in 1940; but the number of farm operators also dropped by 400,000 while the number of day laborers increased by nearly 300,000, and many southerners moved out of agriculture. Although there were more than a million Negro tenants and day laborers in the South, the FSA made less than 2,000 tenant purchase loans to blacks. Nationally, tenant farmers were increasing at the rate of 40,000 per year, and the law allowed the FSA to make fewer than 10,000 loans per year. "Obviously," the director of the budget informed Roosevelt, "this . . . program can be regarded as only an experimental approach to the farm tenancy problem."

The administrator of the FSA, Dr. Will Alexander, had a strong interest in poor blacks as well as poor whites. His agency and the RA distributed a significant share of its benefits to blacks; but these agencies did discriminate against Negroes, dealt cautiously with racial problems, and seldom challenged the system of segregation, fearing that boldness would reduce still further their ability to grapple with the problems of poverty. Yet they were bold enough to arouse opposition. In June 1940, Alexander resigned, in part because his appearances before the congressional appropriations committees were being "made increasingly difficult by the opposition of certain powerful southerners and reactionary northerners who concentrated on FSA their ire against the New Deal and their fear of its threat to white supremacy."

Those who hoped to develop large programs for the rural poor had to struggle against the major pressures of farm politics. As a leading student of the subject has observed, "government agricultural policy . . . is largely designed and administered for the benefit of commercial farmers." Two historians of the rural poor in the 1930's have concluded that "the New Deal definitely preserved more than it changed" in the lives of "the lowest economic level of society—the sharecroppers and the tenant farmers" and "allowed the basic pattern of subsidy for landlords and poverty for rural workers to become permanent." And Leonard J. Arrington has concluded from a careful statistical analysis of the operations of agricultural agencies:

> New Deal expenditures were directed not so much toward the poor farm states but at those states which, though with comparatively high farm incomes, experienced the greatest drops in income as the result of the depression. New Deal loans and expenditures, in other words, were primarily relief-oriented. They were not, at least in their dollar impact, reform-oriented or equality-oriented. The prime goal would seem to have been the restoration of income for individual farmers rather than the achievement of a greater equality.

While the FSA was taking shape, Tolley and other ambitious New Dealers obtained a new opportunity to promote their hopes for agricultural planning. In the fall of 1938, Wallace elevated the Bureau of Agricultural Economics to the role of central planner for the department and appointed Tolley chief of the bureau. During 1939 and 1940, Tolley and his lieutenants, with assistance from Wilson, first as under secretary and then as director of the Extension Service, devoted most of their time and energy to the construction of a planning program involving cooperation among the national agricultural agencies, the agricultural colleges and their extension services, and the farmers.

Tolley and his aides hoped to change both farm policy and the way it was made. The bureau pushed many proposals for change in the AAA. Believing it had not done nearly enough to improve the lot of lower-income groups, the social scientists pushed for changes in this area. Recognizing that AAA officials were interested first of all in making payments to farmers and raising farm prices and farm income, the BAE battled for proposals designed to get more conservation from the program.

The efforts to change the policy-making process included efforts to enlarge the role of the farmers, and was illustrated most significantly by the county planning committees. They were organized by the extension services and composed of farmers and state and national officials serving in the counties. Most members were farmers, and a farmer served as chairman.

One feature of the committees troubled Tolley and others: they did not represent all groups in their communities. The county agent usually selected the farmers who served on the committees, and because those agents tended to work most closely with the more substantial members of their communities, the committees seldom included representatives of the rural poor. Early in 1940, Bushrod W. Allin, the head of the BAE's Division of State and Local Planning, listed efforts to improve representation as one of the "next steps" that could "improve the planning process." He had long been interested in establishing "truly representative" planning committees and regarded elected committees as preferable to ones appointed by county agents. Wallace, Wilson, and Tolley also preferred elected committees.

The promoters of the planning program, however, proceeded cautiously in promoting their theory that all rural groups should be represented in the formulation of agricultural programs. The tendency was to try to influence the extension and farm leaders to take the necessary steps. Frequently, however, these leaders resisted. Allin tolerated slow progress, believing that there were several practical reasons why the less-advantaged groups could not now be adequately represented. Some of them moved too frequently; many were not interested; and social barriers blocked participation. Consequently, farmer membership on the planning committees was drawn "too largely from the ranks of the more prosperous farmers and landowners, particularly in those areas where small farmers, tenants, sharecroppers, and farm laborers comprise a heavy majority of the agricultural population." Although he denied that this prevented the committees from developing an interest in the poor, he believed that "the formulation of plans without participation of the people for whose benefit they are made is not all that might be desired in a democratic process." He and his associates were restrained, however, by fear that vigorous attempts to stimulate mass participation in the committees might only alienate the groups whose cooperation seemed essential.

Although the planning activities failed to conform perfectly with the planners' ideals and many officials in the agricultural agencies and the colleges resisted their efforts, Tolley and his colleagues were optimistic. Farmer participation was growing; planning committees were taking shape and participating actively in the planning process; and various educational programs were at work, seeking to promote participation in, and support for, planning. The work of the planning committees, the schools of philosophy, and the discussion groups might change the ideas of enough farmers, county agents, and administrators and generate enough support for planning to enable it to triumph over hostility and to develop a better farm program. "It may be some time yet before the full significance of this program will be well understood in the majority of the counties, but I believe we are making real progress," Tolley wrote to a college official early in 1940. And he reported later in the year:

> Excellent results have been attained in many of the 1,540 counties where the work had been started by July 1, 1940. These results indicate that the method adopted is a sound one, that the program is developing in the right direction, and that farmers are willing to assume the responsibility and local leadership necessary for the work.

Yet the ambitious efforts to improve the lot of the rural poor and develop a system of agricultural planning had alienated the most influential farm organization, the American Farm Bureau Federation. This organization of rural businessmen had worked hard for the passage of the Agricultural Adjustment Act in 1933 and then had provided strong support for the farm program as it developed during the early years of the New Deal. The president, Edward A. O'Neal, was, Wilson informed a friend, "always Johnny on the spot when it comes to fighting battles in defense of these policies." When a group of prominent businessmen formed the Farmers' Independence Council to try to draw farmers away from the AAA, O'Neal had labeled them men who "farm the farmers" and "Wall Street Hayseeds" masquerading as farmers while trying to defeat legislation real farmers wanted. He had seen "too much rugged individualism" and believed that the nation needed "a national plan for agriculture" and "cooperation instead of competition."

For O'Neal, one of the most attractive features of the New Deal was the many opportunities it provided to strengthen his organization. He applauded the administration's practice of working with farm leaders in drafting the farm laws and claimed credit for obtaining the legislative benefits for the commercial farmers. He liked the use made of the Farm Bureau's allies—the extension services with their agents in each agricultural county—in the administration of the program and the efforts to organize farmers into committees to look after it on the local level, seeing them as "a challenge and an opportunity" for the Farm Bureau and urging Farm Bureau leaders to "take the lead in organizing and coordinating these production control committees and associations." Often, extension officials helped the Farm Bureau recruit new members; and as the committees developed, Farm Bureau members became very influential in them. He also saw the discussion program as an opportunity to increase "the effectiveness of our Farm Bureau units in molding public opinion" and in "stimulating interest and participation in local Farm Bureau meetings." He was alert to every opportunity to increase the size and power of his organization.

In the second half of the 1930's, however, the AFBF grew increasingly unhappy with the New Deal. To the organization's leaders, it seemed that the Roosevelt administration had become dominated by the forces of urban liberalism, especially organized labor, and had become biased against the farmer. Wallace and his department seemed to be drawing away from the Farm Bureau, developing new ties with the Farmers' Union, and rejecting the view that their job was to serve the interests of commercial farmers. The officials seemed too interested in the rural poor and the urban consumers. Furthermore, the department's tendency to develop committees of farmers to plan and administer farm programs seemed capable of creating groups that would replace the farm organizations in the policy-making process, depriving the Farm Bureau of its status as the leading spokesman for the farmer and providing department officials with the power needed to dominate farm politics and alter the orientation of farm policy.

Thus, in the late 1930's, Farm Bureau leaders began to make suggestions for changes in the planning and administration of the farm programs. O'Neal and others criticized the participation of nonfarm groups and called for heavy reliance on the farm organizations and the extension services.

In 1940, the farm organization perfected its proposals. Its Washington office supplied O'Neal with a report charging that the administration of the farm programs was characterized by duplication and overlapping and denying that the planning project had ended duplication. The project, in fact, involved, according to the report, the danger of federal domination of state and county planning and usurped functions of the farmers' own groups by developing new organizations rather than relying on existing ones to deal with problems normally handled by them. The report charged that the project duplicated objectives that earlier had prompted the department to promote the development of the Farm Bureau. Finally, in December, the farm group proposed the establishment of a five-man nonpartisan board, representative of agriculture, to plan and administer farm programs on the national level and reliance on the extension services in handling those functions on the state and local levels.

The farm organization felt both threatened and capable of expanding its power. "The fundamental aim," Christiana Campbell has demonstrated, "was to take control of agricultural programs away from the Department of Agriculture, which was believed to be no longer the farmers' advocate, and give it to the farmers themselves (i.e., the organized farmers)." As a consequence of the power of the Farm Bureau among farm organizations and its influence upon the extension services, the recommendations, if put into effect, would inevitably produce an especially large increase in the power of that farm organization. It did not want to remove the government from agriculture. The organization wanted only to guarantee that it would shape the role that the government played.

The Farm Bureau that had become highly critical of the New Deal was a larger, stronger group than the one that had supported it earlier. Massive membership drives, involving efforts to exploit the organization's ties with the AAA and Extension, had been very successful after 1932, especially in the South. "In all four regions," Campbell writes, "the increase in membership during the New Deal period was striking, but the percentage increase in the South was by far the greatest." In 1933, the organization had but slightly more than 150,000 members; by 1940, it had nearly 450,000. By then, as Grant McConnell had written, it "had established itself in a position of preeminence among farm organizations." In the South especially, George Tindall writes, no farm group "had the durability or influence to offer an alternative to what the *Louisiana Union Farmer* called the 'company union' headed by 'Ed O'Neal, big Alabama cotton planter.'"

The Farm Bureau had become a very substantial obstacle in the path of New Dealers who hoped to serve more than the business interests of commercial farmers, and it could count on very strong support in Congress. The organization had significant links with the conservative coalition that had taken shape there and was strong enough by the end of the 1930's to block major extensions of administration programs. Many members of the coalition were southern Democrats, although not all southerners were conservative and not all conservatives were southern. Most conservatives represented rural areas; resented the sharp increase in the power and influence within the Democratic party and the national administration of urban groups, especially organized labor and northern Negroes; disliked many features of the New Deal, such as deficit spending and welfare programs; and distrusted organized labor and feared prospects for the future, including the possibility that major efforts would be made to alter race relations. Thus, New Dealers who advocated additional innovations faced opponents who offered powerful resistance to further change.

The New Deal for agriculture had, in a sense, created its own strong opponent. The New Deal farm programs had at least created a situation that O'Neal and other hard-driving men were able to exploit successfully in order to develop a large organization.

The growth of the AFBF, like the development of the production control program, represented ways in which the New Deal protected and promoted the development of collective capitalism. Rather than attempt to destroy business organizations and business power, the New Deal tried to fit the farmer into the system. He was advised to organize as other businessmen organized and to regulate production as powerful corporations did. Above all, the New Deal made government much more important in his life. Public organizations such as the AAA and the Soil Conservation Service became very active in rural America and moved the farmer several giant steps farther away from an individualistic economic system. He emerged from the 1930's more dependent on others than ever before. Encouraged to move with rather than against the development of a collectivist type of capitalism, he had done so.

The Roosevelt administration was committed to capitalism. It did not try to break with that aspect of the American past. But the administration did not merely accept the system that had evolved by 1933. It was determined to make changes in it, as well as to preserve it, and the changes in American agriculture were some of the New Deal's more important accomplishments. American agriculture did not welcome all attempts to change it, however. The most ambitious New Dealers discovered that as the period moved forward. By the end of the thirties, their heads were still filled with ideas for change, but the forces of resistance had become very strong. The New Deal for agriculture challenges Barton Bernstein's suggestion that the New Deal "ran out of fuel not because of conservative opposition, but because it ran out of ideas."

Agricultural developments in the 1930's suggest that the New Deal promoted significant though not revolutionary changes. It did not promote a social revolution. Rural poverty remained a large part of American life at the end of the decade as it had been at the beginning. If the New Deal rescued farmers who had been impoverished by the depression, it did not provide much help for rural people who had lived below the poverty line before the depression hit. Furthermore, the New Deal did not replace capitalism with another system. Washington in the 1930's looked upon the farmer as a businessman, worked to make his business profitable, and worked also to persuade him not to move in radical directions. Nevertheless, as its farm policies also suggest, the New Deal did change the structure of American capitalism. This was its most important and fundamental accomplishment. The federal government became much more important in agriculture, and more farmers than ever before were drawn into organizations. Similar changes took place elsewhere. The federal government became more important in many areas of American life, and other groups were organized. The substantial enlargement of the labor movement was one of the most significant developments of the decade. At the same time, business organizations survived the depression crisis. Thus, the New Deal for agriculture was part of a larger story involving, above all, the continued and accelerated evolution of a collectivist or organizational type of capitalism. By 1940, the American farmer worked in a system that was dominated by the interplay among large public and private organizations.

5 The New Deal and the Emergence of Mass-Production Unionism

DAVID BRODY

In the following selection, David Brody, a professor of history at the University of California (Davis) and one of the foremost American labor historians, demonstrates the New Deal's revolutionary impact upon the American worker. He argues persuasively that the Wagner Act and the general prolabor political climate of the New Deal era made it possible to organize the skilled and semiskilled labor of the mass-production industries. By guaranteeing the right of collective bargaining, providing protection for union members and organizers, and establishing procedures for determining bargaining agents, the Wagner Act brought unprecedented change to American labor-management relations. The prolabor attitude of New Deal politicians ensured full and benevolent enforcement of labor's rights; as a result, many of the problems that had destroyed young unions in the past were eliminated.

Yet even the legislation of the New Deal could not compel genuine collective bargaining; nor could it assure that stubborn corporations would grant anything more than union recognition. Unionism in the mass-production industries received its initial impetus from the New Deal, but was made secure only by World War II. Full employment and a friendly federal intervention in the collective bargaining process established the new industrial unionism beyond recall. The war had consolidated and institutionalized labor's New Deal.

* * *

From "The Emergence of Mass-Production Unionism," by David Brody in *Change and Continuity in Twentieth-Century America,* edited by John Braeman, Robert H. Bremner, and Everett Walters, pp. 243–262. Copyright © 1964 by the Ohio State University Press. All rights reserved. Reprinted by permission of the Ohio State University Press.

In the 1930's, a new legal framework for industrial relations emerged. In the past, the right to organize had fallen outside the law; unionization, like collective bargaining, had been a private affair. Within normal legal limits, employers had freely fought the organization of their employees. Now that liberty was being withdrawn. World War I had first raised the point. The National War Labor Board had protected workers from discrimination for joining unions and thus contributed substantially to the temporary union expansion of the war period. The lesson was inescapable. Unionization in the mass-production industries depended on public protection of the right to organize. The drift of opinion in this direction was discernible in the Railway Labor Act of 1926 and the Norris-LaGuardia Act of 1932. But the real opportunity came with the advent of the New Deal. Then key union spokesmen, notably [William] Green and [John L.] Lewis, pressed for the insertion of the famous section 7a in the National Industrial Recovery Act. After an exhilarating start, section 7a foundered; loopholes developed and enforcement broke down long before the invalidation of the NRA. But the intent of section 7a was clear, and it soon received effective implementation.

"If the Wagner bill is enacted," John L. Lewis told the AF of L Executive Council in May 1935, "there is going to be increasing organization. . . ." The measure, enacted on July 5, 1935, heavily influenced Lewis' decision to take the initiative that led to the CIO. For the Wagner Act did adequately protect the right to organize through a National Labor Relations Board clothed with powers of investigation and enforcement. Employer opposition was at long last neutralized.

The Act made it an unfair labor practice for an employer "to interfere with, restrain, or coerce employees in the exercise" of "the right of self-organization." This protection unquestionably freed workers from fear of employer discrimination. Stipulation cases required the posting of such notices as the following at a Sioux City plant:

> The Cudahy Packing Company wants its definitely understood that . . . no one will be discharged, demoted, transferred, put on less desirable jobs, or laid off because he joins Local No. 70 or any other labor organization. . . . If the company, its officers, or supervisors have in the past made any statements or taken any action to indicate that its employees were not free to join Local No. 70 or any other labor organization, these statements are now repudiated.

Even more persuasive was the reinstatement with back pay of men discharged for union activities. The United Auto Workers' cause at Ford was immensely bolstered in 1941 by the rehiring of twenty-two discharged men as the result of an NLRB decision which the company had fought up to the Supreme Court. By June 30, 1941, nearly twenty-

four thousand charges of unfair labor practices—the majority involving discrimination—had been lodged with the NLRB. More important
in the long run, vigorous enforcement encouraged obedience of the
law among employers. Assured of their safety, workers flocked into the
unions.

The law also resolved the knotty problems of determining union
representation. During the NRA period, company unions had been
widely utilized to combat the efforts of outside organizations. The
Wagner Act now prohibited employers from dominating or supporting
a labor union. Legal counsel at first held that "inside" unions could be
made to conform with the law by changing their structure, that is, by
eliminating management participation from the joint representation
plans. The NLRB, however, required the complete absence of company interference or assistance. Few company unions could meet this
high standard, and large numbers were disestablished by NLRB order
or by stipulation. In meat-packing, for instance, the Big Four companies had to withdraw recognition for over fifteen company unions.
Only in the case of some Swift plants did such bodies prevail over
outside unions in representation elections and become legal bargaining
agents. Besides eliminating employer-dominated unions, the law put
the selection of bargaining representatives on the basis of majority rule.
By mid-1941, the NLRB had held nearly 6,000 elections and cross-
checks, involving nearly 2 million workers. Given a free choice, they
overwhelmingly preferred a union to no union (the latter choice resulting in only 6 percent of elections in 1937 and, on the average, in less
than 20 percent up to the passage of the Taft-Hartley Act). Having
proved its majority in an "appropriate" unit, a union became the certi-
fied bargaining agent for all employees in the unit.

An unexpected dividend for union organization flowed from the
Wagner Act. In the past, the crisis of mass-production unions had
occurred in their first stage. Rank-and-file pressure normally built up
for quick action. Union leaders faced the choice of bowing to this
sentiment and leading their organizations into suicidal strikes—as happened on the railroads in 1894, in the stockyards in 1904, and in steel
in 1919—or of resisting the pressure and seeing the membership melt
away or break up in factional conflict—as occurred in meat-packing
after World War I. The Wagner Act, while it did not eliminate rank-
and-file pressures, eased the problem. A union received NLRB certification on proving its majority in a plant. Certification gave it legal
status and rights which could be withdrawn only by formal evidence
that it lacked majority support. Defeat in a strike did not in any way
affect the status of a bargaining agent. Restraint, on the other hand,
became a feasible policy. The CIO unions as a whole were remarkably
successful in resisting workers' demands for national strikes in the early

years, although not in preventing local trouble. The resulting dissidence could be absorbed. The Packinghouse Workers Organizing Committee, for instance, was in continual turmoil from 1939 to 1941 because of the conservative course of Chairman Van A. Bittner; but internal strife did not lead to organizational collapse there or elsewhere. NLRB certification permitted labor leaders to steer between the twin dangers—external and internal—that earlier had smashed vigorous mass-production unionism.

Years later, the efficacy of the Wagner Act was acknowledged by an officer of the most hostile of the major packing firms: ". . . The unions would not have organized Wilson [& Company] if it had not been for the Act." That judgment was certainly general in open-shop circles.

Yet the Wagner Act was not the whole story. For nearly two years while its constitutionality was uncertain, the law was virtually ignored by anti-union employers. And after the Jones and Laughlin decision in April 1937, the effect was part of a larger favoring situation. John L. Lewis was not reacting to a single piece of legislation. He saw developing in the mid-1930's a general shift toward unionization.

The change was partly in the workers themselves. Their accommodation to the industrial system had broken down under the long stretch of depression. The resulting resentment was evident in the sitdown strikes of 1936–37, which involved almost half a million men. These acts were generally not a calculated tactic of the union leadership; in fact President Sherman Dalrymple of the Rubber Workers at first opposed the sitdowns. Spontaneous sitdowns within the plants accounted for the initial victories in auto and rubber. Much of Lewis' sense of urgency in 1935 sprang from his awareness of the pressure mounting in the industrial ranks. A local auto-union leader told Lewis in May 1935 of talk about craft unions' taking skilled men from the federal unions. "We say like h—— they will and if it is ever ordered and enforced there will be one more independent union." Threats of this kind, Lewis knew, would surely become actions under existing AF of L policy, and, as he warned the Executive Council, then "we are facing the merging of these independent unions in some form of national organization." That prophecy, Lewis was determined, should come to pass under his control. The CIO succeeded in large measure because it became the vehicle for channeling the militancy released by the Great Depression.

The second factor that favored union organization was the impact of the depression on the major employers. They had operated on a policy of welfare capitalism: company paternalism and industrial-relations methods were expected to render employees impervious to the blandishments of trade unionism. The depression forced the abandonment of much of this expense and, beyond that, destroyed the workers' faith in the company's omnipotence on which their loyalty rested. Among themselves, as an official of Swift and Company said, industrialists had to admit that grounds existed for "the instances of open dissatisfaction which we see about us, and perhaps with us. . . ."

The depression also tended to undermine the will to fight unionization. Anti-union measures were costly, the La Follette investigation revealed. The resulting labor troubles, in addition, cut deeply into income. The Little Steel companies, Republic in particular, operated significantly less profitably in 1937 than did competitors who were free of strikes. Economic considerations seemed most compelling, not when business was bad, but when it was getting better. Employers then became very reluctant to jeopardize the anticipated return of profitable operations. This apparently influenced the unexpected decision of U.S. Steel to recognize the Steel Workers Organizing Committee. In 1937 the Steel Corporation was earning substantial profits for the first time during the depression; net income before taxes that year ultimately ran to $130 million. And the first British purchases for defense were just then in the offing. During the upswing, moreover, the competitive factor assumed increasing importance. Union firms had the advantage of avoiding the disruptions incident to conflict over unionization. Certainly a decline of 15 percent in its share of the automobile market from 1939 to 1940 contributed to the Ford Company's retreat of the following year.

Finally, the political situation—the Wagner Act aside—was heavily weighted on the side of labor. Management could no longer assume governmental neutrality or, under stress, assistance in the labor arena. The benefits accruing to organized labor took a variety of forms. The Norris-LaGuardia Act limited the use of injunctions that had in the past hindered union tactics. A federal law prohibited the transportation of strike-breakers across state lines. The *Thornhill* decision (1940) declared that antipicketing laws curbed the constitutional right of free speech. Detrimental governmental action, standard in earlier times of labor trouble, was largely precluded now by the emergence of sympathetic officeholders on all levels, from the municipal to the national. Indeed, the inclination was in the opposite direction. The response to the sitdown strike illustrated the change. "Well, it is illegal," Roosevelt commented. "But shooting it out and killing a lot of people because they have violated the law of tresspass . . . [is not] the answer. . . . There must be another way. Why can't those fellows in General Motors meet with the committee of workers?" This tolerance of unlawful labor acts, as sitdowns were generally acknowledged to be, could not have happened at any earlier period of American history. These were negative means of forwarding the labor cause.

But political power was also applied in positive ways. The La Follette investigation* undermined antiunion tactics by exposure and, among other ways, by feeding information on spies to the unions. At critical junctures, there was intercession by public officials ranging from President Roosevelt and Labor Secretary Perkins down to Mayor Kelly of Chicago. Governor Frank Murphy's role in the General Motors controversy is only the best known of a number of such mediating contributions to the union cause. At the start of the CIO steel drive Pennsylvania's Lieutenant-Governor Thomas Kennedy, a Mine Workers' officer, announced that organizers were free to move into steel towns and that state relief funds would be available in the event of a steel strike. The re-election of Roosevelt in 1936 no doubt cast out lingering hopes; many employers bowed to the inevitable after FDR's smashing victory with labor support.

These broader circumstances—rank-and-file enthusiasm, economic pressures on management, and the political condition—substantially augmented the specific benefits flowing from the Wagner Act. In fact, the great breakthroughs at U.S. Steel and General Motors in early 1937 did not result from the law. The question of constitutionality was resolved only some weeks later. And the agreements themselves did not accord with the provisions of the Wagner Act. The unions dared not utilize procedures for achieving certification as bargaining agents in the auto and steel plants. Lee Pressman, counsel for the SWOC, later admitted that recognition could not then have been won "without Lewis' brilliant move" in his secret talks with U.S. Steel's Myron C. Taylor.

> There is no question that [the SWOC] could not have filed a petition through the National Labor Relations Board . . . for an election. We could not have won an election for collective bargaining on the basis of our own membership or the results of the organizing campaign to date. This certainly applied not only to Little Steel but also to Big Steel.

Similarly, the *New York Times* reported on April 4, 1937: "Since the General Motors settlement, the union has been spreading its organization rapidly in General Motors plants, which were weakly organized at the time of the strike." The NLRB could not require either U.S. Steel or General Motors to make agreements with unions under those circumstances. Nor did the companies grant the form of recognition contemplated in the Wagner Act, that is, as *exclusive* bargaining agents. (This would have been illegal under the circumstances.) Only employees who were union members were covered by the two agreements. These initial CIO victories, opening the path as they did for the general

---

*In the late 1930's, a Senate committee headed by Robert La Follette, Jr., extensively investigated antilabor activities in the United States.—Ed.

advance of mass-production unionism, stemmed primarily from the wider pressures favorable to organized labor.

The Wagner Act proved indecisive for one whole stage of unionization. More than the enrollment of workers and the attainment of certification as bargaining agent was needed in unionization. The process was completed only when employers and unions entered bona fide collective bargaining. But this could not be enforced by law. Meaningful bargaining was achievable ultimately only through the interplay of non-legislative forces.

The tactics of major employers had shifted significantly by the 1920's. Their open-shop doctrine had as its declared purpose the protection of workingmen's liberties. "We do not believe it to be the wish of the people of this country," a U.S. Steel official had said, "that a man's right to work shall be made dependent upon his membership in any organization." Since the closed shop was assumed to follow inevitably from collective bargaining, the refusal to recognize unions was the fixed corollary of the open shop. The argument, of course, cut both ways. Open-shop employers insisted that their employees were free to join unions (whether or not this was so). The important fact, however, was that the resistance to unionism was drawn tight at the line of recognition and collective bargaining. That position had frustrated the attempt of the President's Industrial Conference of October 1919 to formulate principles for "genuine and lasting cooperation between capital and labor." The union spokesmen had withdrawn in protest against the insistence of the employer group that the obligation to engage in collective bargaining referred only to shop committees, not to trade unions. In effect, the strategy was to fight organized labor by withholding its primary function.

Federal regulation of labor relations gradually came to grips with the question of recognition and collective bargaining. During World War I, the NWLB only required employers to deal with shop committees. Going further, the NRA granted employees the right to "bargain collectively through representatives of their own choosing. . . ." This was interpreted to imply an obligation of employers to deal with such representatives. The major failing of section 7a was that the NRA did not implement the interpretation. In practice, determined employers were able, as earlier, to escape meaningful negotiation with trade unions. It seems significant that the permanent union gains of the NRA period came in those areas—the coal and garment industries—where collective bargaining did not constitute a line of employer resistance. Profiting by the NRA experience, the Wagner Act established the procedure for determining bargaining agents and the policy of exclusive representation and, by the device of certification, withdrew recognition from the option of an employer.

But recognition did not mean collective bargaining. Section 8 (5) did require employers to bargain with unions chosen in accordance with the law. Compliance, however, was another matter. In the first years, hostile employers attempted to withhold the normal attributes of collective bargaining. When a strike ended at the Goodyear Akron plant in November 1937, for example, the company insisted that the agreement take the form of a "memorandum" signed by the mediating NLRB regional director, not by company and union, and added that "in no event could the company predict or discuss the situation beyond the first of the year." (Although the Rubber Workers' local had already received certification, it would not secure a contract for another four years.) Westinghouse took the position that collective bargaining "was simply an opportunity for representatives of the employees to bring up and discuss problems affecting the working force, with the final decision reserved to the company. It rejected the notion of a signed agreement because business conditions were too uncertain. . . ." Some companies—for instance, Armour in April 1941—unilaterally raised wages while in union negotiations. The contractual forms were resisted: agreements had to be verbal, or take the form of a "statement of policy," or, if in contractual terms, certainly with no signatures. These blatant evasions of the intent of section 8 (5) were gradually eliminated: a series of NLRB and court rulings prohibited the refusal to negotiate or make counteroffers, the unilateral alteration of the terms of employment, and opposition to incorporating agreements into written and signed contracts.

The substance proved more elusive than the externals of collective bargaining. "We have no trouble negotiating with Goodyear," a local union president observed, "but we can never bargain. The company stands firmly against anything which does not give them the absolute final decision on any question." The law, as it was interpreted, required employers to bargain "in good faith." How was lack of good faith to be proved? The NLRB tried to consider the specific circumstances and acts, rather than the words, of the employer in each case. That cumbersome procedure was almost useless from the union standpoint. Delay was easy during the case, and further evasion possible afterward. Barring contempt proceedings after a final court order, moreover, the employer suffered no penalties for his obstruction; there was no counterpart here for the back-pay provisions in dismissal cases. The union weakness was illustrated at Wilson & Co. The Cedar Rapids packing plant had been well organized since the NRA period, but no agreement was forthcoming from the hostile management. In 1938 the union filed charges with the NLRB. Its decision came in January 1940, and another year was consumed by the company's unsuccessful appeal to the Circuit Court. The negotiations that followed (interrupted by a strike which the union lost) led nowhere because, a union official reported, Wilson "as always . . . tried to force the Union to accept the Company's agreement or none at all." The contract which was finally consummated in 1943 resulted neither from an NLRB ruling nor from the free collective bargaining that was the aim of the Wagner Act. Clearly, "good faith" was not to be extracted from recalcitrant employers by government fiat.

The collective-bargaining problem had a deeper dimension. The bitter-enders themselves constituted a minority group in American industry. For every Westinghouse, Goodyear, Ford, and Republic Steel there were several major competitors prepared to abide by the intent of the law and enter "sincere negotiations with the representatives of employees." But, from the union standpoint, collective bargaining was important for the results it could yield. Here the Wagner Act stopped. As the Supreme Court noted in the Sands case, "from the duty of the employer to bargain collectively . . . there does not flow any duty . . . to accede to the demands of the employees." No legal force sustained the objectives of unions either in improving wages, hours, and conditions or in strengthening their position through the union shop, master contracts, and arbitration of grievances.

The small utility of the law in collective bargaining was quickly perceived by labor leaders. The CIO packinghouse union, for instance, did not invoke the Wagner Act at all in its three-year struggle with Armour. The company, in fact, objected to the intercession of Secretary of Labor Perkins in 1939 on the ground that the union had not exhausted, or even utilized, the remedies available through the NLRB. The dispute actually did involve issues which fell within the scope of the Wagner Act. But the union clearly was seeking more effective ways—federal pressure in this case—of countering Armour's reluctance to negotiate and sign contracts. For the prime union objective was a master contract covering all the plants of the company organized by the union, a concession which could only be granted voluntarily by the company. Collective bargaining, both the process itself and the fruits, depended on the working of the other advantages open to the unions in the New Deal era.

Where negotiation was undertaken in "good faith," there were modest initial gains. The year 1937, marking the general beginning of collective bargaining in mass production, saw substantial wage increases as the result of negotiations and/or union pressure. In steel, the advances of November 1936 and March 1937 moved the unskilled hourly rate from 47 cents to 62.5 cents. In rubber, average hourly earnings rose from 69.8 cents to 76.8 cents; in automobiles, from 80 to 93 cents. Other gains tended to be slender. The U.S. Steel agreement, for instance, provided the two major benefits of time-and-a-half after eight hours and a grievance procedure with arbitration. The vacation provision, on the other hand, merely continued an existing arrangement, and silence prevailed on many other questions. The contracts were, in contrast to later ones, very thin documents. Still, the first fruits of collective bargaining were encouraging to labor.

Then the economy faltered again. In 1938 industrial unions had to fight to stave off wage cuts. They succeeded in most, but not all, cases. Rates were reduced 15 percent at Philco after a four months' strike. Less visible concessions had to be granted in some cases. For example, the SWOC and UAW accepted changes which weakened the grievance procedure at U.S. Steel and General Motors. The mass-production unions were, in addition, hard hit by the recession. Employment fell sharply. The UAW estimated that at the end of January 1938, 320,000 auto production workers were totally unemployed and most of the remainder of the normal complement of 517,000 were on short time. The union's membership was soon down to 90,000. It was the same story elsewhere. In the Chicago district of the SWOC, dues payments fell by two-thirds in the twelve months after July 1937 (that is, after absorbing the setback in Little Steel). Declining membership and, in some cases, internal dissension rendered uncertain the organizational viability of the industrial unions. And their weakness in turn further undermined their effectiveness in collective bargaining. They faced a fearful choice. If they became quiescent, they would sacrifice the support of the membership. If they pressed for further concessions, they would unavoidably become involved in strikes. By so doing, they would expose their weakened ranks in the one area in which labor legislation permitted the full expression of employer hostility—and in this period few even of the law-abiding employers were fully reconciled to trade unionism.

Collective bargaining was proving a severe obstacle to the new mass-production unions. The Wagner Act had little value here; and the other favoring circumstances had declining effectiveness after mid-1937. Hostile employers were evading the requirement of negotiating in good faith. For the larger part, the industrial unions achieved the first approximation of collective bargaining. But from 1937 to 1940 very little more was forthcoming. The vital function of collective bargaining seemed stalled. The situation was, in sum, still precarious five years after the formation of the CIO.

John L. Lewis had made something of a miscalculation. The promise of the New Deal era left mass-production unionism short of permanent success. Ultimately, two fortuitous circumstances rescued the industrial unions.

The outbreak of World War II finally ended the American depression. By 1941, the economy was becoming fully engaged in defense production. Corporate profits before taxes leaped from $6.5 billion in 1939 to $17 billion in 1941. The number of unemployed fell from 8.5

million in June 1940 to under 4 million in December 1941. It was this eighteen-month period that marked the turning point for the CIO. Industry's desire to capitalize on a business upswing, noted earlier, was particularly acute now; and rising job opportunities and prices created a new militancy in the laboring ranks. The open-shop strongholds began to crumble. Organization came to the four Little Steel companies, to Ford, and to their lesser counterparts. The resistance to collective bargaining, where it had been the line of conflict, was also breaking down. First contracts were finally being signed by such companies as Goodyear, Armour, Cudahy, Westinghouse, Union Switch and Signal. Above all, collective bargaining after a three-year gap began to produce positive results. On April 14, 1941, U.S. Steel set the pattern for its industry with an increase of ten cents an hour. For manufacturing generally, average hourly earnings from 1940 to 1941 increased over 10 percent and weekly earnings 17 percent; living costs rose only 5 percent. More than wages was involved. Generally, initial contracts were thoroughly renegotiated for the first time, and this produced a wide range of improvements in vacation, holiday, and seniority provisions and in grievance procedure. Mass-production workers could now see the tangible benefits flowing from their union membership. These results of the defense prosperity were reflected in union growth: CIO membership jumped from 1,350,000 in 1940 to 2,850,000 in 1941.

The industrial unions were arriving at a solid basis. That achievement was insured by the second fortuitous change. American entry in the war necessitated a major expansion of the federal role in labor-management relations. To prevent strikes and inflation, the federal government had to enter the hitherto private sphere of collective bargaining. The National War Labor Board largely determined the wartime terms of employment in American industry. This emergency circumstance, temporary although it was, had permanent consequences for mass-production unionism. The wartime experience disposed of the last barriers to viable collective bargaining.

For one thing, the remaining vestiges of anti-unionism were largely eliminated. The hard core of resistance could now be handled summarily. In meat-packing, for instance, Wilson & Co. had not followed Armour, Swift, and Cudahy in accepting collective bargaining. In 1942 the NWLB ordered the recalcitrant firm to negotiate a master contract (Wilson was holding to the earlier Big Four resistance to company-wide bargaining). Years later in 1955, a company official was still insisting that Wilson would not have accepted "a master agreement if it had not been for the war. Such an agreement is an unsatisfactory arrangement; today or yesterday." Subsequent negotiations having yielded no results, a Board panel itself actually wrote the first Wilson contract.

Beyond such flagrant cases, the NWLB set to rest an issue deeply troubling to the labor-management relationship in mass production. With few exceptions, the open shop remained dogma even after the acceptance of unionism. "John, it's just as wrong to make a man join a union," Benjamin Fairless of U.S. Steel insisted to Lewis, ". . . as it is to dictate what church he should belong to." The union shop had been granted in auto by Ford only; in rubber, by the employers of a tenth of the men under contract; in steel, by none of the major producers (although they had succumbed under pressure in the "captive mines"). The issue was profoundly important to the new unions. The union shop meant membership stability and, equally significant, the full acceptance of trade unionism by employers. The NWLB compromised the charged issue on the basis of a precedent set by the prewar National Defense Mediation Board. Maintenance-of-membership prevented members from withdrawing from a union during the life of a contract. Adding an escape period and often the dues checkoff, the NWLB had granted this form of union security in 271 of 291 cases by February 1944. The CIO regarded maintenance-of-membership as a substantial triumph. And, conversely, some employers took the measure, as Bethlehem and Republic Steel asserted, to be a "camouflaged closed shop." Among the expressions of resentment was the indication in contracts, following the example of Montgomery Ward, that maintenance-of-membership was being granted "over protest." This resistance, however, was losing its force by the end of the war. The union shop then generally grew from maintenance-of-membership.

The war experience also served a vital educational function. A measure of collective bargaining remained under wartime government regulation. Both before and after submission of cases to the NWLB, the parties involved were obliged to negotiate, and their representatives had to participate in the lengthy hearings. From this limited kind of confrontation, there grew the consensus and experience essential to the labor-management relationship. Wartime education had another aspect. The wage-stabilization policy, implemented through the Little Steel formula by the NWLB, tended to extend the issues open to negotiation. Abnormal restraint on wages convinced labor, as one CIO man said, that "full advantage must be taken of what leeway is afforded" to achieve "the greatest possible gains. . . ." As a result the unions began to include in their demands a variety of new kinds of issues (some merely disguised wage increases) such as premium pay, geographical differentials, wage-rate inequalities, piece-rate computation, and a host of "fringe" payments. Thus were guidelines as to what was negotiable fixed for use after the war and a precedent set that would help further to expand the scope of collective bargaining. The collapse of economic stabilization then also would encourage the successive wage increases of the postwar rounds of negotiation. However illusory these gains were in terms of real income, they endowed the industrial unions with a reputation for effectiveness.

Finally, the wartime restrictions permitted the groping advance toward stable relations to take place in safety. The danger of strikes that might have pushed the parties back to an earlier stage of hostilities was eliminated. Strikes there were in abundance in the postwar period, but these could then be held to the objective of the terms of employment, not the issue of unionism itself. Nothing revealed more of the new state of affairs than the first major defeat of an industrial union. The packing-house strike of 1948 was a thorough union disaster in an industry traditionally opposed to trade unionism. Yet the United Packinghouse Workers of America recovered and prospered. As one of its officials noted with relief, it was the first time in the history of the industry that a "'lost' strike did not mean a lost union."

Unionization thus ran its full course in mass production. The way had been opened by the New Deal and the Great Depression. The legal right to organize was granted, and its utilization was favored by contemporary circumstances. John L. Lewis seized the unequalled opportunity. Breaking from the bounds of the labor establishment, he created in the CIO an optimum instrument for organizing the mass-production workers. These developments did not carry unionization to completion. There was, in particular, a failure in collective bargaining. In the end, the vital progress here sprang fortuitously from the defense prosperity and then the wartime impact on labor relations. From the half-decade of war, the industrial unions advanced to their central place in the American economy.

6 The New Deal and the Problem of Monopoly

ELLIS W. HAWLEY

In this selection from his brilliant monograph, *The New Deal and the Problem of Monopoly*, Ellis W. Hawley, a professor of history at the University of Iowa, argues that New Deal policy toward business was economically illogical yet politically successful because it reflected the divided yearnings of the American people. Americans, he believes, had accepted the benefits and practical necessity of corporate bigness but longed for the simplicity and opportunity of an old competitive order. Roosevelt's approach to the question of monopoly was highly inconsistent but, "his mixed emotions so closely reflected the popular mind that they were a political asset rather than a liability." This inconsistency, this divided mind, Hawley argues, characterized the New Deal from beginning to end.

Hawley does feel that there was a rough shift in emphasis from a First New Deal built around the concept of central economic planning to a Second New Deal based on antitrust sentiment. But the First New Deal failed to impose any real central planning on the economy; indeed the American tradition of competitive individualism made genuine central planning impossible. Acting through the NRA, the First New Deal instead gave government sanction to many disjointed and uncoordinated monopolistic agreements; it also maintained a rhetorical commitment to the competitive ethic.

On the other hand, when the New Deal emphasis moved to antimonopoly, the shift was sharply limited by practical considerations. However much Americans might idealize the past, they appreciated the progress that bigness had brought. In addition, a serious antitrust program might well have caused deflationary business disruptions and worsened the depression. Consequently, the effort that developed was ritualistic. Thurman Arnold's program "made no real effort to rearrange the underlying industrial structure itself, no real attempt to dislodge vested interests, disrupt controls that were actual checks against deflation, or break up going concerns." And the creation of the Temporary National Economic Committee in Congress was a method of avoiding decisions rather than arriving at definite programs.

In the end, the New Deal made little change in the structure of American business. It instead attempted to restore prosperity by organizing agriculture and labor as countervailing powers and by moving toward a policy of compensatory government spending. These were rather radical departures, but they allowed the nation to continue its evasion of an even more fundamental decision.

* * *

"Two souls dwell in the bosom of this Administration," wrote Dorothy Thompson in 1938, "as indeed, they do in the bosom of the American people. The one loves the Abundant Life, as expressed in the cheap and plentiful products of large-scale mass production and distribution. . . . The other soul yearns for former simplicities, for decentralization, for the interests of the 'little man,' revolts against high-pressure salesmanship, denounces 'monopoly' and 'economic empires,' and seeks means of breaking them up." "Our Administration," she continued, "manages a remarakable . . . stunt of being . . . in favor of organizing and regulating the Economic Empires to greater and greater efficiency, and of breaking them up as a tribute to perennial American populist feeling."

Dorothy Thompson was a persistent critic of the Roosevelt administration; yet her remarks did show considerable insight into the dilemma that confronted New Dealers, and indeed, the dilemma that confronted industrial America. The problem of reconciling liberty and order, individualism and collective organization, was admittedly an ancient one, but the creation of a highly integrated industrial system in a land that had long cherished its liberal, democratic, and individualistic traditions presented the problem in a peculiarly acute form. Both the American people and their political leaders tended to view modern industrialism with mingled feelings of pride and regret. On one hand, they tended to associate large business units and economic organization with abundance, progress, and a rising standard of living. On the other, they associated them with a wide variety of economic abuses, which, because of past ideals and past standards, they felt to be injurious to society. Also, deep in their hearts, they retained a soft spot for the "little fellow." In moments of introspection, they looked upon the immense concentrations of economic power that they had created and accused them of destroying the good life, of destroying the independent businessman and the satisfactions that came from owning one's own business and working for oneself, of Americans to a race of clerks and machine tenders, of creating an impersonal, mechanized world that destroyed man as an individual.

The search in twentieth-century America, then, was for some solution that would reconcile the practical necessity with the individualistic ideal, some arrangement that would preserve the industrial order, necessarily based upon a high degree of collective organization, and yet would preserve America's democratic heritage at the same time. Americans wanted a stable, efficient industrial system, one that turned out a large quantity of material goods, insured full employment, and provided a relatively high degree of economic security. Yet at the same time they wanted a system as free as possible from centralized direction, one in which economic power was dispersed and economic opportunity was really open, one that preserved the dignity of the individual and adjusted itself automatically to market forces. And they were unwilling to renounce the hope of achieving both. In spite of periodic hurricanes of anti-big-business sentiment, they refused to follow the prophets that would destroy their industrial system and return to former simplicities. Nor did they pay much attention to those that would sacrifice democratic ideals and liberal traditions in order to create a more orderly and more rational system, one that promised greater security, greater stability, and possibly even greater material benefits.

There were times, of course, when this dilemma was virtually forgotten. During periods of economic prosperity, when Americans were imbued with a psychological sense of well-being and satiated with a steady outflow of material benefits, it was hard to convince them that their industrial organization was seriously out of step with their ideals. During such periods, the majority rallied to the support of the business system; so long as it continued to operate at a high level, they saw no need for any major reforms. So long as the competitive ideal was embodied in statutes and industrial and political leaders paid lip service to it, there was a general willingness to leave it at that. If there were troubled consciences left, these could be soothed by clothing collective organizations in the attributes of rugged individuals and by the assurances of economic experts that anything short of pure monopoly was "competition" and therefore assured the benefits that were supposed to flow from competition.

In a time of economic adversity, however, Americans became painfully aware of the gap between ideal and reality. Paradoxically, this awareness produced two conflicting and contradictory reactions. Some pointed to the gap, to the failure of business organizations to live by the competitive creed, and concluded that it was the cause of the economic debacle, that the breakdown of the industrial machine was the inevitable consequence of its failure to conform to competitive standards. Others pointed to the same gap and concluded that the ideal itself was at fault, that it had prevented the organization and conscious direction of a rational system that would provide stability and security. On one hand, the presence of depression conditions seemed to intensify anti-big-business sentiment and generate new demands for antitrust crusades. On the other, it inspired demands for planning, rationalization, and the creation of economic organizations that could weather deflationary forces. The first general effect grew directly out of the loss of confidence in business leadership, the conviction that industrial leaders had sinned against the economic creed, and the determination that they should be allowed to sin no more. The second grew out of the black fear of economic death, the urgent desire to stem the deflationary tide, and the mounting conviction that a policy of laissez-faire or real implementation of the competitive ideal would result in economic disaster.

During such a period, moreover, it would seem practically inevitable that the policy-making apparatus of a democracy should register both streams of sentiment. Regardless of their logical inconsistency, the two streams were so intermixed in the ideology of the average man that any administration, if it wished to retain political power, had to make concessions to both. It must move to check the deflationary spiral, to provide some sort of central direction, and to salvage economic groups through the erection of cartels and economic controls. Yet while it was doing this, it must make a proper show of maintaining competitive ideals. Its actions must be justified by an appeal to competitive traditions, by showing that they were designed to save the underdog, or if this was impossible, by an appeal to other arguments and other traditions that for the moment justified making an exception. Nor could antitrust action ever be much more than a matter of performing the proper rituals and manipulating the proper symbols. It might attack unusually privileged and widely hated groups, break up a few loose combinations, and set forth a general program that was presumably designed to make the competitive ideal a reality. But the limit of the program would, of necessity, be that point at which changes in business practice or business structures would cause serious economic dislocation. It could not risk the disruption of going concerns or a further shrinkage in employment and production, and it would not subject men to the logical working out of deflationary trends. To do so would amount to political suicide.

To condemn these policies for their inconsistency was to miss the point. From an economic standpoint, condemnation might very well be to the point. They were inconsistent. One line of action tended to cancel the other, with the result that little was accomplished. Yet from the political standpoint, this very inconsistency, so long as the dilemma persisted, was the safest method of retaining political power. President Roosevelt, it seems, never suffered politically from his reluctance to choose between planning and antitrust action. His mixed emotions so closely reflected the popular mind that they were a political asset rather than a liability.

II

That New Deal policy was inconsistent, then, should occasion little surprise. Such inconsistency, in fact, was readily apparent in the National Industrial Recovery Act, the first major effort to deal with the problems of industrial organization. When Roosevelt took office in 1933, the depression had reached its most acute stage. Almost every economic group was crying for salvation through political means, for some sort of rationalization and planning, although they might differ as to just who was to do the planning and the type and amount of it that would be required. Pro-business planners, drawing upon the trade association ideology of the 1920's and the precedent of the War Industries Board, envisioned a semi-cartelized business commonwealth in which industrial leaders would plan and the state would enforce the decisions. Other men, convinced that there was already too much planning by businessmen, hoped to create an order in which other economic groups would participate in the policy-making process. Even under these circumstances, however, the resulting legislation had to be clothed in competitive symbols. Proponents of the NRA advanced the theory that it would help small businessmen and industrial laborers by protecting them from predatory practices and monopolistic abuses. The devices used to erect monopolistic controls became "codes of fair competition." And each such device contained the proper incantation against monopoly.

Consequently, the NRA was not a single program with a single objective, but rather a series of programs with a series of objectives, some of which were in direct conflict with each other. In effect, the National Industrial Recovery Act provided a phraseology that could be used to urge almost any approach to the problem of economic organization and an administrative machine that each of the conflicting economic and ideological groups might possibly use for their own ends. Under the circumstances, a bitter clash over basic policies was probably inevitable.

For a short period these inconsistencies were glossed over by the summer boomlet of 1933 and by a massive propaganda campaign appealing to wartime precedents and attempting to create a new set of cooperative symbols. As the propaganda wore off, however, and the economic indices turned downward again, the inconsistencies inherent in the program moved to the forefront of the picture. In the code-writing process, organized business had emerged as the dominant economic group, and once this became apparent, criticism of the NRA began to mount. Agrarians, convinced that rising industrial prices were canceling out any gains from the farm program, demanded that businessmen live up to the competitive faith. Labor spokesmen, bitterly disillusioned when the program failed to guarantee union recognition and collective bargaining, charged the administration had sold out to management. Small businessmen, certain that the new code authorities were only devices to increase the power of their larger rivals, raised the ancient cry of monopolistic exploitation. Antitrusters, convinced that the talk about strengthening competition was sheer hypocrisy, demanded that this disastrous trust-building program come to a halt. Economic planners, alienated by a process in which the businessmen did the planning, charged that the government was only sanctioning private monopolistic arrangements. And the American public, disillusioned with rising prices and the failure of the program to bring economic recovery, listened to the criticisms and demanded that its competitive ideals be made good.

The rising tide of public resentment greatly strengthened the hand of those that viewed the NRA primarily as a device for raising the plane of competition and securing social justice for labor. Picking up support from discontented groups, from other governmental agencies, and from such investigations as that conducted by Clarence Darrow's National Recovery Review Board, this group within the NRA had soon launched a campaign to bring about a reorientation in policy. By June 1934 it had obtained a formal written policy embodying its views, one that committed the NRA to the competitive ideal, renounced the use of price and production controls and promised to subject the code authorities to strict public supervision. By this time, however, most of the major codes had been written, and the market restorers were never able to apply their policy to codes already approved. The chief effect of their efforts to do so was to antagonize businessmen and to complicate the difficulties of enforcing code provisions that were out of line with announced policy.

The result was a deadlock that persisted for the remainder of the agency's life. Putting the announced policy into effect would have meant, in all probability, the complete alienation of business support and the collapse of the whole structure. Yet accepting and enforcing the codes for what they were would have resulted, again in all probability, in an outraged public and congressional opinion that would have swept away the whole edifice. Thus the NRA tended to reflect the whole dilemma confronting the New Deal. Admittedly, declared policy was inconsistent with practice. Admittedly, the NRA was accomplishing little. Yet from a political standpoint, if the agency were to continue at all, a deadlock of this sort seemed to be the only solution. If the Supreme Court had not taken a hand in the matter, the probable outcome would have been either the abolition of the agency or a continuation of the deadlock.

The practical effect of the NRA, then, was to allow the erection, extension, and fortification of private monopolistic arrangements, particularly for groups that already possessed a fairly high degree of integration and monopoly power. Once these arrangements had been approved and vested interests had developed, the administration found it difficult to deal with them. It could not move against them without alienating powerful interest groups, producing new economic dislocations, and running the risk of setting off the whole process of deflation again. Yet, because of the competitive ideals, it could not lend much support to the arrangements or provide much in the way of public supervision. Only in areas where other arguments, other ideals, and political pressure justified making an exception, in such areas as agriculture, natural resources, transportation, and to a certain extent labor, could the government lend its open support and direction.

Moreover, the policy dilemma, coupled with the sheer complexity of the undertaking, made it impossible to provide much central direction. There was little planning of a broad, general nature, either by businessmen or by the state; there was merely the half-hearted acceptance of a series of legalized, but generally uncoordinated, monopolistic combinations. The result was not over-all direction, but a type of partial, piecemeal, pressure-group planning, a type of planning designed by specific economic groups to balance production with consumption regardless of the dislocations produced elsewhere in the economy.

III

There were, certainly, proposals for other types of planning. But under the circumstances, they were and remained politically unfeasible, both during the NRA period and after. The idea of a government-supported business commonwealth still persisted, and a few men still felt that if the NRA had really applied it, the depression would have been over. Yet in the political context of the time, the idea was thoroughly unrealistic. For one thing, there was the growing gap between businessmen and New Dealers, the conviction of one side that cooperation would lead to bureaucratic socialism, of the other that it would lead to fascism or economic oppression. Even if this quarrel had not existed, the administration could not have secured a program that ran directly counter to the anti-big-business sentiment of the time. The monopolistic implications in such a program were too obvious, and there was little that could be done to disguise them. Most industrial leaders recognized the situation, and the majority of them came to the conclusion that a political program of this sort was no longer necessary. With the crisis past and the deflationary process checked, private controls and such governmental aids as tariffs, subsidies, and loans would be sufficient.

The idea of national economic planning also persisted. A number of New Dealers continued to advocate the transfer of monopoly power from businessmen to the state or to other organized economic groups. Each major economic group, they argued, should be organized and allowed to participate in the formulation of a central plan, one that would result in expanded production, increased employment, a more equitable distribution, and a better balance of prices. Yet this idea, too, was thoroughly impractical when judged in terms of existing political realities. It ran counter to competitive and individualistic traditions. It threatened important vested interests. It largely ignored the complexities of the planning process or the tendency of regulated interests to dominate their regulators. And it was regarded by the majority of Americans as being overly radical, socialistic, and un-American.

Consequently, the planning of the New Deal was essentially single-industry planning, partial, piecemeal, and opportunistic, planning that could circumvent the competitive ideal or could be based on other ideals that justified making an exception. After the NRA experience, organized business groups found it increasingly difficult to devise these justifications. Some business leaders, to be sure, continued to talk about a public agency with power to waive the antitrust laws and sanction private controls. Yet few of them were willing to accept government participation in the planning process, and few were willing to come before the public with proposals that were immediately vulnerable to charges of monopoly. It was preferable, they felt, to let the whole issue lie quiet, to rely upon unauthorized private controls, and to hope that these would be little disturbed by antitrust action. Only a few peculiarly depressed groups, like the cotton textile industry, continued to agitate for government-supported cartels, and most of these groups lacked the cohesion, power, and alternative symbols that would have been necessary to put their programs through.

In some areas, however, especially in areas where alternative symbols were present and where private controls had broken down or proven impractical, it was possible to secure a type of partial planning. Agriculture was able to avoid most of the agitation against monopoly, and while retaining to a large extent its individualistic operations, to find ways of using the state to fix prices, plan production, and regularize markets. Its ability to do so was attributable in part to the political power of the farmers, but it was also due to manipulation of certain symbols that effectively masked the monopolistic implications in the program. The ideal of the yeoman farmer—honest, independent, and morally upright—still had a strong appeal in America, and to many Americans it justified the salvation of farming as a "way of life," even at the cost of subsidies and the violation of competitive standards. Agriculture, moreover, was supposed to be the basic industry, the activity that supported all others. The country, so it was said, could not be prosperous unless its farmers were prosperous. Finally, there was the conservation argument, the great concern over conservation of the soil, which served to justify some degree of public planning and some type of production control.

Similar justifications were sometimes possible for other areas of the economy. Monopolistic arrangements in certain food-processing industries could be camouflaged as an essential part of the farm program. Departures from competitive standards in such natural resource industries as bituminous coal and crude oil production could be justified on the grounds of conservation. Public controls and economic cartelization in the fields of transportation and communication could be justified on the ground that these were "natural monopolies" in which the public had a vital interest. And in the distributive trades, it was possible to turn anti-big-business sentiment against the mass distributors, to brand them as "monopolies," and to obtain a series of essentially anti-competitive measures on the theory that they were designed to preserve competition by preserving small competitors.* The small merchant, however, was never able to dodge the agitation against monopoly to the same extent that the farmer did. The supports granted him were weak to begin with, and to obtain them he had to make concessions to the competitive ideal, concessions that robbed his measures of much of their intended effectiveness.

In some ways, too, the Roosevelt administration helped to create monopoly power for labor. Under the New Deal program, the government proceeded to absorb surplus labor and prescribe minimum labor standards; more important, it encouraged labor organization to the extent that it maintained a friendly attitude, required employer recognition of unions, and restrained certain practices that had been used to break unions in the past. For a time, the appeals to social justice, humanitarianism, and anti-big-business sentiment overrode the appeal of business spokesmen and classical economists to the competitive ideal and individualistic traditions. The doctrine that labor was not a commodity, that men who had worked and produced and kept their obligations to society were entitled to be taken care of, was widely accepted.

---

*The Robinson-Patman Act (1936) and the Miller-Tydings Act (1937) were designed to protect small business by prohibiting wholesalers from practicing price discrimination and by establishing "fair trade" price floors on numerous items. Neither bill received the active support of the Roosevelt administration.—Ed.

Along with it went a growing belief that labor unions were necessary to maintain purchasing power and counterbalance big business. Consequently, even the New Dealers of an antitrust persuasion generally made a place in their program for social legislation and labor organization.

The general effect of this whole line of New Deal policy might be summed up in the word counterorganization, that is, the creation of monopoly power in areas previously unorganized. One can only conclude, however, that this did not happen according to any preconceived plan. Nor did it necessarily promote economic expansion or raise consumer purchasing power. Public support of monopolistic arrangements occurred in a piecemeal, haphazard fashion, in response to pressure from specific economic groups and as opportunities presented themselves. Since consumer organizations were weak and efforts to aid consumers made little progress, the benefits went primarily to producer groups interested in restricting production and raising prices. In the distributive trades, the efforts to help small merchants tended, insofar as they were successful, to impede technological changes, hamper mass distributors, and reduce consumer purchasing power. In the natural resource and transportation industries, most of the new legislation was designed to restrict production, reduce competition, and protect invested capital. And in the labor and agricultural fields, the strengthening of market controls was often at the expense of consumers and in conjunction with business groups. The whole tendency of interest-group planning, in fact, was toward the promotion of economic scarcity. Each group, it seemed, was trying to secure a larger piece from a pie that was steadily dwindling in size.

From an economic standpoint, then, the partial planning of the post-NRA type made little sense, and most economists, be they antitrusters, planners, or devotees of laissez-faire, felt that such an approach was doing more harm than good. It was understandable only in a political context, and as a political solution, it did possess obvious elements of strength. It retained the antitrust laws and avoided any direct attack upon the competitive ideal or competitive mythology. Yet by appealing to other goals and alternative ideals and by using these to justify special and presumably exceptional departures from competitive standards, it could make the necessary concessions to pressure groups interested in reducing competition and erecting government-sponsored cartels. Such a program might be logically inconsistent and economically harmful. Perhaps, as one critic suggested at the time, it combined the worst features of both worlds, "an impairment of the efficiency of the competitive system without the compensating benefits of rationalized collective action." But politically it was a going concern, and efforts to achieve theoretical consistency met with little success.

Perhaps the greatest defect in these limited planning measures was their tendency toward restriction, their failure to provide any incentive for expansion when an expanding economy was the crying need of the time. The easiest way to counteract this tendency, it seemed, was through government expenditures and deficit financing; in practice, this was essentially the path that the New Deal took. By 1938 Roosevelt seemed willing to accept the Keynesian arguments for a permanent spending program, and eventually, when war demands necessitated pump-priming on a gigantic scale, the spending solution worked. It overcame the restrictive tendencies in the economy, restored full employment, and brought rapid economic expansion. Drastic institutional reform, it seemed, was unnecessary. Limited, piecemeal, pressure-group planning could continue, and the spending weapon could be relied upon to stimulate expansion and maintain economic balance.

IV

One major stream of New Deal policy, then, ran toward partial planning. Yet this stream was shaped and altered, at least in a negative sense, by its encounters with the antitrust tradition and the competitive ideal. In a time when Americans distrusted business leadership and blamed big business for the prevailing economic misery, it was only natural that an antitrust approach should have wide political appeal. Concessions had to be made to it, and these concessions meant that planning had to be limited, piecemeal, and disguised. There could be no over-all program of centralized controls. There could be no government-sponsored business commonwealth. And there could be only a minimum of government participation in the planning process.

In and of itself, however, the antitrust approach did not offer a politically workable alternative. The antitrusters might set forth their own vision of the good society. They might blame the depression upon the departure from competitive standards and suggest measures to make industrial organization correspond more closely to the competitive model. But they could never ignore or explain away the deflationary and disruptive implications of their program. Nor could they enlist much support from the important political and economic pressure groups. Consequently, the antitrust approach, like that of planning, had to be applied on a limited basis. Action could be taken only in special or exceptional areas, against unusually privileged groups that were actively hated and particularly vulnerable, in fields where one business group was fighting another, in cases where no one would get hurt, or against practices that violated common standards of decency and fairness.

This was particularly true during the period prior to 1938. The power trust, for example, was a special demon in the progressive faith, one that was actively hated by large numbers of people and one that had not only violated competitive standards but had also outraged accepted canons of honesty and tampered with democratic political ideals. For such an institution, nothing was too bad, not even a little competition; and the resulting battle, limited though its gains might be, did provide a suitable outlet for popular antitrust feeling. Much the same was also true of the other antitrust activities. Financial reform provided another outlet for antitrust sentiment, although its practical results were little more than regulation for the promotion of honesty and facilitation of the governmental spending program. The attacks upon such practices as collusive bidding, basing-point pricing,* and block-booking† benefited from a long history of past agitation. And the suits in the petroleum and auto-finance industries had the support of discontented business groups. The result of such activities, however, could hardly be more than marginal. When the antitrusters reached for real weapons, when they tried, for example, to use the taxing power or make drastic changes in corporate law, they found that any thorough-going program was simply not within the realm of political possibilities.

Under the circumstances, it appeared, neither planning nor antitrust action could be applied in a thorough-going fashion. Neither approach could completely eclipse the other. Yet the political climate and situation did change; and, as a result of these changes, policy vacillated between the two extremes. One period might see more emphasis on planning, the next on antitrust action, and considerable changes might also take place in the nature, content, and scope of each program.

Superficially, the crisis of 1937 was much like that of 1933. Again there were new demands for antitrust action, and again these demands were blended with new proposals for planning, rationalization, and monopolistic controls. In some respects, too, the results were similar. There was more partial planning in unorganized areas, and eventually, this was accompanied by a resumption of large-scale federal spending. The big difference was in the greater emphasis on an antitrust approach, which could be attributed primarily to the difference in political circumstances. The alienation of the business community, memories of NRA experiences, and the growing influence of antimonopolists in the Roosevelt administration made it difficult to work

---

*A practice followed by several major industries. The delivered price of a product was calculated by adding freight charges from an agreed-upon "basing point," rather than the actual point from which the shipment originated. The Federal Trade Commission began to move against this system in 1937.—Ed.

†A system by which the major motion picture companies forced independent theaters to accept their entire output of films. Thurman Arnold, head of the Antitrust Division in the Department of Justice, began a relatively mild campaign against the practice in 1938.—Ed.

out any new scheme of business-government cooperation. These same factors, coupled with the direct appeal of New Dealers to the competitive ideal, made it difficult for business groups to secure public sanction for monopolistic arrangements. The political repercussions of the recession, the fact that the new setback had occurred while the New Deal was in power, made it necessary to appeal directly to anti-big-business sentiment and to use the administered price thesis* to explain why the recession had occurred and why the New Deal had failed to achieve sustained recovery. Under the circumstances, the initiative passed to the antitrusters, and larger concessions had to be made to their point of view.

One such concession was the creation of the Temporary National Economic Committee. Yet this was not so much a victory for the antitrusters as it was a way of avoiding the issue, a means of minimizing the policy conflict within the administration and postponing any final decision. Essentially, the TNEC was a harmless device that could be used by each group to urge a specific line of action or no action at all. Antimonopolists hoped that it would generate the political sentiment necessary for a major breakthrough against concentrated economic power, but these hopes were never realized. In practice, the investigation became largely an ineffective duplicate of the frustrating debate that produced it, and by the time its report was filed, the circumstances had changed. Most of the steam had gone out of the monopoly issue, and antitrust sentiment was being replaced by war-induced patriotism.

The second major concession to antimonopoly sentiment was Thurman Arnold's revival of antitrust prosecutions, a program that presumably was designed to restore a competitive system, one in which prices were flexible and competition would provide the incentive for expansion. Actually, the underlying assumptions behind such a program were of doubtful validity. Price flexibility, even if attainable, might do more harm than good. The Arnold approach had definite limitations, even assuming that the underlying theories were sound. It could and did break up a number of loose combinations; it could and did disrupt monopolistic arrangements that were no necessary part of modern industrialism. It could and, in some cases, did succeed in convincing businessmen that they should adopt practices that corresponded a bit more closely to the competitive model. But it made no real effort to rearrange the underlying industrial structure itself, no real attempt to dislodge vested interests, disrupt controls that were actual checks against deflation, or break up going concerns. And since the practices and policies complained of would appear in many cases to be the out-

---

*Many leading figures within the Roosevelt administration, including apparently Roosevelt himself for a time, attributed the recession of 1937–1938 to artificially high prices "administered" by corporate monopoly.—Ed.

growth of this underlying structure, the Arnold program had little success in achieving its avowed goals.

Even within these limits, moreover, Arnold's antitrust campaign ran into all sorts of difficulties. Often the combinations that he sought to break up were the very ones that the earlier New Deal had fostered. Often, even though the arrangements involved bore little relation to actual production, their sponsors claimed that they did, that their disruption would set the process of deflation in motion again and impair industrial efficiency. Arnold claimed that his activities enjoyed great popular support, and as a symbol and generality they probably did. But when they moved against specific arrangements, it was a different story. There they succeeded in alienating one political pressure group after another. Then, with the coming of the war, opposition became stronger than ever. As antitrust sentiment was replaced by wartime patriotism, it seemed indeed that the disruption of private controls would reduce efficiency and impair the war effort. Consequently, the Arnold program gradually faded from the scene.

It is doubtful, then, that the innovations of 1938 should be regarded as a basic reversal in economic policy. What actually happened was not the substitution of one set of policies for another, but rather a shift in emphasis between two sets of policies that had existed side by side throughout the entire period. Policies that attacked monopoly and those that fostered it, policies that reflected the underlying dilemma of industrial America, had long been inextricably intertwined in American history, and this basic inconsistency persisted in an acute form during the 1930's. Policy might and did vacillate between the two extremes; but because of the limitations of the American political structure and of American economic ideology, it was virtually impossible for one set of policies to displace the other. The New Deal reform movement was forced to adjust to this basic fact. The practical outcome was an economy characterized by private controls, partial planning, compensatory governmental spending, and occasional gestures toward the competitive ideal.

III | FDR and the New Deal

7 FDR: Pragmatist-Democrat

ARTHUR M. SCHLESINGER, JR.

Few historians have combined careers in scholarship and politics so remarkably as Arthur Schlesinger, Jr. The son of an eminent Harvard historian, Schlesinger won the Pulitzer Prize at the age of twenty-eight for his brilliant and controversial book, *The Age of Jackson* (1945). After a brief career as a Washington journalist, he returned to Harvard as a faculty member and began a study of the era of Franklin D. Roosevelt, three volumes of which are now in print. His active interest in public affairs and liberal politics found expression in his roles as a founder of the Americans for Democratic Action; as an aide and adviser to Adlai E. Stevenson, John F. Kennedy, and Robert F. Kennedy; and as author of such works as *The Vital Center* (1949), *A Thousand Days: John F. Kennedy in the White House* (1965), *The Imperial Presidency* (1973), and *Robert Kennedy and His Times* (1978). Since 1966, Schlesinger has been Albert Schweitzer Professor of Humanities at the City University of New York.

Schlesinger is a strong and articulate believer in the ability of great men to influence history. He pictures Roosevelt as a towering individual who determined the basic character of the New Deal and probably preserved American democracy. FDR, he believes, was a pragmatist who rejected the absolute systems that attracted so many social thinkers of the 1930's. Roosevelt felt that Herbert Hoover's philosophy of absolute individualism had failed to meet the problems of the depression and at the same time saw himself and the New Deal as fighters against the absolute totalitarianisms of fascism and communism. He sought to lead America down a middle way, establish a nonsystematic, mixed economy, preserve democracy, and provide security for all. In so doing, he established himself as the international leader of democracy, a "trustee for those in every country" who believed in freedom and democratic experimentation.

Schlesinger's critics, including James MacGregor Burns, question his designation of Roosevelt as a real pragmatist. They argue that FDR rejected not simply ideological systems but also systematic thinking. They feel that his vague affirmations of democracy, freedom, and security failed to provide a basis for the kind of reform movement that would have ended the depression and rebuilt American society. The argument is, one should remember, between two types of liberals, those who prefer to stress Roosevelt's accomplishments and those who think he should have accomplished much more.

* * *

Was no middle way possible between freedom and tyranny—no mixed system which might give the state more power than Herbert Hoover would approve, enough power, indeed, to assure economic and social security; but still not enough to create a Hitler or a Stalin? This was the critical question.

To this question the Hoovers, no less than the Hitlers and Stalins, had long since returned categorical answers. They all—the prophets of individualism and the prophets of totalitarianism—agreed on this if on nothing else: no modified capitalism was possible, no mixed economy, no system of partial and limited government intervention. One could have one thing or the other, but one could never, never, never mix freedom and control. There was, in short, no middle way.

If this conclusion were true, it would have the most fateful consequences for the future of the world.

The assumption that there were two absolutely distinct economic orders, capitalism and socialism, expressed, of course, an unconscious Platonism—a conviction that reality inhered in theoretical essences of which any working economy, with its compromises and confusions, could only be an imperfect copy. If in the realm of essences capitalism and socialism were wholly separate phenomena based on wholly separate principles, then they must be rigorously kept apart on earth. Thus abstractions became more "real" than empirical reality: both doctrinaire capitalists and doctrinaire socialists fell victim to what Whitehead called the "fallacy of misplaced concreteness." Both ideological conservatism and ideological radicalism dwelt in the realm of either-or. Both preferred essence to existence.

The distinction of the New Deal lay precisely in its refusal to approach social problems in terms of ideology. Its strength lay in its preference of existence to essence. The great central source of its energy was the instinctive contempt of practical, energetic, and compassionate people for dogmatic absolutes. Refusing to be intimidated by abstractions or to be overawed by ideology, the New Dealers responded by doing things. Walt Whitman once wrote, "To work for Democracy is good, the exercise is good—strength it makes and lessons it teaches." The whole point of the New Deal lay in its faith in "the exercise of Democracy," its belief in gradualness, its rejection of catastrophism, its denial of either-or, its indifference to ideology, its conviction that a managed and modified capitalist order achieved by piecemeal experiment could best combine personal freedom and economic growth. "In a world in which revolutions just now are coming easily," said Adolf Berle, "the New Deal chose the more difficult course of moderation and rebuilding." "It looks forward toward a more stable social order," said Morgenthau, "but it is not doctrinaire, not a complete cut-and-dried program. It involves the courage to experiment." "The course that the new administration did take," wrote Ickes, "was the hardest course. It conformed to no theory, but it did fit into the American system—to meet concrete needs, a system of courageous recognition of change." Tugwell, rejecting laissez faire and Communism, spoke of the "third course." *Hold Fast the Middle Way* was the title of a book by John Dickinson.

Roosevelt hoped to steer between the extreme of chaos and tyranny by moving always, in his phrase, "slightly to the left of center." "Unrestrained individualism" had proved a failure; yet "any paternalistic system which tries to provide for security for everyone from above only calls for an impossible task and a regimentation utterly uncongenial to the spirit of our people." He deeply agreed with Macaulay's injunction to reform if you would preserve. Once, defending public housing to a press conference, he said, "If you had knowledge of what happened in Germany and England and Vienna, you would know that 'socialism' has probably done more to prevent Communism and rioting and revolution than anything else in the last four or five years."

Roosevelt had no illusions about revolution. Mussolini and Stalin seemed to him "not mere distant relatives" but "blood brothers." Whem Emil Ludwig asked him his "political motive," he replied, "My desire to obviate revolution. . . . I work in a contrary sense to Rome and Moscow." He said during the 1932 campaign:

> Say that civilization is a tree which, as it grows, continually produces rot and dead wood. The radical says: "Cut it down." The conservative says: "Don't touch it." The liberal compromises: "Let's prune, so that we lose neither the old trunk nor the new branches." This campaign is waged to teach the country to march upon its appointed course, the way of change, in an orderly march, avoiding alike the revolution of radicalism and the revolution of conservatism.

His "speech material" file contained a miscellany of material indexed according to the random categories of the President's mind. One folder bore the revealing label: "Liberalism vs. Communism and Conservatism."

As Roosevelt saw it, he was safeguarding the constitutional system by carrying through reforms long overdue. "The principal object of every Government all over the world," he once said, "seems to have been to impose the ideas of the last generation upon the present one. That's all wrong." As early as 1930 he had considered it time for America "to become fairly radical for at least one generation. History shows that where this occurs occasionally, nations are saved from revolution." In 1938 he remarked, "In five years I think we have caught up twenty years. If liberal government continues over another ten years we ought to be contemporary somewhere in the late nineteen forties."

For Roosevelt, the technique of liberal government was pragmatism. Tugwell talked about creating "a philosophy to fit the Roosevelt method"; but this was the aspiration of an intellectual. Nothing attracted Roosevelt less than rigid intellectual systems. "The fluidity of change in society has always been the despair of theorists," Tugwell once wrote. This fluidity was Roosevelt's delight, and he floated upon it with the confidence of an expert sailor, who could detect currents and breezes invisible to others, hear the slap of waves on distant rocks, smell squalls beyond the horizon and make infallible landfalls in the blackest of fogs. He respected clear ideas, accepted them, employed them, but was never really at ease with them and always ultimately skeptical about their relationship to reality.

His attitude toward economists was typical. Though he acknowledged their necessity, he stood in little awe of them. "I brought down several books by English economists and leading American economists," he once told a press conference. ". . . I suppose I must have read different articles by fifteen different experts. Two things stand out: The first is that no two of them agree, and the other thing is that they are so foggy in what they say that it is almost impossible to figure out what they mean. It is jargon; absolute jargon." Once Roosevelt remarked to Keynes of Leon Henderson, "Just look at Leon. When I got him, he was only an economist." (Keynes could hardly wait to repeat this to Henderson.) Roosevelt dealt proficiently with practical questions of government finance, as he showed in his press conferences on the budget; but abstract theory left him cold.

Considering the state of economic theory in the 1930's, this was not necessarily a disabling prejudice. Roosevelt had, as J. K. Galbraith has suggested, what was more important than theory, and surely far more useful than bad theory, a set of intelligent economic attitudes. He believed in government as an instrument for effecting economic change (though not as an instrument for doing everything: in 1934, he complained to the National Emergency Council, "There is the general feeling that it is up to the Government to take care of everybody . . . they should be told all the different things the Government can not do"). He did not regard successful businessmen as infallible reposito- ries of economic wisdom. He regarded the nation as an estate to be improved for those who would eventually inherit it. He was willing to try nearly anything. And he had a sense of the complex continuities of history—that special intimacy with the American past which, as Frances Perkins perceptively observed, signified a man who had talked with old people who had talked with older people who remembered many things back to the War of the Revolution.

From this perspective, Roosevelt could not get excited about the debate between the First and Second New Deals. No one knew what he really thought about the question of the organic economy versus the restoration of competition. Tugwell, perhaps the most vigilant student of Roosevelt's economic ideas, could in one mood pronounce Roosevelt "a progressive of the nineteenth century in economic matters" (1946) who "clung to the Brandeis-Frankfurter view" (1950) and "could be persuaded away from the old progressive line only in the direst cir- cumstances" (1950); in another, he could speak of Roosevelt's "prefer- ence for a planned and disciplined business system" (1957) and for "overhead management of the whole economy" (1940), and question whether he ever believed in Brandeis (1957). Corcoran and Cohen, who helped persuade Roosevelt to the Second New Deal, thought he never really abandoned the NRA dream of directing the economy through some kind of central economic mechanism. Roosevelt himself, confronted with a direct question, always wriggled away ("Brandeis is one thousand percent right in principle but in certain fields there must be a guiding or restraining hand of Government because of the very nature of the specific field"). He never could see why the United States has to be all one way or all the other. "This country is big enough to experiment with several diverse systems and follow several different lines," he once remarked to Adolf Berle. "Why must we put our econom- ic policy in a single systematic strait jacket?"

Rejecting the battle between the New Nationalism and the New Free- dom which had so long divided American liberalism, Roosevelt equably defined the New Deal as the "satisfactory combination" of both. Reject- ing the platonic distinction between "capitalism" and "socialism," he led the way toward a new society which took elements from each and rendered both obsolescent. It was this freedom from dogma which outraged the angry, logical men who saw everything with dazzling certitude. Roosevelt's illusion, said Herbert Hoover, was "that any eco- nomic system would work in a mixture of others. No greater illusions ever mesmerized the American people." "Your President," said Leon

Trotsky with contempt, "abhors 'systems' and 'generalities.' . . . Your philosophic method is even more antiquated than your economic system." But the American President always resisted ideological commitment. His determination was to keep options open within the general frame of a humanized democracy; and his belief was that the very diversity of systems strengthened the basis for freedom.

Without some critical vision, pragmatism could be a meaningless technique; the flight from ideology, a form of laziness; the middle way, an empty conception. For some politicians, such an approach meant nothing more than splitting the difference between extremes; the middle of the road was thus determined by the clamor from each side. At times it appeared to mean little more than this to Roosevelt. But at bottom he had a guiding vision with substantive content of its own. The content was not, however, intellectual; and this was where he disappointed more precise and exacting minds around him. It was rather a human content, a sense of the fortune and happiness of people. In 1936 a Canadian editor asked him to state his objectives. Roosevelt's off-the-cuff reply defined his goal in all its naïveté and power:

> . . . to do what any honest Government of any country would do; try to increase the security and the happiness of a larger number of people in all occupations of life and in all parts of the country; to give them more of the good things of life, to give them a greater distribution not only of wealth in the narrow terms, but of wealth in the wider terms; to give them places to go in the summer time—recreation; to give them assurance that they are not going to starve in their old age; to give honest business a chance to go ahead and make a reasonable profit, and to give everyone a chance to earn a living.

The listing was neither considered nor comprehensive, but the spirit was accurate. "The intellectual and spiritual climate," said Frances Perkins, "was Roosevelt's general attitude that *the people mattered*." Nothing else would count until ordinary people were provided an environment and an opportunity "as good as human ingenuity can devise and fit the children of God."

Developed against the backdrop of depression, his philosophy of compassion had a particular bias toward the idea of security—"a greater physical and mental and spiritual security for the people of this country." "Security," he once said,

> means a kind of feeling within our individual selves that we have lacked all through the course of history. We have had to take our chance about our old age in days past. We have had to take our chance with depressions and boom times. We have had to take chances on buying our homes. I have believed for a great many years that the time has come in our civilization when a great many of these chances should be eliminated from our lives.

The urgencies of depression carried the concern for security to a degree which later generations, who thought they could assume abundance and move on to problems of opportunity and self-fulfillment, would find hard to understand. The old American dream, Roosevelt told a collection of young people in 1935, was the dream of the golden ladder—each individual for himself. But the newer generation would have a different dream: "Your advancement, you hope, is along a broad highway on which thousands of your fellow men and women are advancing with you." In many ways this was a dispiriting hope. In the longer run, security, while indispensable as a social minimum, might be cloying and perhaps even stultifying as a social ideal.

But this was a nuance imposed by depression. His essential ideals had an old-fashioned flavor. He was unconsciously seeing America in the Jeffersonian image of Dutchess County and Hyde Park. He hoped, as he said, to extend "to our national life the old principal of the local community, the principle that no individual, man, woman, or child, has a right to do things that hurt his neighbors." "Our task of reconstruction does not require the creation of new and strange values. It is rather the finding of the way once more to known, but to some degree forgotten ideals." He wanted to make other people happy as he had been happy himself. Lifting his right hand high, his left hand only a little, he would say, "The difference is too big, it must become smaler—like this. . . . Wasn't I able to study, travel, take care of my sickness? The man who doesn't have to worry about his daily bread is securer and freer." He spoke of his philosophy as "social-mindedness." He meant by this essentially the humanization of industrial society.

A viewpoint so general provided no infallible guide to daily decision. Roosevelt therefore had to live by trial and error. His first term had its share of error: the overextension of NRA; the fumbling with monetary policy; the reluctant approach to spending; the waste of energy in trying to achieve the communitarian dream; the bungling of the London Economic Conference; the administrative confusion and conflict; the excessive reliance on ballyhoo and oratory. At times Roosevelt seemed almost to extemporize for the joy of it; his pragmatism appeared an addition to playing by ear in the nervous conviction that any kind of noise was better than silence. "Instead of being alarmed by the spirit of improvisation," wrote George Creel, "he seemed delighted by it, whooping on the improvisers with the excitement of one riding to hounds."

The chronic changing of front exposed the New Deal to repeated charges that it had no core of doctrine, that it was improvised and opportunistic, that it was guided only by circumstance. These charges were all true. But they also represented the New Deal's strength. For the advantage enjoyed by the pragmatists over the ideologists was their exceptional sensitivity to social and human reality. They measured results in terms not of conformity to *a priori* models but of concrete impact on people's lives. The New Deal thus had built-in mechanisms of feed-back, readjustment, and self-correction. Its incoherences were considerably more faithful to a highly complicated and shifting reality than any preconceived dogmatic system could have been. In the welter of confusion and ignorance, experiment corrected by compassion was the best answer.

Roosevelt's genius lay in the fact that he recognized—rather, rejoiced in—the challenge to the pragmatic nerve. His basic principle was not to sacrifice human beings to logic. Frances Perkins describes him as "in full revolt against the 'economic man.'" He had no philosophy save experiment, which was a technique; constitutionalism, which was a procedure; and humanity, which was a faith.

The depression, the Social Science Research Council Committee on Studies in Social Aspects of the Depression declared in unwontedly nonacademic language, "was like the explosion of a bomb dropped in the midst of society." It shook and strained the American community in a multitude of ways and profoundly challenged the nation's will to survive. The American people, in recording in 1936 so astonishing a vote of confidence in the New Deal, were by no means endorsing everything that had taken place in the tumultuous years since March 4, 1933. But they were voting unmistakably for the capacity of a representative democracy under strong leadership to produce energetic, resourceful, and free government in the face of an economic holocaust. And their vote came at a time when, throughout the west, faith in government by the people—faith in free society itself—was flickering and fading. While the men of Washington wrote their laws and established their agencies and set out to make America over, other men in Berlin and in Moscow looked confidently forward to the collapse of free institutions—and too few in free countries dared say them nay. In a real sense, the New Deal was testing the resources of democracy, not just for Americans, but for all mankind. Roosevelt's victory, said *The Times* of London, "is a matter of supreme importance at the moment when English-speaking nations are becoming more isolated as the champions of democracy in a world 'blown about by all the winds of doctrine.'"

Could the pragmatic experiment possibly work? Would not its failure hurtle the nation—and perhaps the western world—into darker and more desperate experiments? "I can hardly describe," said Winston Churchill, "with what eagerness, not only our working people, but all those who think about social problems in this island are watching the results of President Roosevelt's valiant effort to solve the riddle of the sphinx." "My whole impression," wrote Sir Stafford Cripps after visiting Roosevelt in 1935, "is of an honest anxious man faced by an impossible task—humanising capitalism and making it work." "It takes an opportunist and a moderate liberal to wreck capitalism in an hour of crisis and to prepare the way for the radical dictator," said Lawrence Dennis hopefully, adding, "Mr. Roosevelt is the Kerensky of American capitalism." Roosevelt sometimes used to make the Kerensky joke himself. No one can guess to what extent such jokes ventilated the interior doubts and fears which might well surge up in rare moments of solitude, when the shouting died away and he could not longer evade the ultimates. But Roosevelt had had private agonies before, and had conquered doubts and fears. There were historical consolations, too: Tugwell has compared the ordeal of Roosevelt's struggle against depression with the ordeal of Lincoln's struggle against disunion—the generals tried and dismissed, the strategic plans adopted and discarded, the troubles with Congress and the Supreme Court, the resistance of the faint of heart and the stubborn of mind, the waste and the tears, until at last national energies came into focus and produced victory.

Whatever might haunt Roosevelt in the dark of night, he showed nothing in the daylight but confidence and decision. He well knew that more was at stake than America—that the challenge of achieving economic security within a framework of freedom offered civilized society a decisive test. No one stated the challenge more exactly than John Maynard Keynes in his letter to Roosevelt at the end of 1933.

"You have made yourself," Keynes said, "the trustee for those in every country who seek to mend the evils of our condition by reasoned experiment within the framework of the existing social system.

"If you fail, rational choice will be gravely prejudiced throughout the world, leaving orthodoxy and revolution to fight it out.

"But, if you succeed, new and bolder methods will be tried everywhere, and we may date the first chapter of a new economic era from your accession to office."

He was apparently succeeding; and people could start to believe again in the free state and its capacity to solve problems of economic stability and social justice. Free society, in consequence, might not yet be finished; it had a future; it might have the strength and steadfastness to surmount the totalitarian challenge. Franklin Roosevelt and Adolf Hitler had come to power together in 1933. Four years later their two images were more sharply juxtaposed than ever, symbolizing a conflict between profoundly different views of society and humanity.

When Roosevelt was re-elected in 1936, the French Chamber of Deputies passed, without dissent, a resolution of congratulations. "Henceforth democracy has its chief!" said *Paris-Soir*. "After his brilliant triumph President Roosevelt has become the statesman on whom every hope is to be pinned if the great liberal and democratic civilization of the west is one day threatened, either by Bolshevism or by autocracy." "No dictator, whether Fascist or Communist," said *The Times* of London, "can challenge the solid basis of his backing. None can afford so securely to take the course which he believes to be right without regard for any need of a spell-bound popularity."

In England, Winston Churchill, roused from his pessimism of 1930, took a new look at the prospects of freedom. "His impulse," Churchill wrote of Roosevelt, "is one which makes toward the fuller life of the masses of the people in every land, and which, as it glows the brighter, may well eclipse both the lurid flames of German Nordic self-assertion and the baleful unnatural lights which are diffused from Soviet Russia."

For all his absorption in the struggle for American recovery during these years, Roosevelt had watched the spread of fascism and aggression with increasing apprehension. The only answer, he felt, was the strengthened vitality of democracy. When he accepted renomination at Franklin Field on June 27, 1936, he seemed also to accept a larger challenge. There were, he said, people in other lands who had once fought for freedom, but who now appeared too weary to carry on the fight, who had "sold their heritage of freedom for the illusion of a living."

"I believe in my heart," Roosevelt said, "that only our success can stir their ancient hope. They begin to know that here in America we are waging a great and successful war. It is not alone a war against want and destitution and economic demoralization. It is more than that: it is a war for the survival of democracy. We are fighting to save a great and precious form of government for ourselves and for the world.

"I accept the commission you have tendered me. I join with you. I am enlisted for the duration of the war."

8 | FDR: Unsuccessful Improviser

JAMES MacGREGOR BURNS

James MacGregor Burns, a professor of political science at Williams College, has, like Arthur Schlesinger, Jr., combined a distinguished academic career with a commitment to liberal political activity. His scholarly work has focused on two special concerns—the ways in which American political institutions have blocked progressive leadership, and the nature of creative political leadership. The first theme pervades his books *Congress on Trial* (1949) and *The Deadlock of Democracy* (1963); the second is central to his studies *Presidential Government* (1966) and *Leadership* (1978). The two themes come together in his superb two-volume biography of FDR, *Roosevelt: The Lion and the Fox* (1956) and *Roosevelt: The Soldier of Freedom* (1970. *The Lion and the Fox*, perhaps the most original of all Burns' books, was the first important critique of FDR by a liberal historian.

Burns argues, first of all, that Roosevelt failed to end the depression despite the fact that the formula for doing so, Keynesian economic policy, was available and was being urged upon the President by its brilliant creator. Burns believes that Roosevelt's mind was too undisciplined, too unsystematic, to accept even a program that so perfectly embodied the "middle way" between individualistic capitalism and socialism. Keynesian economics called for a complete commitment; the depression could be ended if the government were willing to inject enough money into the economy; but a little bit of deficit spending, while it might improve economic conditions, could not bring complete recovery. FDR could not grasp this point. His idea of the middle way

From *Roosevelt: The Lion and the Fox* by James MacGregor Burns, pp. 328–336, 375–380, 400–404. Copyright © 1956 by James MacGregor Burns. Reprinted by permission of the publishers, Harcourt Brace Jovanovich, Inc.

was a compromise between diametrically opposed solutions. Consequently, the New Deal never undertook the program of massive spending the nation needed, and its inability to end the depression was "a major failure of American democracy."

Even more critical was Roosevelt's failure to reorganize the party system and establish the Democratic party as a positive liberal force in American politics. During the years when his prestige was at its peak, he worked with a regular party organization dominated by southern conservatives and nonideological city bosses. He made no effort to undertake the difficult but necessary job of rebuilding the party structure from the bottom up. By 1938, when he attempted to "purge" several leading conservatives in Democratic party primary elections, it was too late. (A subsequent effort in the fall of 1944 to attract Wendell Willkie and his liberal Republican following into the party was aborted by Willkie's sudden death.) As a result, the Democratic party remained a loose coalition of conflicting groups incapable of continuing and enlarging the New Deal.

Unable to make basic commitments at key moments, "captive to his habit of mediating among pressures rather than reshaping them," FDR "was less a great creative leader than a skillful manipulator and a brilliant interpreter." Whatever his successes, "he failed to achieve that combination of tactical skill and strategic planning that represents the acme of political leadership."

Burns actually has a large degree of sympathy for Roosevelt; nevertheless, his critique is a harsh one. Those who disagree would argue that the author undervalues the many accomplishments of the New Deal, underestimates the many problems and pressures that diverted Roosevelt from party realignment, fails to grasp the novelty of Keynesian economics in the 1930's, and exaggerates the powers of the Presidency. Still, *Roosevelt: The Lion and the Fox* expresses the most important and convincing critique of its subject yet made. It is securely established as one of the great books on FDR and the New Deal.

* * *

Roosevelt as an Economist

One day late in Roosevelt's second term Marriner Eccles reported at the White House to raise some pressing economic questions with the President. He had been promised an hour-long luncheon engagement—a prize that an administrator might spend weeks conniving for. To his dismay, he found that Senator McAdoo was cutting into his time. When Eccles finally got into the President's study the burly old

Californian was standing over Roosevelt and declaiming about the political situation back home.

"Bring up a chair, Marriner," the President said. To McAdoo he added: "Marriner and I are just about to have lunch."

McAdoo was too engrossed in his problems to take the hint. "Oh, that's all right," he said, "you two boys go right ahead—I'll talk while you eat."

Reaching to a warming oven next to his chair, Roosevelt pulled out a plate. It was burning hot. Juggling it awkwardly, he managed to place it before Eccles. While the President shook his scorched fingers and Eccles burned inside, McAdoo continued to talk. He finally wound up:

"Now, remember, Franklin. I want to leave one last thought with you. When it comes to appointing any of those federal judges in California, I wish you would take the matter up with me instead of with that son-of-a-bitch Downey. . . ."

McAdoo finally left. Marveling at Roosevelt's good humor through all this, Eccles leaned forward to talk. But as the waiter rolled away the tray there was a new diversion. Fala bounded in, Roosevelt took a ball out of his desk, and for several minutes the dog played retriever for his master, while Eccles feebly voiced words of praise.

"That's enough now," Roosevelt said to Fala. "I've got to get back to work." Eccles started talking, but after a few minutes he saw that he had lost his audience. Roosevelt was looking around the room for Fala. Suddenly the President burst out: "Well, I'll be God-damned! Marriner, do you see what I see?"

Eccles did. Over in a corner Fala was committing an indiscretion on the rug. Several more minutes elapsed while Roosevelt summoned a guard, had Fala's nose rubbed in the mess, and delivered a post mortem. By now Eccles' time was almost up. He left in a blind rage. To his associates awaiting him expectantly at the Federal Reserve Building he could report only on California politics and on the doings of Fala.

This sort of thing happened many times. People were amazed at Roosevelt's governmental habits—at his way of running through a series of wholly unrelated conferences like a child in a playroom turning from toy to toy, at his ability seemingly to put one matter out of his head when he turned to another, above all at his serenity and even gaiety under the pitiless pressures of men and events. The methods, of course, reflected the man. Roosevelt's mental agility and flexibility were well suited to the experimental phase of the New Deal. In 1938 Roosevelt was still the improviser, still the pragmatist.

Was practicality enough? Roosevelt's fumbling and indecisiveness during the recession showed his failings as an economist and thinker. His distrust of old and doctrinaire theories freed him from slavery to ideas that would have been risky in the 1930's. But at the same time, that distrust helped cut him off from the one economist and the one economic idea that might have provided a spectacular solution to Roosevelt's chief economic, political, and constitutional difficulties.

The man was the noted British economist John Maynard Keynes. An academician who was yet a leader in the bizarre Bloomsbury set, an economist who had won and lost fortunes as a speculator, a Cambridge don who also ran insurance companies, a prickly intellectual who was close to men of affairs throughout the world, a reformer who believed in liberal capitalism, Keynes for two decades had been provoking British opinion with his unorthodox views of economics, industry, and international affairs. In 1936 he had published the capstone of his economic thought, *The General Theory of Employment, Interest, and Money*. Bristling with critical references to cherished theories and honored names, filled with strange terms and equations, punctuated by lengthy appendixes, the *General Theory* had been read by few. But its impact on liberal economists in America was already making itself felt.

For, out of all the complexities and involutions of Keynes's writings, there emerged a central idea that was dazzling in its stark simplicity. Classical economics dictated that in bad times governments must permit if not encourage lower wages, lower prices, and rigorously balanced budgets. Purged and cleansed by this stringent process, the economy could then right itself and once again march up the long foothills to the mountain peaks of the business cycle. Keynes boldly assaulted this notion. The nub of his advice to government in time of depression was to unbalance the budget deliberately by heavy spending and low taxes. Only through heavy spending by consumers and investing by government or private capitalists could the economy right itself.

To call any single doctrine a "solution" is, of course, dangerous business. Keynesianism, moreover, is still a highly controversial topic among economists and policy makers; its usefulness is sharply limited depending on the nature of an economy, the people, the condition, and the time. Yet it seems clear that if ever the idea of deficit financing had urgent applicability, it was to the America of the 1930's, with its huge army of unemployed, its vast raw materials, and the state of its industrial arts.

In the first place, deficit spending was constitutional. When at a social gathering Justice Stone whispered to Miss Perkins, "My dear, the taxing power is sufficient for everything you want and need," he was in effect reminding the administration of its plentitude of power in the whole fiscal realm as compared with other avenues that could be blocked off by judicial action. Indeed, a great authority on the Constitution, Professor Edward S. Corwin of Princeton, had predicted the "twilight of the Supreme Court" because the Court, by making difficult a legal challenge to federal appropriations, had left to Congress power over spending and taxing.

Massive deficit spending was politically feasible too. Despite the ceaseless talk of economy on the Hill, Congress, at least during Roosevelt's first five years, was eager to spend. It is an old political bromide that congressmen want to vote for all spending bills and against all taxing bills—which happens to be just the right combination for deficit spending. The President often had to throw his weight *against* the congressional spenders, as in the case of the veterans' bonus. If Roosevelt had urged spending programs on Congress rather than the Court plan and certain reform measures in 1937, he probably could have both met his commitments to the one-third ill-housed, ill-fed, and ill-clothed and achieved substantial re-employment.

Deficit spending was ideally suited to Roosevelt's ideology and program. He was no doctrinaire capitalist; twenty years before his presidency he was a New Deal state senator favoring a host of governmental controls and reforms, and he had stood for progressivism as a Wilson lieutenant and as governor. He was no doctrinaire socialist; he had never embraced the idea of central state ownership of the means of production. Rejecting both doctrinaire solutions, Keynesian economics was a true middle way—at a time when New Dealers were groping for a middle way that worked.

As a practical man, Roosevelt liked to apply the test, "Will it work?" Deficit spending *had* worked in 1935 and 1936 with the huge relief programs, veterans' bonus payments, and monetary expansion. Then had come a shift to the opposite policy: relief spending had been cut, reserve requirements for commercial banks raised, holdings of securities by banks reduced, and the growth of loans slowed. This shift from deficit spending had *not* worked. Both experiments had been fairly conclusive, each in its way; Roosevelt might have wanted the chance to experiment further, but a nation can hardly be expected to serve indefinitely as a laboratory.

Why did this most practical of men miss out on what probably would have been the ideal solution for his economic, political, and judicial problems?

Not because Keynes had failed to reach him. The Englishman had corresponded with the President, and he had talked with him in 1934. The two men liked each other, but the intellectual and the politician were cut from different cloth: Roosevelt was dubious about Keynes's "rigmarole of figures" and seemed surprised to find him a mathematician rather than a political economist; for his part Keynes was disappointed that the President was not more literate in economics.

From England, Keynes had watched the sharp decline of late 1937 with mounting anxiety. On February 1, 1938, he had written the President a long and eloquent letter. "You received me so kindly when I visited you some three years ago that I make bold to send you some bird's eye impressions. . . ." After a disclaimer of omniscience, Keynes delivered a polite but candid attack on the administration's recent economic policies. There had been an "error of optimism," he said, in 1936. Recovery was possible only through a large-scale recourse to public works and other investments. The administration had had an unexampled opportunity to organize increased investment in durable goods such as housing, public utilities and transport.

Could the administration, asked Keynes, escape criticism for the failure of increased investment? "The handling of the housing problem has been really wicked," and housing could be the best aid to recovery. As for utilities, their litigation against the government was senseless. But as for the allegedly wicked holding companies, no one had suggested a way to unscramble the eggs. The President should either make peace with the utilities or be more drastic. Keynes leaned toward nationalizing them, but if public opinion was not yet ripe for that, what was the point of "chasing the utilities around the lot every other week"? As for railroads, either take them over or have pity on the overwhelming problems of the managers.

Keynes even tried to educate the President on the nature of businessmen. They had a different set of delusions from politicians, he warned, and thus required different handling. "They are, however, much milder than politicians, at the same time allured and terrified by the glare of publicity, easily persuaded to be 'patriots,' perplexed, bemused, indeed terrified, yet only too anxious to take a cheerful view, vain perhaps but very unsure of themselves, pathetically responsive to a kind word. You could do anything you liked with them, if you would treat them (even the big ones), not as wolves and tigers, but as domestic animals by nature, even though they have been badly brought up and not trained as you would wish."

It was a mistake, Keynes went on, to think that businessmen were more immoral than politicians. "If you work them into the surly, obstinate, terrified mood of which domestic animals, wrongly handled, are so capable, the nation's burden will not get carried to market; and in the end, public opinion will veer their way. . . ."

"Forgive the candour of these remarks," Keynes had concluded. He listed half a dozen administration policies he supported with enthusiasm. "But I am terrified lest progressive causes in all the democratic countries should suffer injury, because you have taken too lightly the risk to their prestige which would result from a failure measured in terms of immediate prosperity. There *need* be no failure. But the maintenance of prosperity in the modern world is extremely *difficult;* and it is so easy to lose precious time."

The eloquent appeal had not moved the President. He asked Morgenthau to write a reply to Keynes for him, and the President signed as written the banal little letter that Morgenthau produced. Two months later Roosevelt did resume spending, of course, but it was not the kind of massive spending that Keynes was calling for.

Part of the reason for Roosevelt's failure to exploit Keynes and his ideas lay in the web of political circumstances. Lacking a coherent economic philosophy in 1932, Roosevelt had opportunistically pummeled Hoover from both right and left, attacking him both for do-nothing government *and* for unbalancing the budget. Roosevelt had thus committed himself to a balanced budget, at least in the long run, and during his presidential years he mired himself further in this swamp. The more he unbalanced the budget, the more—literally scores of times—he insisted that eventually he would balance it. The more he promised, the more he gave hostages to the conservatives on the Hill and in his party. His personal stand became party policy in both the 1932 and 1936 platforms.

Another reason for the failure lay with Roosevelt's advisers. Some of them, of course, opposed any type of heavy spending; but even those who leaned toward a new economic program were unable to exploit the full potential of Keynes's idea. Some of them were mainly concerned about price rigidity—so concerned, indeed, that they wished to make this the main basis of a campaign against big business. Some were more worried about inflation than continuing unemployment. Some wanted to penalize business by raising taxes—good politics, perhaps, but a contradiction of the Keynesian idea of lowering taxes while increasing spending. Some, lacking faith in the long-term prospects of capitalism in America, believed in a theory of secular stagnation that did not admit that Keynesian economics was a basic solution. Some were believers only in pump priming; the government could pour heavy doses of purchasing power into the economy, as it had in 1935 and 1936, but after that business was supposed to man the pumps.

These splits even among his liberal advisers reflected to some extent the haphazard fashion in which Roosevelt had assembled his brain trust. Even so, there were few out-and-out Keynesians in the government, and most of these were in the lower echelons and lacked access to the President. And Keynesian theory was so new that certain statistical and analytical tools were lacking.

The main reason for Roosevelt's failure in the economic sphere, however, lay neither in the political situation nor in his divided advisers. With his immense political resourcefulness and volatility Roosevelt could always have broken out of the party and congressional web, at least in 1936 and early 1937. He could always have changed his advisers. His main trouble was intellectual. Roosevelt was simply unable as a thinker to seize the opportunity that Keynesian economics gave him. His failure as an economist was part of a broader intellectual failure.

What was the nature of this failure? Roosevelt's mind was an eminently operative one, quick, keen, fast, flexible. It showed in his intellectual habits. He disdained elaborate, fine-spun theories; he paid little attention to the long and abstract briefs that academic people were always sending him on ways of improving administration, on strengthening the cabinet as an institution, on dealing with Congress. He hated abstractions. His mind yearned for the detail, the particular, the specific. Invariably he answered general questions in terms of examples—in terms of an individual business, of a farmer in Kansas, of a problem in Hyde Park, of a situation during the Wilson administration. He had a passion for the concrete.

His working habits bespoke his mind. From the start of his day to the end, from his skimming through a half-dozen newspapers at breakfast through a schedule of quick conferences on a score of different subjects to his playing with his stamps before bedtime, his mind sped from topic to topic, picking them up, toying with them, and dropping them. His intellectual habits were not disorderly; they were staccato.

Roosevelt's mental way of life was nourished by its own successes. He liked to outwit the reporters in fast repartee. He liked to show off the incredible knowledge of a wide variety of specific matters that he carried in his head. Sometimes there was a touch of fakery in this, for the President could steer a conversation toward a subject on which he was newly briefed. But to an extraordinary extent he grasped an immediate, specific situation in all its particulars and complexity. He knew, for example, the tangled political situations and multitude of personalities in each of the states; he could talk for hours about the housing, roads, people, and history of Hyde Park; he could describe knowledgeably the activities and problems of a host of businesses and industries; he could pull out of his head hundreds of specific prices, rents, wages; he could identify countless varieties of fish, birds, trees; he could not be stumped on geography.

His self-esteem as a practical man must have been fed, too, by the ignorance of so many of his critics. Many men of affairs were slaves to the theories of defunct economists, and Roosevelt could puncture their pretensions with his knowledge of their own business and its relation to the rest of the world. His indignant complaints to his friends about the businessmen's failure to advance specific constructive suggestions was the lament of the practitioner against the theorist. Undoubtedly Roosevelt's emphasis on his own practicality had an element of overcompensation too. Cartoonists in 1938 were still picturing him as a fuzzy theorist surrounded by bemused brain trusters; and a friend who had romped with him as a child in the Hyde Park nursery, and who had evidently learned little since those days, rebuked him with the words: "You are not an essentially practical person."

And now, by a supreme irony, fate placed before this man of practicality an economic theory that seemed to embody only uncommon sense. The idea of boosting spending and holding down taxes and of doing this year after year as a deliberate policy, the idea of gaining prosperity by the deliberate creation of huge debts—this idea in its full dimensions seemed but another fanciful academic theory, and Roosevelt by 1938 had had a bellyful of such theories. Pump priming as a temporary emergency measure he could understand—but not deficit spending as the central, long-term approach to full-scale economic recovery.

Deficit spending posed a special intellectual problem for the President. If there had been consistency in his handling of economic affairs, it was his habit of trying to make economic decisions by combining opposites. "Lock yourself in a room and don't come out until you agree," he would say blithely to people who differed hopelessly in their economic premises—to free traders and nationalists, to deflationists and inflationists, to trust busters and collectivists, to spenders and economizers. The trouble with deficit spending was that halfway application did not work. It had utility only through full and determined use; otherwise it served only to antagonize and worry business by increasing the public debt without sufficiently raising spending and investment.

A Keynesian solution, in short, involved an almost absolute commitment, and Roosevelt was not one to commit himself absolutely to any political or economic method. His mind was a barometric reflection of the personal and policy pressures around him. "We are at one of those uncommon junctures of human affairs," Keynes said in the 1930's, "when we can be saved by the solution of intellectual problems and in no other way." But Roosevelt's mind was attuned to the handling of a great variety of operational and tactical matters, not to the solving of intellectual problems.

Roosevelt's deficiencies as an economist were as striking as his triumphs as a politician. It was a major failure of American democracy that it was not able in the late 1930's to show that a great nation could provide jobs for its workers and food, clothes, and houses for its people. What Roosevelt could not achieve World War II would achieve as a by-product enabling Republicans to charge later that the New Deal could end depression only through war. It was a personal failure for Roosevelt too. Halfway through his second term the man who had ousted Hoover on the depression issue knew that eight or nine million people were walking the streets. He knew that millions were still living in shanties and tenements, and that some were not far from starvation. Would the great promise of January 1937 become a mockery?

Roosevelt as a Party Leader

The New Deal, wrote historian Walter Millis toward the end of 1938, "has been reduced to a movement with no program, with no effective political organization, with no vast popular party strength behind it, and with no candidate." The passage of time has not invalidated this judgment. But it has sharpened the question: Why did the most gifted campaigner of his time receive and deserve this estimate only two years after the greatest election triumph in recent American history?

The answer lay partly in the kind of political tactics Roosevelt had used ever since the time he started campaigning for president. In 1931 and 1932, he had, like any ambitious politician, tried to win over Democratic leaders and groups that embraced a great variety of attitudes and interests. Since the Democratic party was deeply divided among its sectional and ideological splinter groups, Roosevelt began the presidential campaign of 1932 with a mixed and ill-assorted group backing. Hoover's unpopularity with many elements in his own party brought various Republican and independent groups to Roosevelt's support. Inevitably the mandate of 1932 was a highly uncertain one, except that the new President must do something—anything—to cope with the depression.

Responding to the crisis, Roosevelt assumed in his magnificent way the role of leader of all the people. Playing down his party support he mediated among a host of conflicting interest groups, political leaders, and ideological proponents. During the crisis atmosphere of 1933 his broker leadership worked. He won enormous popularity, he put through his crisis program, he restored the morale of the whole nation. The congressional elections of 1934 were less a tribute to the Democratic party than a testament of the President's wide support.

Then his ill-assorted following began to unravel at the edges. The right wing rebelled, labor erupted, Huey Long and others stepped up their harrying attacks. As a result of these political developments, the cancellation of part of the New Deal by the courts, and the need to put through the waiting reform bills, Roosevelt made a huge, sudden, and unplanned shift leftward. The shift put him in the role of leader of a great, though teeming and amorphous, coalition of center and liberal groups; it left him, in short, as party chief. From mid-1935 to about the end of 1938 Roosevelt deserted his role as broker among all groups and assumed the role as party leader commanding his Grand Coalition of the center and left.

This role, too, the President played magnificently, most notably in the closing days of the 1936 campaign. During 1937 he spoke often of Jefferson and Jackson and of other great presidents who, he said, had served as great leaders of popular majorities. During 1938 he tried to perfect the Democratic party as an instrument of a popular majority. But in the end the effort failed—in the court fight, the defeat of effective recovery measures, and the party purge.

That failure had many causes. The American constitutional system had been devised to prevent easy capture of the government by popular majorities. The recovery of the mid-1930's not only made the whole country more confident of itself and less dependent on the leader in the White House, but it strengthened and emboldened a host of interest groups and leaders, who soon were pushing beyond the limits of New Deal policy and of Roosevelt's leadership. Too, the party system could not easily be reformed or modernized, and the anti-third-term custom led to expectations that Roosevelt was nearing the end of his political power. But the failure also stemmed from Roosevelt's limitations as a political strategist.

The trouble was that Roosevelt had assumed his role as party or majority leader not as part of a deliberate, planned political strategy but in response to a conjunction of immediate developments. As majority leader he relied on his personal popularity, on his *charisma* or warm emotional appeal. He did not try to build up a solid, organized mass base for the extended New Deal that he projected in the inaugural speech of 1937. Lacking such a mass base, he could not establish a rank-and-file majority group in Congress to push through his program. Hence the court fight ended as a congressional fight in which the President had too few reserve forces to throw into the battle.

Roosevelt as party leader, in short, never made the strategic commitment that would allow a carefully considered, thorough, and long-term attempt at party reorganization. The purge marked the bankruptcy of his party leadership. For five years the President had made a fetish of his refusal to interfere in "local" elections. When candidates—many of them stalwart New Dealers—had turned desperately to the White House for support, McIntyre or Early had flung at them the "unbreakable" rule that "the President takes no part in local elections." When the administration's good friend Key Pittman had faced a coalition of Republicans and McCarran Democrats in 1934, all Roosevelt could say was "I wish to goodness I could speak out loud in meeting and tell Nevada that I am one thousand per cent for you!" but an "imposed silence in things like primaries is one of the many penalties of my job." When cabinet members had asked during the 1934 elections if they could make campaign speeches, Roosevelt had said, No, except in their own states.

After all this delicacy Roosevelt in 1938 completely reversed himself and threw every ounce of the administration's political weight—money, propaganda, newspaper influence, federal jobholders as well as his own name—into local campaigns in an effort to purge his foes. He mainly failed, and his failure was due in large part to his earlier policy. After five years of being ignored by the White House, local candidates and party groups were not amenable to presidential control. Why should they be? The White House had done little enough for them.

The execution of the purge in itself was typical of Roosevelt's improvising methods. Although the problem of party defections had been evident for months and the idea of a purge had been taking shape in the winter of 1938, most of the administration's efforts were marked by hurried, inadequate, and amateurish maneuvers at the last minute. In some states the White House interfered enough to antagonize the opponent within the party but not enough to insure his defeat. Roosevelt's own tactics were marked by a strange combination of rashness and irresolution, of blunt face-to-face encounters and wily, backscene stratagems.

But Roosevelt's main failure as party leader lay not in the purge. It involved the condition of the Democratic party in state after state six years after he took over as national Democratic chief. Pennsylvania, for example, was the scene of such noisy brawling among labor, New Dealers, and old-line Democrats that Roosevelt himself compared it to Dante's Inferno. A bitter feud wracked the Democracy in Illinois. The Democrats in Wisconsin, Nebraska, and Minnesota were still reeling under their ditchings by the White House in 1934 and 1936. The party in California was split among organization Democrats, $30 every Thursday backers, and a host of other factions.

In New York the condition of the Democratic party was even more significant, for Roosevelt had detailed knowledge of politics in his home state and had no inhibitions about intervening there. He intervened so adroitly and indirectly in the New York City mayoralty elections of 1933 that politicians were arguing years later as to which Democratic faction he had aided, or whether he was intent mainly on electing La Guardia. In 1936 he encouraged the formation of the Labor party in New York State to help his own re-election, and he pooh-poohed the arguments of Farley, Flynn, and other Democrats that the Labor party would some day turn against the state Democracy—as indeed it later did. By 1938 the Democratic party in New York State was weaker and more faction-ridden than it had been for many years.

It was characteristic of Roosevelt to interpret the 1938 election setbacks largely in terms of the weakness of local Democratic candidates and leaders. Actually the trouble lay much deeper. The President's failure to build a stronger party system at the grass roots, more directly responsive to national direction and more closely oriented around New Deal programs and issues, left a political vacuum that was rapidly filled by power groupings centered on state and local leaders holding office or contending for office. Roosevelt and his New Deal had vastly strengthened local party groups in the same way they had organized interest groups. And just as, nationally, the New Deal jolted interest groups out of their lethargy and mobilized them into political power groups that threatened to disrupt the Roosevelt coalition, so the New Deal stimulated local party groups to throw off the White House apron strings.

"If our beloved leader," wrote William Allen White to Farley early in the second term, "cannot find the least common multiple between John

Lewis and Carter Glass he will have to take a maul and crack the monolith, forget that he had a party and build his policy with the pieces which fall under his hammer." The perceptive old Kansan's comment was typical of the hopes of many liberals of the day. The President had pulled so many rabbits out of his hat. Could he not produce just one more?

The purge indicated that he could not. The hat was empty. But White's suggestion posed the cardinal test of Roosevelt as party leader. How much leeway did the President have? Was it ever possible for him to build a stronger party? Or did the nature of the American party system, and especially the Democratic party, preclude the basic changes that would have been necessary to carry through the broader New Deal that the President proclaimed in his second-term inaugural?

On the face of it the forces of inertia were impressive. The American party system does not lend itself easily to change. In its major respects the national party is a holding company for complex and interlacing clusters of local groups revolving around men holding or contending for innumerable state and local offices—governors, sheriffs, state legislators, mayors, district attorneys, United States senators, county commissioners, city councilmen, and so on, all strung loosely together by party tradition, presidential leadership, and, to some extent, common ideas. As long as the American constitutional system creates electoral prizes to hold and contend for in the states and localities, the party is likely to remain undisciplined and decentralized.

Long immersed in the local undergrowth of American politics, Roosevelt was wholly familiar with the obstacles to party change. His refusal to break with some of the more unsavory local bosses like Hague and Kelly is clear evidence that he had no disposition to undertake the most obvious kind of reform. Perhaps, though, the President underestimated the possibility of party invigoration from the top.

Some New Dealers, worried by the decay of the Democratic party as a bulwark for progressive government, wanted to build up "presidential" factions pledged to the New Deal, factions that could lift the party out of the ruck of local bickering and orient it toward its national program. Attempts to build such presidential factions were abortive. They might have succeeded, however, had the President given them direction and backing. The New Deal had stimulated vigorous new elements in the party that put programs before local patronage, that were chiefly concerned with national policies of reform and recovery. By joining hands with these elements, by exploiting his own popularity and his control over the national party machinery, the President could have challenged anti-New Deal factions and tried to convert neutralists into backers of the New Deal.

Whether such an attempt would have succeeded cannot be answered because the attempt was never made. Paradoxically enough, however, the purge itself indicates that a long-run, well-organized effort might have worked in many states. For the purge did succeed under two conditions—in a Northern urban area, where there was some planning rather than total improvisation, and in those Southern states where the White House was helping a well-entrenched incumbent rather than trying to oust a well-entrenched opponent. The first was the case of O'Connor, the second the cases of Pepper and of Barkley.* Indeed, the results of the purge charted a rough line between the area within the presidential reach and the area beyond it. Undoubtedly the former area would have been much bigger had Roosevelt systematically nourished New Deal strength within the party during his first term.

But he did not. The reasons that the President ignored the potentialities of the great political organization he headed were manifold. He was something of a prisoner of the great concessions he had made to gain the 1932 nomination, including the admission of Garner and other conservatives to the inner circle. His first-term success had made his method of personal leadership look workable; overcoming crisis after crisis through his limitless resourcefulness and magnetism, Roosevelt did not bother to organize the party for the long run. As a politician eager to win, Roosevelt was concerned with his own political and electoral standing at whatever expense to the party. It was much easier to exploit his own political skill than try to improve the rickety, sprawling party organization.

The main reason, however, for Roosevelt's failure to build up the party lay in his unwillingness to commit himself to the full implications of party leadership, in his eternal desire to keep open alternative tactical lines of action, including a line of retreat. The personal traits that made Roosevelt a brilliant tactician—his dexterity, his command of a variety of roles, his skill in attack and defense, above all his personal magnetism and *charisma*—were not the best traits for hard, long-range purposeful building of a strong popular movement behind a coherent political program. The latter would have demanded a continuing intellectual and political commitment to a set strategy—and this kind of commitment Roosevelt would not make.

He never forgot the great lesson of Woodrow Wilson, who got too far ahead of his followers. Perhaps, though, he never appreciated enough Wilson's injunction that "if the President leads the way, his party can hardly resist him." If Roosevelt had led and organized the party toward well-drawn goals, if he had aroused and tied into the party the masses of farmers and workers and reliefers and white-collar

---

*John J. O'Connor, a conservative New York Democrat who chaired the House Rules Committee, was successfully "purged" in the 1938 Democratic primary. Pro–New Deal Senators Claude Pepper (Florida) and Alben Barkley (Kentucky) received White House assistance in their successful campaigns for renomination.—Ed.

workers and minority religious and racial groups, if he had met the massed power of group interests with an organized movement of his own, the story of the New Deal on the domestic front during the second term might have been quite different.

Thus Roosevelt can be described as a great party leader only if the term is rigidly defined. On the one hand he tied the party, loosely perhaps, to a program; he bought it glorious victories; he helped point it in new ideological directions. On the other hand, he subordinated the party to his own political needs; he failed to exploit its full possibilities as a source of liberal thought and action; and he left the party, at least at its base, little stronger than when he became its leader.

Roosevelt as a Political Leader

No leader is a free agent. Even Hitler had to cope with grumbling and foot dragging among the military; even Stalin had to deal with backward peasants and with party rivals grasping for power. Roosevelt's plight was far more difficult. He was captain of the ship of state, but many hands reached for the tiller, and a rebellious crew manned the sails. It was only natural that this vessel should move ahead by hugging the shore, threading its way past shoal and reef, putting into harbor when the storm roared. The test of great political leadership is not whether the leader has his way; it is, first, whether the leader makes the most of existing materials he has to work with, and, second, whether he creates new materials to help him meet his goals.

At the end of 1939, as Roosevelt neared the last year of his second term, it was time to apply to him both tests of leadership. His goal had always been clear in broad outline—a prosperous people in a secure nation. By the end of 1939 this goal was still far off. Economic conditions had improved since the recession, but not back to the uncertain levels of the mid-1930's, with millions out of work. And as the President himself saw more clearly than most Americans, the nation was in grave peril.

The ship of state had not reached port; neither had it foundered. How had the captain done?

Undeniably the reefs and shoals were formidable. Any attempt to chart a clear course to port—in this case to build a liberal program for New Deal objectives—ran head on into the absence of a cohesive liberal tradition in America. Any effort to shape long-term economic programs ran up against limited understanding of economic problems. Any effort to build a consistent foreign policy that would throw the country's weight toward peace and against the aggressors encountered the fierce isolationism of most Americans. The political and governmental means to these ends were equally hard to forge. Attempts to build a stronger "presidential party" behind the New Deal fell afoul of the federal, factional make-up of the existing party system. Any effort to establish a cohesive rank-and-file group for New Deal policies in Congress splintered against the entrenched power of seniority. Even the attempt to fashion a more cohesive executive branch ran into the centrifugal tendencies of the American system and the pervasive popular fear of executive power.

But what was the factor of creative leadership in these lost battles? Could it be said that Roosevelt had tried and failed? Was it bad luck, or a rebellious crew, or a flimsy ship that had kept him from reaching port? Or was the blame his alone?

There is an important difference between the politician who is simply an able tactician, and the politician who is a creative political leader. The former accepts political conditions as given and fashions a campaign and a set of policies best suited to the existing conditions. The latter tries consciously to change the matrix of political forces amid which he operates, in order that he may better lead the people in the direction he wants to go. The former operates within slender margins; the latter, through sheer will and conviction as well as political skill, tries to widen the margins within which he operates. He seeks not merely to win votes but consciously to alter basic political forces such as public opinion, party power, interest-group pressure, the governmental system.

There were times—most notably in 1935—when Roosevelt brilliantly capitalized on every opportunity to convert New Deal aims into law. There were times—most notably in the court fight—when he tested and found the outer limits of his power. But sometimes he made no effort at all—especially in gaining lasting influence in Congress. Sometimes he tried too little and too late. And sometimes—as in the case of party consolidation and realignment and of economic program—he seemed to lack the intellectual qualities necessary to the task.

During his second term Roosevelt seemed to forget the great lesson of his inaugural speech of 1933—that courageous affirmation in itself changes the political dimensions of a situation. That speech was more than a speech—it was an act that loosened a tidal wave of support behind the new administration. The most important instrument a leader has to work with is himself—his own personality and its impact on other people. When the people's opinions are vaguely directed the way the leader is headed but lack depth and solidity, action by the leader can shift opinion in his own favor. In the parallelogram of forces in which the leader operates, such action alters the whole equation. To be sure, more than speeches was needed after 1937, for the feeling of crisis had gone and popular attitudes had hardened. But the inaugural speech of 1933 stood as an index of the leader's influence when he takes a posture of bold affirmation.

Roosevelt's failure to build a liberal coalition and a new party behind the New Deal is a further case in point. For here the materials were available for the right shaping and mixing. To be sure, most Americans during the mid-1930's as an abstract matter opposed realigning the parties along liberal and conservative lines. But when confronted in 1938 with the question of following "President Roosevelt's" proposal that old party lines be disregarded and that liberals of all parties unite to support liberal candidates for Congress, twice as many people favored as opposed the idea. The missing key was long-term and effective organization by Roosevelt of firmer support for realignment. Despite its failure, the purge showed the great potential of party realignment in the North and in the border states.

As for foreign policy, at potential turning points of public opinion—most notably in 1935 and 1936, when the people's fear of war might have been directed toward internationalist policies rather than isolationist ones—the President had failed to give the cue the people needed. Roosevelt did not exploit his superior information about the foreign situation and his understanding of foreign policy in order to guide popular attitudes.

Indeed, Roosevelt to a surprising degree was captive to the political forces around him rather than their shaper. In a democracy such must ever be the case. But democracy assigns a place for creative political leadership too. The forces handcuffing Roosevelt stemmed as much from his own actions and personality as from the unyielding political environment. He could not reshape his party, reorient foreign policy attitudes, reorganize Congress and the bureaucracy, or solve the economic problem largely because he lacked the necessary intellectual commitment to the right union of ends and means.

A test of Roosevelt's creative leadership, of his willingness to alter the environment—the pressures working on him—when he had the capacity to do so, was provided by the inner circle of his advisers. Haphazardly brought together, embracing conservatives and liberals, isolationists and internationalists, his brain trust helped him mediate among opposing policies and ideas during his first term. But, despite the comings and goings of individuals, the brain trust remained an amorphous and divided group during Roosevelt's later period of party leadership, at a time when he needed program guidance more directly and clearly pointed toward the aims of an expanded New Deal at home and toward firmer action abroad. Instead of compelling his advisers to serve his new needs, he allowed them unduly to define his own purposes. Fearing commitment to any one adviser or faction, he became overly involved in the divisions among all of them.

Roosevelt, in a sense, was captive to himself as well as to his political environment. He was captive to his habits of mediating among pressures rather than reshaping them, of responding eclectically to all the people around him, of balancing warring groups and leaders against one another, of improvising with brilliance and gusto. Impatient of theory, insatiably curious about people and their ideas, sensitively attuned to the play of forces around him, he lacked that burning and almost fanatic conviction that great leadership demands.

Roosevelt was less a great creative leader than a skillful manipulator and a brilliant interpreter. Given the big, decisive event—depression at home or naked aggression abroad—he could dramatize its significance and convey its import to the American people. But when the crisis was less striking but no less serious, and when its solution demanded a union of intellectual comprehension and unified and continuing strategic action, Roosevelt saw his efforts turn to dust, as in the cases of court packing, the purge, and putting his country behind efforts toward collective security. He was always a superb tactician, and sometimes a courageous leader, but he failed to achieve that combination of tactical skill and strategic planning that represents the acme of political leadership.

IV | The Politics of the New Deal

9 The Roosevelt Coalition

SAMUEL LUBELL

Samuel Lubell, a noted political analyst who supplements statistical study with personal interviewing, has done more than any other student of American politics to explain the ways in which the New Deal affected American voting patterns. His important book, *The Future of American Politics,* originally published in 1951, is still the major point of departure for historians who seek to understand the nature of the overwhelming electoral support which sustained Franklin D. Roosevelt and the New Deal.

The Roosevelt coalition, as Lubell sees it, began to take shape in the 1920's as urban immigrant groups, unable to identify with the leadership or ideology of the Republican party, moved away from the GOP. The magnetic appeal of Al Smith brought these minorities to the Democratic party in 1928 and gave it a solid majority in the twelve largest cities. Consolidating this support, Roosevelt added to the coalition old-stock Americans from the lower and lower-middle classes and vast numbers of blacks. These elements, normally antagonistic, could unite behind the New Deal because of the benefits it distributed to them. Its job programs for the unemployed and its mortgage programs for hard-pressed homeowners, if not as spectacular as the NRA or the AAA, were more crucial to the lives of many. Equally important was the New Deal's encouragement of labor, and the new Congress of Industrial Organizations, whose membership largely reflected the new coalition, assumed an active role in politics and became a major rallying point for New Deal supporters.

From *The Future of American Politics* by Samuel Lubell, 3d rev. ed. (Colophon), pp. 43–68. Copyright © 1951, 1952, 1956, 1965 by Samuel Lubell. Reprinted by permission of Harper & Row, Publishers.

World War II, as Lubell observes, somewhat altered the Roosevelt coalition. Americans of German and Italian descent tended to fall away from the Democratic party, but other groups, such as Jews and Polish-Americans, gave Roosevelt heavier support than ever. The author's analysis is a reminder that deeply held ethnic loyalties may be as important as rational individual self-interest in determining political commitments.

Lubell agrees with several other writers that beginning about 1935 there was an important shift in the tone and emphasis of the New Deal—one which he defines as a shift from concentration on simple economic recovery to the promotion of far-reaching reforms. It was this change that assured the emergence of the Roosevelt coalition in 1936. Lubell also argues that it was the war, not the New Deal, which brought back prosperity. Despite the defection of some German- and Italian-Americans, the defense boom and FDR's third-term campaign of 1940 essentially solidified the new political divisions which the New Deal had brought into being.

Lubell's assertion that important population shifts necessarily lead to political realignments seems somewhat simplistic, but whatever the shortcomings of his general theory, no writer has told us more about the politics of the New Deal.

*   *   *

A Little Matter of Birth Rates

In the winter of 1910 Congress received the longest report ever submitted by a government investigating body up to that time. From early 1907 a special commission had been studying almost every imaginable aspect of immigration, filling forty-two fat volumes with its findings. Buried in that statistical mountain was at least one table of figures which was to prove peculiarly prophetic for our own times.

This table showed that a majority of the children in the schools of thirty-seven of the nation's leading cities had foreign-born fathers. In cities like Chelsea, Fall River, New Bedford, Duluth, New York and Chicago more than *two out of every three* school children were the sons and daughters of immigrants.

Viewed in today's perspective, it is clear that those figures forecast a major political upheaval some time between 1930 and 1940. By then all of these children, plus baby brothers and sisters not enrolled in school, would have grown to voting age. Massed as they were in the states commanding the largest electoral vote, their sheer numbers would topple any prevailing political balance.

No matter what else had happened, the growing up of these children of the 13 million immigrants who poured into the country between 1900 and 1914 was bound to exert a leveling pull on American society. As it was, the Great Depression—striking when most of them had barely entered the adult world—sharpened all their memories of childhood handicaps. When Roosevelt first took office, no segment of the population was more ready for "a new deal" than the submerged, inarticulate urban masses. They became the chief carriers of the Roosevelt Revolution.

The real revolutionary surge behind the New Deal lay in this coupling of the depression with the rise of a new generation, which had been malnourished on the congestion of our cities and the abuses of industrialism. Roosevelt did not start this revolt of the city. What he did do was to awaken the climbing urban masses to a consciousness of the power in their numbers. He extended to them the warming hand of recognition, through patronage and protective legislation. In the New Deal he supplied the leveling philosophy required by their sheer numbers and by the hungers stimulated by advertising. In turn, the big-city masses furnished the votes which re-elected Roosevelt again and again—and, in the process, ended the traditional Republican majority in this country.

In the elections that followed this same big-city generation would stand like a human wall between the Republicans and their past dominance. It was this generation—now grown to parenthood and in many cases to home-owning, but still bound by common underdog attitudes—which the Republicans had to crack to win and hold the Presidency.

Twice before in American history a majority party has been transformed into a minority party. Each time the change was prefaced by a dramatic reshuffling of population. Jacksonian democracy tramped in to the echoes of the oxcarts which had rolled westward in the twenty years before. In 1800 only one of twenty Americans lived west of the Appalachians; when Jackson was inaugurated the transmountain country claimed one of every three Americans.

Similarly, the formation of the Republican party was preceded by a tremendous westward expansion into the Great Lakes and Midwest regions. Between 1840 and 1860 the nation's population almost doubled, swelling another 60 percent by 1880. If it is true that the pre–Civil War parties were overwhelmed by their inability to dam back the passions stirred by the slavery controversy, it is also true that they were unable to channel the floor of new voters.

There were two population currents which cleared the way for the New Deal:

Between 1910 and 1930 for the first time a majority of the American people came to live in cities. The second population shift might be described as the triumph of the birth rates of the poor and underprivileged over those of the rich and well-born.

Searching for families of five or more, the U.S. Immigration Commission's investigators found two-and-a-half times as many among unskilled laborers as among businessmen. In Minneapolis, for example, the second generation of English stock—the backbone of Republican strength—celebrated a blessed event on the average of one every five years. Among the foreign born a new baby arrived every three years.

As late as 1925 wives of miners and laborers were still having twice as many children as the wives of bankers.

Nor was it the birth rates of the immigrants alone which were threatening the Republican majority. The other prolific baby patches were in the farming areas, particularly in the Appalachian hills and in the South. When World War I shut off the flow of European immigrants, it was into these areas of high human fertility and low living standards that industry sent its recruiting agents searching for cheap labor. Whites and Negroes were sucked north into the cities, especially after 1920 when immigration was curtailed sharply.

Between 1920 and 1930 more than 6.5 million persons were drawn off the farms and hills; 4.5 million came into New York, Chicago, Detroit and Los Angeles alone. They hit the cities at roughly the same time that the children of the immigrants were growing up and bestirring themselves. The human potential for a revolutionary political change had thus been brought together in our larger cities when the economic skies caved in.

Through the entire Roosevelt era the Republicans labored on the wrong side of the birth rate. Nor was there anything they could do about it, since the birth rates frustrating them were those of 1910 to 1920. During the last years of Republican victory, from 1920 through 1928, roughly 17 million potential new voters passed the age of twenty-one. From 1936 through 1944, the number ran over 21 million, most of them coming from poorer, Democratically inclined families.

Whatever inroads into Roosevelt's popularity the Republicans made was offset largely by these new voters. In 1936, for example, nearly 6 million more ballots were cast than in 1932. While the Republicans gained just under 1 million, Roosevelt's vote swelled by almost 5 million.

Except for the Polish-Americans and Italo-Americans, the wave of new voters among the immigrant groups passed its crest by 1945. Not until the late 1960's will the record number of births of recent years register politically. Until then the nation's basal political metabolism is likely to remain more sluggish than during the Roosevelt years. The issues of realignment will have to be fought out primarily among existing population elements, whose instinctive voting attitudes are already largely formed.

This prospect, of no abrupt change in the make-up of the electorate, re-emphasizes the decisive importance of the bit-city generation, which came of age through the Roosevelt years. Without their overwhelming urban pluralities the Democrats would not have won in either 1940, 1944 or 1948. The 1948 election was so close because Truman's vote in the twelve largest cities fell nearly 750,000 below Roosevelt's 1944 plurality.

Not only does this generation hold the balance of political power in the nation. It also constitutes a radically new political force in American history. The old Republican dominance was rooted in the Civil War and the transcontinental expansion which followed. Most of the immigrants who peopled our larger cities came to these shores long after the Civil War, even after the exhaustion of free lands in the West. To their children and grandchildren the loyalties of Appomattox and the Homestead Act were details in history books rather than a family experience passed down from grandfather to grandson.

Never having known anything but city life, this new generation was bound to develop a different attitude toward the role of government from that of Americans born on farms or in small towns. To Herbert Hoover the phrase "rugged individualism" evoked nostalgic memories of a rural self-sufficiency in which a thrifty, toiling farmer had to look to the marketplace for only the last fifth of his needs. The Iowa homestead on which Hoover grew up produced all of its own vegetables, its own soap, its own bread. Fuel was cut and hauled from the woods ten miles away, where one could also gather walnuts free. "Sweetness" was obtained from sorghums. Every fall the cellar was filled with jars and barrels which, as Hoover observes in his memoirs, "was social security in itself."

To men and women who regulated their labors by the sun and rain, there was recognizable logic in talking of natural economic laws—although even among farmers the murmur for government intervention grew louder, as their operations became more commercialized and less self-sufficient.

In the city, though, the issue has always been man against man. What bowed the backs of the factory worker prematurely were not hardships inflicted by Mother Nature but by human nature. He was completely dependent on a money wage. Without a job, there were no vegetables for his family, no bread, no rent, no fuel, no soap, no "sweetness." Crop failures, plagues of grasshoppers or searing drought could be put down as acts of God. Getting fired or having one's wages cut were only too plainly acts of the Boss.

A philosophy that called for "leaving things alone" to work themselves out seemed either unreal or hypocritical in the cities, where nearly every condition of living groaned for reform. The wage earner had to look to the government to make sure that the milk bought for his baby was not watered or tubercular; he had to look to government to regulate the construction of tenements so all sunlight was not blocked out. If only God could make a tree, only the government could make a park.

Neither the Republicans nor the New Dealers seem to have appreciated how sharp a wrench from the continuity of the past was involved in the rise of this big-city generation. GOP leaders persisted in regarding Roosevelt's popularity as a form of hero worship, abetted by the radio. Only Roosevelt's personal magnetism and political skill were holding together the varied Democratic elements, reasoned the Republicans. With "that voice" quieted, the coalition would fall apart. The nation would then return to safe and sane Republicanism. What this reasoning overlooked was that the Roosevelt generation had no tradition of Republicanism to go back to. For them the weight of tradition was such that if they were undecided about rival Presidential candidates, they instinctively would give the Democrats preference.

The basic weakness of the Republican party stems from this fact, that it has remained rooted in an earlier historical era in which it was dominant. The resilient Democratic strength springs from being so alive—clumsily perhaps, but definitely alive—to the problems with which the newer generation has grown up.

Between the Republican and Democratic appeals, as we shall see, the issue has been less one of conservatism versus liberalism than one of timeliness.

The Forgotten Warrior

At the height of Roosevelt's popularity, Republicans used to lament over the youthfulness of so many of the nation's voters. Since they had come of age after 1928, the complaint ran, the only Presidents they knew were Roosevelt and Hoover, who were hopelessly linked with the depression. Still, it would be a mistake to regard the Roosevelt coalition as strictly a product of the depression.

The startling fact—generally overlooked—is that through the booming twenties Republican pluralities in the large industrial centers were dropping steadily. Even when the stock market tickers were clicking most gratifyingly the forces of urban revolt were gathering momentum.

Consider the waning Republican strength revealed in the table below which totals the vote in our twelve largest cities (New York, Chicago, Philadelphia, Pittsburgh, Detroit, Cleveland, Baltimore, St. Louis, Boston, Milwaukee, San Francisco and Los Angeles). In 1920 the Republicans had 1,638,000 more votes than the Democrats in these twelve cities. This net Republican plurality dropped in 1924 and was turned into a Democratic plurality by 1928.

Year	Net Party Plurality
1920	1,540,000 Republican
1924	1,308,000 Republican
1928	210,000 Democratic
1932	1,791,000 Democratic
1936	3,479,000 Democratic
1940	2,112,000 Democratic
1944	2,230,000 Democratic
1948	1,481,000 Democratic

Two things stand out from those figures. First, it was not the depression which made Roosevelt the champion of the urban masses but what he did after he came to the Presidency. Between 1932 and 1936 the Democratic plurality in these cities leaped 80 percent, the biggest change in any single election. Second, the Republican hold on the cities was broken not by Roosevelt but by Alfred E. Smith. Before the Roosevelt Revolution there was an Al Smith Revolution.

In many ways, Smith's defeat in 1928, rather than Roosevelt's 1932 victory, marked off the arena in which today's politics are being fought. The Happy Warrior and four-time governor of New York first hacked out the rural-city cleavage which generates so much of the force behind the present struggle between Congress and the President. It was Smith who first slashed through the traditional alignments that had held so firmly since the Civil War, clearing the way for the more comprehensive realignment which came later.

Smith split not only the Solid South but the Republican North as well. While Hoover was carrying more than 300 Southern and border state counties which had not gone Republican since Reconstruction, Smith was swinging 122 Northern counties out of the GOP column.

Seventy-seven of these counties are predominantly Catholic. But more than religious sympathy inspired their support of Smith. This is shown clearly by the way these counties have voted since. Fifty-seven have remained staunchly Democratic in every Presidential election from 1928 through 1948. Included are some of our heaviest voting areas—New York, Boston, Providence, St. Louis, San Francisco, Cleveland, Milwaukee and St. Paul, also Butte, Montana, and Burlington, Vermont.

Of the sixty-two Smith counties whose allegiance has wavered, most are German-American in background and therefore broke against Roosevelt in 1940 because of the war. In 1948 Truman gained over

Roosevelt in fifty of these counties, with eighteen returning to the Democratic party.

Smith may be today's "Forgotten Warrior" but the line he drew across the map of American politics has never been erased.

How profound a social upheaval stirred beneath the Smith vote can be seen most clearly in the industrial East, where one finds the heaviest concentration of counties which have been Democratic since 1928. Before Smith, no other part of the country was more religiously Republican. None had a heavier proportion of foreign born. Nor were these two factors unrelated.

During the twenty years of heaviest immigration, from 1890 to 1910, coal production tripled and steel output multiplied seven times. It was in the cities with the most immigrants that Bryan's free silver crusade was beaten. To a considerable extent, in short, both the expansion of industry and Republican political dominance rested on the immigrant.

The conditions under which these immigrants worked and lived hardly requires description here. Coming to this country after the free lands were gone, they were thrust into the sectors of the economy with the sorest tensions, into the sweatiest jobs, where wages were not much above subsistence level and where labor unions were feeble. The foreign born made up 60 percent of the workers in the packing-house plants described by Upton Sinclair's *The Jungle;* 57 percent of those in iron and steel, 61 percent of our miners, nearly 70 percent of those toiling in textiles or clothing.

Probably of greater long-run political significance than their low wages was the segregation in which they lived. In one-industry coal and steel towns the separation of laborers and managers was as complete as that between serfs and lord on a feudal manor. In the larger cities, even where Gold Coast and slum were hardly a block apart, they still constituted two separate worlds. Roosevelt has often been accused of ranging class against class, as if class antagonism did not exist before the New Deal. Yet, certainly since the turn of the century our urban social structure had been a class structure.

For a long time, though, the resentment of the "other half" against those on top merely smoldered submissively. Even had the immigrants been inclined to political activity, they would have found it difficult. In 1910 one of every five among the foreign born spoke no English. Until 1920 the twelve-hour working day, still the rule in iron and steel, left little leisure time. As late as 1933, when the NRA codes were being considered, Secretary of Labor Frances Perkins had to go out into the mill towns to drum up interest among the steel workers. At Homestead a Catholic priest arranged a meeting with some Polish-American workers, all of whom came scrupulously scrubbed. They spoke no English, and the meeting had to be conducted through an interpreter. Mrs. Perkins was visibly touched when several workers rose and spoke and it developed they were asking God to bless the President, much as peasants in Russia might have blessed the czar.

The rise in the educational level is a revealing index to the quickening political pulse of the urban masses. At the turn of the century only one of every fifteen youngsters was going beyond the elementary school. By 1930 every second child of high school age was in high school.

At first, this rising generation found little real identification with either of the major parties. In exchange for a favor or a two-dollar bill the newly naturalized voter would vote the way the political machine instructed. But he was as likely to follow the dictates of a Republican boss in Philadelphia as of Tammany Hall in New York. None of the Republican Presidents stirred that most vital of all political assets: vicarious identification. It was not a matter of postwar disillusionment. Far from feeling like a lost generation, the children of the immigrants were intensely idealistic. But with whom could they identify this idealism? Harding was a dirty story. Calvin Coolidge might be untouched by scandal, but the same Puritanical, small-town qualities which endeared him to Main Street made "Silent Cal" a chilling, pedagogic figure to city kids.

On the Democratic side, Woodrow Wilson had captured the imagination of some of these underdog elements through favorable labor legislation, through his dream of peace and by championing the cause of Europe's minorities. For years afterward, in appealing to Czechs and Poles, Democratic politicians found it effective to invoke Wilson's memory. But this enthusiasm did not carry over to either James M. Cox, an Ohio publisher, or John W. Davis, a Wall Street lawyer. As for William Jennings Bryan, his revivalist oratory might inflame the Bible belt—but in the city he was a repellent, even comic figure. When the "Great Commoner" rose before the 1924 Democratic Convention in New York to oppose denouncing the Ku Klux Klan by name, contending "We can exterminate Ku Kluxism better by recognizing their honesty and teaching them that they are wrong," he was hissed and booed by the galleries.

By 1924, "the enemy's country," as Bryan called the East, had flung up its own Great Commoner in Al Smith. Prohibition and the Klan were the immediate weapons in the duel Smith and Bryan fought; but behind each antagonist were ranged the habits and prejudices, hopes and frustrations, prides and hatreds of two different cultures and two historical eras.

The very eccentricities and mannerisms of the two men were symbolic. The brown derby and rasping East Side accent, which stamped Smith as "one of our boys" to the sidewalk masses, sent shivers down the spine of Protestant respectability. In turn, the traits which made Bryan seem like the voice of pious morality to his Prohibitionist, rural,

Protestant following—the liberal use of Biblical phrases, the resonant Chautauqua tones, the heaven-stomping energy—made him sound like the voice of bigotry to the urban masses.

Both men were mouthpieces of protest—Bryan of the over-mortgaged Bible belt, Smith of the underpaid melting pot. Whether either was understood in the other's country is doubtful. Could the factory worker really share the despair of the farmer watching a sheriff tack a foreclosure notice on the barn door? Could the farmer feel the vicarious terror of the factory masses reading of a shirtwaist-factory fire in which 145 women were trapped and burned alive?

The year of this Triangle factory fire, 1911, was the year Smith first went to Albany. It marked the beginning of his fight to improve factory conditions, reduce the hours of labor for women and other social legislation. After his relations with Roosevelt had curdled, Smith came to denounce the New Deal's "socialism." But during the 1920's he was the means by which the Democratic party absorbed the agitations—and votes—of the Socialists and their sympathizers.

What Smith really embodied was the revolt of the underdog, urban immigrant against the top dog of "old American" stock. His Catholicism was an essential element in that revolt. The so-called "old" immigration which settled the farms was drawn largely from Protestant countries, England, Norway, Sweden and Germany. The "new" immigrant after 1885 which crowded the teeming cities, came mainly from Italy, Poland, Russia, Greece and the disintegrating Hapsburg Empire. The larger part of these new immigrants were Catholic. They also included perhaps 1.5 million Jews.

Because they came to this country late, these immigrants and their children were concentrated in the lower economic rungs. Moreover, they resented what seemed to them efforts to force conformity to an Anglo-Saxon, Protestant culture, through Sunday Blue Laws, Prohibition and the Klan.

Throughout the industrialized East, the make-up of society was such that Protestantism coincided largely with the Republican party, with millowners and financiers, with the snobbish members of exclusive clubs—in short, with the upper class. Catholicism, in turn, coincided largely with discrimination and sweated labor, with immigrant minorities who were looked down upon as inferior beings—in short, the lower class.

In his campaign Smith did not draw the line of class conflict. His campaign manager, John S. Raskob, was a millionaire. So were other ardent supporters like Pierre Du Pont, Herbert Lehman and William F. Kenny, who was reputed to have made $30 million as a contractor. Still, the class and cultural cleavage was there, like a deep fault, in the granite of our national life. Smith's candidacy unavoidably split the rock along that fault.

Before Smith the Democrats were little more of an urban party than were the Republicans. In Pennsylvania, for example, the three counties the Democrats won in 1920 and 1924—Columbia, Green and Monroe—were largely rural and native born. These counties swung for Hoover in 1928. In their place, the Democrats captured three mining and industrial counties—Elk, Lucerne and Lackawanna—which had not gone Democratic since 1892. In Pennsylvania, Smith pushed the Democratic vote above the million mark for the first time. Throughout New England, whole voting elements such as the French-Canadian and Italo-Americans were swung out of the Republican party never to return.

Smith also made women's suffrage a reality for the urban poor. In better income families, women started voting in 1920 as soon as they were granted the privilege; but among the urban masses the tradition that a woman's place was in the home still held strong until 1928. That year in Massachusetts (which Smith carried along with Rhode Island) the outpouring of women lifted the number of voters by 40 percent over 1924. The turnout in Boston was 44 percent heavier.

Although the issues of 1928 have long passed off, the cleavage which Smith's candidacy laid bare persisted. If New England remained the most Republican of the major regions, it was also where the line between unwaveringly Republican and unwaveringly Democratic voters was most rigidly drawn. Between 1932 and 1944, New England's Democratic vote did not shift by more than 2 percent in any election, while other parts of the country were fluctuating by 5 and 10 percent.

There were Catholic Republicans, of course, as there were Yankee Democrats, but the bedrock cleavage in the East remains a Catholic-Protestant one. . . .

But if Smith lifted the Democratic vote to new heights in some cities, he lost such Democratic strongholds as Oklahoma City, Atlanta, Birmingham, Dallas, Houston. In virtually all the Southern cities, Smith's vote fell off, as well as in cities with heavy Scandinavian populations, reflecting Lutheran distrust of Catholicism; he also lost ground wherever the population was mainly native born or Ku Klux in sympathy.

To sum up, by 1928 the masses in the cities with the most foreign born were already in political revolt. But that part of the urban population which was drawn from native American stock had still to be roused.

The Year of Decision

Bowls of red roses graced the speakers' table while American flags and tricolored bunting draped the walls of the banquet hall. The occasion was the first annual dinner of the Muncie, Indiana, Chamber of Com-

merce since the depression. Its immediate inspiration had been the
news that General Motors, which had stripped its local plant three
years before, was moving back. Mindful that the company was returning to escape a strike in Toledo, the Mayor assured the banqueters that
"the citizens of Muncie are in no mood for outsiders to come in and
agitate."

Returning to the city that June week in 1935 to begin their study of
"Middletown in Transition," Robert and Helen Lynd were struck by
the eagerness with which Muncie's community leaders were hailing the
return of the "good old days."

But if Muncie's businessmen were ready to forget the depression as
"just a bad bump in the road," that was not the feeling across the
railroad tracks "in the other world of wage-earners." Predominantly
native born, drawn mainly from nearby farms, Muncie's "corn-feds," as
the local workers were called, had seen no point in labor unions before
the depression. Out of a working force of 13,000, hardly 700 had
carried union cards, fewer than joined the Klan. Al Smith won a lone
precinct in the city, losing one of the two precincts which went Democratic in 1924. With every fourth Muncie worker jobless in 1932,
Roosevelt carried thirteen precincts, but still lost the city.

As in so many other communities, the NRA brought a rush among
Muncie's workers to join labor unions. At the Ball glass factory and the
automotive plants—Muncie's two strongest antiunion citadels—the
American Federation of Labor was petitioned to send in organizers.
But the AF of L was fumbling and inept, while the business community
was militantly efficient. The local police force was secretly increased.
Persons distributing handbills advertising a union meeting were picked
up. One local newspaper front-paged a photograph of a picket in
Oregon being dragged through the streets under the caption THIS PICK-
ET HAD REAL "DRAG" WITH COPS.

By the time the 1936 Presidential campaign opened, the drive to
unionize Muncie had been broken. But the workers still had the ballot.
To the Lynds the 1936 campaign "witnessed perhaps the strongest
effort in the city's history by the local big businessmen (industrialists
and bankers) to stampede local opinion in behalf of a single Presidential candidate." When the ballots were in, Muncie had gone for a
Democratic President for the first time since the Civil War. Exulted one
worker to the Lynds, "We certainly licked the big bosses."

Muncie was not the only Republican citadel which resisted Roosevelt
in 1932 but fell in 1936. Twenty-three other counties, which the Republicans held in 1932, swung four years later and—like Muncie—
stayed Democratic. Among these was "Bloody" Harlan in southeast
Kentucky, where efforts to organize the miners in the 1930's exploded
in assassinations and pitched battles; also the cities of Philadelphia and
Wilmington, the home of the Du Ponts. To defeat Roosevelt, various

members of the Du Pont clan contributed more than $500,000 to the Republicans, in addition to their donations to the American Liberty League. The net effect seems only to have advertised more sharply who was on whose side.

So overwhelming was Roosevelt's 1936 victory, that its political decisiveness is often overlooked. With only Maine and Vermont remaining Republican, Roosevelt's re-election seemed primarily a vote of gratitude for lifting the country out of a desperate economic crisis. Certainly many people favored him for that reason. But 1936 was also the year of realignment in which the Democrats became the nation's normal majority party. The traditional dominance which the Republicans had enjoyed since the Civil War was washed away and a new era in American politics began.

The depression vote of 1932 still mirrored the orbit of conflict of the old Republican order. The GOP cleavage had been mainly a struggle between the "progressives," of the Midwest and Far West against the industrial East. Roosevelt's first campaign was directed primarily toward splitting off this "progressive" vote. His best showing came in the Western and Mountain states. All six states he lost—Pennsylvania, Delaware, Connecticut, Vermont, New Hampshire and Maine—were in the East.

The shift in the basis of Roosevelt's appeal "from acreage to population," to use Raymond Moley's phrase, occurred in 1935. Moley credits the change to Huey Long's "Share Our Wealth" agitation and to Roosevelt's ire over the Supreme Court's declaring the NRA unconstitutional. To steal Long's thunder, Roosevelt proposed a "soak the rich" tax bill, which, Moley feels, marked the beginning of the conservative-liberal split inside the Democratic party. Whatever the exact turning point, 1935 saw more social legislation enacted than in any other year in the nation's history—the "wealth tax," the Wagner Labor Relations Act, the Social Security Law, the creation of WPA, the Public Utilities Holding Law, the start of the Rural Electrification Administration.

Not only in Washington but throughout the country 1935 was the year of decision. To go back to the old order or to move forward to something different? That was the question posed for decision in 1935, in countless different ways, in every phase of life.

In the early New Deal days how things were done had been less important than getting the stalled economy going again. By 1935 recovery had progressed to the point where there no longer was any question that the country would be saved. The new issue was: Would the "good old days" of unchallenged business dominance be restored? Or was America to be reshaped?

The more articulate business groups had one answer. As in Muncie, they were ready to resume their annual Chamber of Commerce dinners as if there never had been a depression. But the same processes of recovery which restored the courage of businessmen also enabled the leaders of organized labor to recover their nerve. Early in 1933 John L. Lewis, Phil Murray and Tom Kennedy lamented to Roosevelt that the United Mine Workers had barely enough members to pay the union's expenses. "Go home and have a good night's sleep," Roosevelt consoled them. "If I don't do anything else in my administration I am going to give the miners an opportunity to organize in the United Mine Workers of America."

Taking Roosevelt at his word, Lewis nearly emptied the UMW treasury to hire organizers, sending them out to tell the miners, "The President wants you to join a union." By 1934 Lewis could stand before the AF of L convention and boast that the UMW was again a fighting force of 400,000 miners. By 1935 he was ready to demand that the AF of L embrace the principle of industrial unionism or let a new labor movement organize the mass production industries.

When the first sit-down strike broke in November 1935, it came—significantly—not among workers of immigrant origin, but among the rubber workers of Akron. That city had drawn so many hillbillies from near-by states that it was often jokingly called "the capital of West Virginia." Before taking their place in the picket line, some rubber workers knelt in prayer. After the last "Amen," they picked up their baseball bats and lead pipes and moved into formation around the factories.

This fervor for unions which swept the native American workers—some observers likened it to a religious revival—was of crucial political importance. Al Smith, as we have seen, stirred a new sense of political consciousness among workers of immigrant and Catholic origin. But the native workers of the farms and hills had always held suspiciously aloof from those of immigrant stock.

The hillbillies had their own sense of group solidarity. Flint, Michigan, had its "Little Missouri" and "Little Arkansas" residential settlements. In Akron, the West Virginia State Society had 25,000 members and put on an annual West Virginia day picnic. Marked off from the older inhabitants by their accents, manners and dress, the "snake-eaters" were the butt of ridicule and jokes, which were fiercely resented. A judge in Akron suspended sentence on one man on condition that he return to West Virginia. A newspaper reporter wrote up the incident, "Judge Sentences Man to West Virginia for Life." At the next election the hapless judge was badly beaten by the votes of outraged mountaineers.

The formation of the CIO marked the fusing of the interests of the immigrant and native-stock workers, both Negro and white. That, I believe, is perhaps the most telling accomplishment of the CIO. Its political importance can hardly be exaggerated. The mass production industries had been the ones in which racial and religious antagonisms among the workers were most divisive. Carnegie, Illinois, had sprinkled clusters of different nationalities in each of its mines, reasoning correctly that a Balkanized working force would be more difficult to unionize. In some industries immigrants and Negroes had first been introduced as strikebreakers or because they would work for lower wages than native-born workers. The failure of the Knights of Labor in the 1880's was largely a failure to unite the immigrant working groups. Much of the AF of L's reluctance to embark on a real organizing drive in the mass production industries reflected the dislike of the "aristocrats of labor" in the skilled crafts for the immigrant "rubbish."

By 1935, of course, the immigrants had made considerable progress toward Americanization. But the key to the change was the rise of a common class consciousness among all workers. The depression, in making all workers more aware of their economic interests, suppressed their racial and religious antagonisms. Put crudely, the hatred of bankers among the native American workers had become greater than their hatred of the Pope or even of the Negro.

This struggle between the old nativist prejudices and the newer class consciousness still remains one of the crucial behind-the-scenes battles in the mass production unions. Class feeling or racial-religious feeling? The future of American labor rests largely on which holds the ascendancy.

The rise in class consciousness among native-American workers was a nation-wide development. In Muncie the Lynds reported the first evidences of class-feeling among the workers, stirred by the sense that the government could do something for them. In "Yankee City" (Newburyport, Mass.) W. Lloyd Warner tells of a similar change among the so-called "Riverbrookers," the proud, clannish, Yankee-stock workers who had always refused to join unions with immigrant workers. When the new shoe union staged the first successful strike in Yankee City's history, the Riverbrookers supplied the leadership.

Negroes were another voting element which was determined to go forward rather than back. In some cities as many as four out of five Negro families were on relief. "Don't Buy Where You Can't Work" campaigns were being pressed to force white storeowners to hire Negroes. In Harlem the accumulated tensions of the depression years were exploded suddenly by a trivial incident.

On March 19, 1935, a sixteen-year-old boy snatched a ten-cent bread knife from a five-and-ten-cent counter—"just for fun" he later told the police. Two white clerks and the white manager chased the boy to the rear of the store. When they grabbed him, he bit their hands and broke away.

The boy was a Puerto Rican, yet the rumor spread that a Negro had been lynched in the store. Pickets appeared. A soapbox orator on one street corner attracted a growing crowd. When a funeral hearse happened to drive by a woman shrieked, "They've come to take the boy's body!" The Negro mob went on a rampage. When the riot was over, one man was dead—three others died later of injuries—and a hundred or more whites and Negroes had been shot, stabbed or stoned.

The grisly tragedy was lightened only by the action of a Chinese laundryman. When he saw the mob surging through the streets, heaving stones into store windows, he hastily thrust a sign into his window, "Me colored too."

New York City had four previous race riots, without anything much happening afterward. The 1935 riot, however, set off a series of far-reaching changes. Harlem's shopowners hastily put on Negro employees. Before the year was out Tammany Hall had named its first Negro district leader. Mayor Fiorello La Guardia had appointed the first Negro magistrate. In 1932 most Negro voters in the country were still Republican. In 1936, in many cities two of every three Negro voters were for Roosevelt.

And so it went all through the country. It would be impossible to trace in full all the different ways in which the question—whether to go back or forward—was being asked of the American people. Sometimes the query was put bluntly in so many words. More often it was implicit in the logic of events or in reminders of the depression. At the end of 1935, more than $780 million was still tied up in closed banks, 3 million persons were still on relief; one survey of a group of garment workers showed that half of them had not bought a new coat for four years.

Lifelong Socialists had to ask themselves—did they return to the ivory tower of a futile third party or did they defend their immediate interests by rallying behind Roosevelt? Sidney Hillman and David Dubinsky, whose unions had been saved by the NRA, formed a new American Labor party to enable New Yorkers to vote for Roosevelt and still remain independent of the Democrats. Norman Thomas polled 884,000 Socialist votes nationally in 1932 but only 187,000 votes four years later.

On the other side of the political barricades the realignment was equally sharp. In 1932 one fourth of the Democratic campaign funds was contributed by bankers. In 1936 bankers accounted for a mere 3 percent of the Democratic party's war chest. (Their total contributions to the Democrats were only about a third of the $750,000 spent by organized labor.)

Particularly in rural areas, the 1936 vote showed that sizable numbers of voters were ready to return to the Republicanism of their ancestors. Winston County, which had seceded from Alabama during the Civil War to remain loyal to the union, swung back to the Republican party in 1936; so did thirty-two counties in Missouri, all but eight bone-dry by tradition. Less than a dozen wheat counties in the whole country had stayed Republican in 1932. Four years later, most of the wheat counties were on their way back to the Republican party.

In the industrial centers, however, the political allegiances that had grown out of the Civil War were uprooted for good. In New York, New Jersey and Pennsylvania, alone, the Democratic vote leaped by roughly 1.8 million. Despite the depression, in 1932, Roosevelt failed to carry a dozen cities with 100,000 or more population—Philadelphia, Scranton and Reading in Pennsylvania; Canton, Youngstown and Columbus in Ohio; Gary, Duluth, Des Moines, Grand Rapids and Springfield, Massachusetts. Every one swung for Roosevelt in 1936 and except for Grand Rapids have remained Democratic since.

A dramatic glimpse into the nature of this hidden political revolution will be found by comparing the 1928 and 1936 vote in our major cities. While Smith won six of every ten voters in some cities, in others he drew only three out of ten. This disparity had narrowed by 1932, but wide divergences in voting still prevailed in different parts of the country. With the 1936 election, as the table below shoes, the voting of nearly all our major cities hit a common level.

Whether the cities are heavily foreign born or native American in make-up, Catholic or Protestant, with large numbers of Negroes or of whites up from the South, did not make too much difference in their 1936 vote. Nor whether the city had a strong labor tradition like San Francisco or an open shop tradition like Los Angeles, nor whether it was located on the East or West coast or in the Midwest.

A new nationalizing force had clearly been injected into American politics. In the past American political realignments have always fol-

CITIES HIGH SMITH			CITIES LOW SMITH		
City	Dem. % 1928	Dem. % 1936	City	Dem. % 1928	Dem. % 1936
Lawrence	71	73	Flint	19	72
Boston	67	63	Wichita, Kan.	24	64
Lowell	64	61	Los Angeles	28	67
Fall River	64	67	Akron	31	71
New York	60	75	Des Moines	31	55
New Haven	57	65	San Diego	32	65
Milwaukee	53	76	Seattle	32	64
New Bedford	52	65	Duluth	32	71
Cleveland	52	76	Canton	34	66
St. Louis	51	66	Spokane	35	71
San Francisco	49	72	Detroit	37	65
Chicago	48	65	Indianapolis	39	57
Pittsburgh	47	67	Philadelphia	39	60
Baltimore	47	67	Youngstown	39	74

lowed sectional lines. The Revolt of the City, however, had drawn the same class-conscious line of economic interest across the entire country, overriding not only regional distinctions but equally strong cultural differences.

This development was not without its irony. In drawing the line of cleavage between worker and "economic royalists," Roosevelt unquestionably sharpened the sense of class division in American society. Yet, in doing so, he subordinated the old nativistic prejudices of race and religion, which had divided the lower half of American society for so long, bringing to these lower income elements a greater degree of social unity than they had ever shared before. Was Roosevelt dividing or unifying the country? . . .

By Fire and Water

If the 1936 vote marked the emergence of the new Roosevelt coalition, the third term election brought the crucial trial by fire and water which demonstrated the coalition's durability.

In both 1932 and 1936 Roosevelt would still have been elected without his heavy urban pluralities. In 1940, however, with the war and the third-term issue cutting heavily into his rural strength, the margin of victory that accounted for at least 212 electoral votes was supplied by the dozen largest cities in the country.

In every city I visited while doing postelection survey I found that the Roosevelt vote broke at virtually the same economic level, between $45 and $60 a month rent. Below that line his pluralities were overwhelming. Above it, they faded away. In Pittsburgh, for example, Roosevelt got three fourths of the vote in wards whose rentals averaged under $40 a month and only four tenths of the vote where rentals were above $65 a month. Minneapolis, whose social make-up contrasts sharply with Pittsburgh, showed much the same results—about 40 percent of the vote for Roosevelt in the highest income ward, but seven of every ten voters in the lower rental areas.

The sharpness with which the balloting stratified in city after city—Chicago, Boston, St. Louis, Seattle, Cleveland—left little room for any appreciable shift of votes because of the campaign put on by Wendell Willkie. When I asked one auto unionist in Detroit why the third-term issue had made so little difference he replied, "I'll say it even though it doesn't sound nice. We've grown class conscious." With other unions there may have been less bitterness but the division between worker and "economic royalist" was as sharply drawn. In a Minneapolis ward, inhabited largely by teamsters, the pastor of one church had been outspoken in condemning the third term. He admitted bitterly, "I don't suppose I changed a single vote." John Lewis, who had endorsed Willkie, could have echoed him.

This class consciousness, it should be noted, was not confined to workers. The balloting revealed as much class feeling among the higher income Republicans. If Roosevelt solidified the lower classes, he also welded the upper class.

The one sharp break from "economic voting" came on the basis of ethnic background, reflecting the varying impact upon different groups of Hitler's War. Roosevelt's heaviest losses came in German-American and Italo-American wards, where resentment was strong against his "stab in the back" reference to Mussolini's attack on France. The highest income areas voting for Roosevelt were Jewish. In Brooklyn he carried streets with $15,000 homes—a comfortable valuation in 1940—and apartment houses with doormen. Where low income status coincided with the nationality background of a country invaded by Germany, the vote for Roosevelt was prodigious. Polish-American wards in Buffalo went Democratic nine to one, with individual precincts running as high as twenty to one, his heaviest pluralities in the whole country.

Curiously, the ethnic elements most bitterly antagonized by Hitler were largely those contributing the heaviest numbers of new voters. In Buffalo, in 1940, the Polish-Americans mustered enough votes to elect a Polish-American judge for the first time. One Democratic ward leader, John Kryzinski, a tavern keeper, was foaming with enthusiasm at the significance of this victory.

"Out in ritzy Humboldt Park they get two voters to a family," he snorted contemptuously. "I get six out of my house. I got neighbors who give me eight. We elected a judge this year. The way things are going in eight years we'll elect a mayor."

Nine years later Buffalo did elect Joseph Mruc its first Polish-American mayor.

In every city one could see the same inexorable spread of numbers and the same leveling pressures. Almost it seemed, in fact, that the Republicans had decided to abandon the cities to the Democratic masses, taking refuge in the suburbs. In St. Louis the Twenty-eighth Ward had stayed Republican in 1932. By 1940 this GOP stronghold had been reduced to three precincts. Along Lindell Boulevard and Skinker Road, "For Sale" signs were propped in front of mansionlike homes with graveled driveways, flagstone walks and antique-fabricated lampposts. Some of the more imposing residences were being razed to make way for apartment houses. In the old days at the Pageant, the neighborhood movie house, seats were reserved. When I saw it, the lobby was placarded with handbills advertising double features on Wednesday and Thursdays, with three features for a quarter on Fridays and Saturdays.

In Harlem, as well, the spirit of 1936 had quickened. Along 125th Street Negroes were working in hundreds of establishments which as late as 1935 had been manned completely by whites. Garment workers, janitors, bartenders, waiters and waitresses, Pullman porters, laundry workers, newspaper men, retail clerks and redcaps were flocking into labor unions with a sense of deliverance. To the Negro, unionism promised more than a wage boost. It also seemed the trumpet which would eventually tumble the Jericho walls of discrimination. Some Harlem unions were holding daily classes to teach Negroes selling, typing and stenography, to be able to rebuff employers who protested, "I can't hire Negroes, they're not experienced."

Probably 50 percent of Harlem's Negroes were still getting relief of some kind. Older Negroes, clinging to the Republican party, might shake their graying heads and mutter, "Our people are selling their birthrights for a mess of pottage." Younger Negroes had a different slant on WPA. "The really important thing about WPA is that it is a guarantee of a living wage," explained Carl Lawrence, a reporter on the *Amsterdam News*. "It means Negroes don't have to work for anything people want to give them. This helps life the standards of all Negroes, even those not on WPA."

The fall of France in 1940 had spurted the armament program, and the defense boom had been building up steadily in the months before the election. With the boom in employment, a highly significant thing was happening. Older people, who had been thrown out of work during the depression, were not being re-employed. The jobs were going to their children, while the older folk stayed on relief or lived on their savings, plus some help from their children. It hardly had been planned that way, but the New Deal was cushioning a wholesale shift in the working population, by easing the older generation of depression casualties out of the way to make room for a new generation.

In the Charlestown area of Boston one half of the voters were under forty. The ward leader himself, William Galvin, was thirty-six. Two younger brothers had got out of high school during the depression and had gone into the CCC camps. When employment in the Boston Navy Yard expanded, they got jobs as electrician's and pipe fitter's helpers. From the CCC to the Navy Yard—to these two youths, the government had brought advancement as real as any they could have achieved under a private employer.

As a reporter in Washington I had shared the general belief that the New Deal was hastily improvised and animated by no coherent philosophy. When one translated its benefits down to what they meant to the families I was interviewing in 1940, the whole Roosevelt program took on a new consistency.

The depression had thrown grave strains upon lower income families. Many family heads had lost their jobs, never to be employed regularly again. In some instances, the children were old enough to take over the bread-winning, which often robbed the deposed patriarch of his self-respect. In other families the parents had to struggle along until the children grew of age and took over.

In varied ways the New Deal eased these family strains. Through the HOLC* a million homes were saved. Many homeowners were too old to have been able to buy a new home, if they had lost their old ones. With their children grown older, I found, many were renting out part of the house, often to a married son or daughter.

Into the CCC camps went 2.75 million sons of the cities. No longer a drain on the family larder, they even sent some money back home. Children in high school might get NYA† aid. Those who went to work usually did so in low-wage industries where the effects of the wage-hour law were most noticeable.

These and other New Deal benefits did not solve all the family problems by any means. They did ease the adjustments that had to be made as the unfortunates of one generation grew unemployable and another generation finally found its opportunity in defense employment.

The recovery from the depression low helped Roosevelt politically with all groups. It was particularly important in the cities because that recovery coincided with the hatching out of the birth rates of 1910 to 1920 and the rise of a new generation. The very size of the Democratically inclined families helped knit them to the New Deal. Even persons who had done rather well for themselves were likely to have a less fortunate family member lower down the economic ladder being benefited by the New Deal. Old-age pensions and other aid eased the burden of having to care for parents too old to work. Instead of being dragged by family burdens, the rising generation was able to solidify its gains.

How much of all this was "planned that way" and how much of it just happened can be speculated upon endlessly. One can also speculate about what might have happened if Roosevelt had not run for a third term and if the war in Europe had not broken out when it did.

Both Garner and Farley have written that they opposed a third term to keep the Democratic party from degenerating into a personal vehicle for Roosevelt and Roosevelt alone. If Roosevelt runs again, Garner told Bascom Timmons, his biographer, "after he is off the ticket the Democratic party will fall to pieces." Despite Garner's deserved reputation for political shrewdness, he seems to have misjudged the forces at work. But for the third term, it is questionable whether many of the elements who had thrown their strength to the Democrats for the first time in 1936 would have solidified in the party. Early in 1940, for example, Ralph Bunche was still writing of the Negro vote as being "essentially Republican."

Paradoxically, the New Deal also appears to have grown stronger politically after it was abandoned. The outbreak of the war put an end

---

*Home Owners Loan Corporation.—Ed.
†National Youth Administration.—Ed.

to social reform. But the war boom made unnecessary any additional New Deal measures. In fact, the war succeeded in doing what the New Deal never could accomplish; it brought the country out of the depression.

Unemployment never fell below 8 million in 1939 and growing numbers of people wondered whether there ever would be full employment. In the "little steel" strike of 1937 organized labor suffered a serious setback. If the recession of 1938 had dragged on, labor might have had to retreat, instead of entrenching itself as a permanent force in the mass production industries. All through the 1930's surplus sons and daughters had been held back on the farms because of a lack of opportunities in the cities.

The defense boom sparked anew the migration from farm to city. It also sparked new vigor into the marriage rate. In the middle 1930's one of four youths in their late teens and early twenties had never had regular work. By 1939 the marriage rate had risen from the depression low of eight to nearly eleven per thousand population. In 1941 it leaped to almost thirteen per thousand.

Economically speaking, then, the defense boom was the happy ending which saved the New Deal and made it a success story. The years of full employment which followed the outbreak of Hitler's War solved the economic problem of the Roosevelt generation, solidifying them in the Democratic party. But in the process this generation changed markedly. Not only had it aged and taken on new responsibilities, but much of this generation had climbed from poverty into the middle class. . . .

10 The Conservative Coalition

JAMES T. PATTERSON

James T. Patterson, a professor of history at Brown University, studied at Williams College with James MacGregor Burns and at Harvard with Frank Freidel. Perhaps the foremost historian of recent American conservatism, he is the author of *Congressional Conservatism and the New Deal* (1967), which received the Prize Studies Award of the Organization of American Historians, and of *Mr. Republican: A Biography of Robert A. Taft* (1972). *Congressional Conservatism* was the first effort to explore in depth the nature of the conservative coalition that stalemated the New Deal and dominated congressional politics until 1964; this article is a concise presentation of its findings.

The coalition, he asserts, was not made up of old men living in the past, though its leaders did have considerable congressional seniority. It was never well organized, and its membership shifted from issue to issue. Generally, however, its most consistent participants came from "safe" districts and tended to represent rural areas. The coalition crystallized as Roosevelt's prestige dropped because of the Court-packing plan, the sitdown strikes, the recession of 1937–1938, and the President's failure to "purge" key conservatives in 1938. At the same time, a partial economic recovery reduced the sense of urgency which had impelled many congressmen to vote for New Deal measures earlier in the decade. Finally, Roosevelt's urban coalition by its own excesses and lack of unity helped bring the conservative coalition into being. As the author sees it, the coalition grew out of a series of uncontrollable cir-

From "A Conservative Coalition Forms in Congress, 1933–1939" by James T. Patterson, *Journal of American History*, LII (March, 1966), 757–772. Copyright © 1966 by the Organization of American Historians. Reprinted by permission of the Editor of the *Journal of American History*.

cumstances, not bad presidential leadership. The result in any case was a rebirth of the urban-rural antagonism that had disrupted the Democratic party in the 1920's and that now brought an effective end to the New Deal.

* * *

Few political developments in recent American history have been more significant than the creation of a conservative coalition in Congress. Formed by Republicans and conservative Democrats to combat the New Deal, this "unholy alliance" operated effectively as early as 1937, and by 1939 it was strong enough to block extensions of the administration's program. It has functioned with varying degrees of success since that time, harassing and alarming Presidents of both parties.

Certain aspects of the coalition are well known and open to little question. Undoubtedly, both houses of Congress were more cantankerous in President Franklin D. Roosevelt's second term than they had been in his first, and most of the uncooperative congressmen were conservative on key issues. They tended to favor balanced budgets, to oppose welfare programs, to be suspicious of organized labor, and to speak favorably of states rights and limited government.

But historians have seldom ventured beyond these generalizations. They have not identified the members of the coalition. They have not tried to generalize about them as a group. They have not probed into the questions of why or when the coalition began. Finally, they have not shown whether the coalition was consciously organized, well disciplined, or coherent on crucial roll calls. These matters deserve attention.

Actually, the conservative leaders were well known. In the House the focus of conservative strength was the Rules Committee, dominated after 1938 by Edward E. Cox, a fiery Georgian who was a ranking Democratic member, and by Howard W. Smith, a Jeffersonian Democrat from Virginia. These two men, with three other southern Democrats and four Republicans, composed a majority of the fourteen-man committee after 1936. Cox was friendly with Joseph W. Martin, Jr. of Massachusetts, the leading Republican member of the committee in 1937–1938 who became House minority leader in 1939. When controversial issues arose, Cox and Martin usually conferred. If they agreed—which was often—Martin instructed his Republican colleagues on the committee to vote with Cox and the southern Democrats. Martin said later that he and Cox were the "principal points of contact between the northern Republicans and the southern Democratic conservatives."

Conservative leadership in the Senate was more diverse. The official Republican leader was Charles L. McNary of Oregon. The popular McNary was neither an orator nor a conservative by nature; indeed, he had voted for most New Deal measures before 1937. Though McNary participated in GOP strategy conferences, the most aggressive Republican senator after 1936 was the moderately conservative Arthur H. Vandenberg of Michigan. Other well-known Republicans who usually voted against major administration proposals included Henry Cabot Lodge, Jr. of Massachusetts, Warren R. Austin of Vermont, and Hiram W. Johnson of California, who became one of the most vitriolic foes of the New Deal after 1936.

Democratic conservatives in the Senate were a varied group. On the extreme right was a cluster of irreconcilables who had voted against most New Deal programs since 1933. These included Carter Glass and Harry F. Byrd of Virginia and Josiah W. Bailey of North Carolina. Bailey was particularly pungent in his criticism of Roosevelt. The President, he wrote,

> figures on hard times and does not wish for recovery. He would perish like a rattlesnake in the sun under conditions of prosperity. Pardon the illustration. Mr. Roosevelt is not a rattlesnake. He rattles a great deal, but that is all I am willing to say. Perhaps you know the rattlesnake must stay in the swamp for the reason that he does not have any means of sweating or panting. His heat accumulates. Mr. Roosevelt belongs to that type of man who lives on hard times and discontent.

Other Democrats, equally irreconcilable, joined Bailey in 1935–1936. These included Edward R. Burke of Nebraska, Peter G. Gerry of Rhode Island, Walter F. George of Georgia, and Ellison D. ("Cotton Ed") Smith of South Carolina. Such powerful veterans as Byron ("Pat") Harrison of Mississippi and James F. Byrnes of South Carolina, early supporters of the New Deal, also voted consistently against New Deal spending, tax, and labor programs after 1937. Vice-President John N. Garner of Texas, an influential figure in both houses, was another Democrat who by 1937 was counselling Roosevelt to move in a conservative direction.

While these men were unquestionably the most prominent congressional conservatives, it is not easy to generalize about them as a group. In the main they were not simply old men who had outlived their times. True, some like "Cotton Ed" Smith and Glass undoubtedly had. "Perhaps I am a relic of constitutional government," Glass admitted in 1938. "I entertain what may be the misguided notion that the Constitution of the United States, as it existed in the time of Grover Cleveland, is the same Constitution that exists today. . . ." But others, such as Byrd, Martin, and Howard Smith, were relatively young men. The average age of the most conservative Democratic senators in 1937 was precisely that of the Senate as a whole, while the most conservative Democratic representatives in 1937 averaged fifty years of age, two years less than the entire House.

Furthermore, the conservatives were by no means all veterans whose congressional service preceded the New Deal. Glass, George, and some others fitted this category, but many more first served in 1933 or thereafter, and the percentage of veteran and "coat-tail" Democrats who opposed the New Deal on most crucial roll calls was very much the same. Moreover, the most senior Republicans after 1935 included the moderately progressive McNary, William E. Borah of Idaho, and Arthur Capper of Kansas, while newcomers Austin of Vermont and H. Styles Bridges of New Hampshire tended to be among the most consistent opponents of the New Deal. Democratic veterans included not only conservatives of the Glass variety but New Deal regulars Alben W. Barkley of Kentucky, Hugo L. Black of Alabama, and Robert F. Wagner of New York. As Arthur S. Link has pointed out, the Congresses of the 1920's contained many relics of the progressive era; some of these veteran congressmen became reliable supporters of the New Deal in the 1930's.

Similarly, it is not entirely accurate to say that conservative strength in Congress derived from chairmanships of key committees. In the House, committee chairmen John J. O'Connor of New York and Hatton W. Sumners of Texas occasionally blocked administration proposals. So did "Cotton Ed" Smith, Glass, and Harrison in the Senate. But these men were counterbalanced by such liberal chairmen as Senators Black, Wagner, and Elbert D. Thomas of Utah and Representatives Sam Rayburn of Texas, Adolph J. Sabath of Illinois, and Sol Bloom of New York. More often than not, committee chairmen cooperated with the administration.

Roosevelt's congressional troubles after 1936 stemmed not so much from uncooperative committee chairmen as from more widespread opposition to his programs. In the House, for example, his three most painful defeats on domestic legislation from 1937 through 1939 were the recommittal of the fair labor standards bill in 1937, the recommittal of executive reorganization in 1938, and the defeat of his lending program in 1939. All three came at the hands of the entire House. In the Senate he lost three successive battles for increased relief expenditures in 1939, and each time the reason was the adverse vote of the entire Senate. It is too easy—and too misleading—to blame the seniority rule for Roosevelt's congressional problems.

At first glance it would appear that the conservative bloc was composed of Republicans and southern Democrats, but such was not always the case. It is undeniable that Republicans, especially in the House, opposed the administration with remarkable solidarity after 1936, but the stance of southerners was less easy to determine. Occasionally, it seemed that Cox and Bailey were representative southern spokesmen. For instance, when the House recommitted the fair labor standards bill by a vote of 216–198 in December 1937, 81 of the 99 southern Democrats voted for recommittal, as opposed to but 51 of the remaining 230

Democrats in the House. And when the Senate in August 1937 adopted, 44–39, the so-called Byrd amendment aimed at damaging the Wagner housing bill, 10 of the 22 southern Democrats supported the amendment, while only 19 of the remaining 54 Senate Democrats were with the majority.

Two factors dispel much of this seeming clarity. First, voting alignments depended upon the issue. The labor bill, by proposing to destroy southern competitive wage advantages, upset southerners of all persuasions. Walter Lippmann, in fact, called the bill "sectional legislation disguised as humanitarian reform." On other crucial votes in the House, however, such as those which recommitted reorganization in 1938 and defeated the death sentence provision of the utility holding company bill in 1935, representatives from the South divided as did Democrats from other sections. Secondly, southerners were seldom united. As V. O. Key put it, "while individual southern Senators may frequently vote with the Republicans, a majority rarely does; and when it does, the group as a whole is badly split more than half the time." The New Deal Congresses had their Glasses and Baileys, but they also had their Blacks and Rayburns. Except on race legislation, southern congressmen were never "solid."

Three things, nonetheless, were generally true of the congressional conservatives as a group. First of all, most of the vocal conservatives came from safe states or districts. The Glass-Byrd machine in Virginia, for instance, was able not only to keep veterans like Glass in the Senate but to send new conservatives to the House throughout the period. With all his power and prestige Roosevelt was too often unable to influence congressional nominations; the result was the nomination and election of many conservative Democrats during the New Deal years. In 1935 alone, new Senate Democrats included Rush D. Holt of West Virginia, Gerry of Rhode Island, and Burke of Nebraska, all of whom were soon to become staunch foes of the New Deal. That such men could be nominated in a year of unusually restive and liberal politics indicates both the limitations of presidential political power and the continuing strength of local political organizations.

Second, most of the effective Democratic conservatives, though not committee chairmen, were ranking or near-ranking members of important committees. Cox was the most strategically placed of these men, but there were several others. In the House they included Martin Dies, Jr. of Texas on the Rules Committee and Clifton A. Woodrum of Virginia on appropriations. In the Senate Bailey, George, William H. King of Utah, and many others comprised this group. Those conservative Democrats without responsibility, it seemed, often felt free to act as they pleased.

Thirdly, most conservative congressmen after 1936 were from rural districts or states. Too much should not be made of this fact: so, too, were many liberals. There were also many conservative Democrats from urbanized states, such as Senators Gerry of Rhode Island and Millard E. Tydings of Maryland. The nature of opposition to administration programs depended greatly upon the type of issue: New Deal farm bills, for example, often aroused considerable hostility among urban congressmen. Generally, however, rural congressmen voted against New Deal programs more consistently than did urban congressmen. The coalition was composed not so much of Republicans and southern Democrats as of Republicans and rural Democrats; urban southerners were often more favorably disposed to administration programs than their rural counterparts.

The existence of this urban-rural split upon many economic issues after 1936 was indisputable. Democratic votes in the House against administration measures in the 1937–1939 period were: investigation of sit-downs, 82 percent rural; recommit fair labor standards, 74 percent rural; investigate National Labor Relations Board, 77 percent rural; lending bill, 69 percent rural; and housing bill, 83 percent rural. Since the percentage of Democrats who represented rural districts was 54 in 1937 and 57 in 1939, it is clear that the Democratic opposition on these bills was heavily rural in character.*

It is difficult to say that any given issue or year "created" the conservative group. Rather, different groups of inherently conservative men switched at different times from unhappy allegiance to the New Deal to open hostility. In most cases these men changed their positions because they discovered that they could oppose the administration without fear of electoral extinction. The state of the President's prestige, as much as the nature of his program, determined the kind of reception he received on Capitol Hill.

Roosevelt's great popularity before 1937 was undeniable. Even Republicans bowed before it. "There can be no doubt," wrote one Republican senator in 1933, "that at the moment the President has an extraordinary support throughout the country and is able to do with the Congress as he wills. I suppose prudence dictates that one should not attempt to swim against the tide." Thus, Republicans through 1936 split sharply on final votes on major pieces of legislation. Cautious men like Vandenberg supported part of the administration program; others, not so astute, lost in 1934 or 1936. Many congressmen of both

---

*An urban congressman is one who represented a district in which 50 percent or more of its inhabitants lived in areas identified as urban by the *Sixteenth Census of the United States, 1940, Population*, I (Washington, 1942), 10. This definition admittedly does not differentiate among the different types of urban districts nor does it take into account the fact that some urban districts were represented by men with rural backgrounds and values— or vice versa. But it seems the fairest way to deal with the often rather haphazardly defined concepts of "rural" and "urban."

parties were unhappy with the New Deal well before 1937, but few dared to publicize their discontent with adverse votes.

Nevertheless, Democratic disaffection in Congress grew ominously as early as 1935. In that year the House three times defeated the death sentence clause of the utility holding company bill, and in the Senate the "wealth tax" bill antagonized not only the Democratic irreconcilables but also moderates like Harrison and Byrnes. Roosevelt's success with his 1935 Congress was indeed remarkable, but it cost him some political capital. Even if he had not thrown Congress into turmoil in 1937 with his court reform plan, he probably would have had great difficulty with the many congressmen who had already chafed at his relentless leadership and who considered the reform era at an end.

The court reform plan, presented in February 1937, provided these fractious congressmen with the ideal occasion for open rebellion. While Harrison and some other leaders remained outwardly loyal, the plan caused many formerly dependable Democrats to oppose the President openly. In addition, it united progressive and conservative Republicans, created intense personal rancor, and left all but the "100 percent New Dealers" suspicious of the President's motives. Above all, it emboldened congressmen who had not dared speak out before.

Other events after 1936 increased congressional courage. The wave of sit-down strikes in 1937 caused many to blame the New Deal for the growth of labor "radicalism." The recession of 1937–1938 convinced others that the New Deal had failed. The President's plan to reorganize the executive branch, a divisive issue in 1938, provided another occasion for successful coalition effort. And Roosevelt's unsuccessful attempt to purge his conservative opponents in 1938 encouraged disenchanted congressmen to become still more outspoken.

The election of 1938 solidified this trend. Republicans gained 80 seats in the House and 8 in the Senate, increasing their numbers to 169 and 23 respectively. Since unreliable Democrats already numbered some 40 in the House and 20 in the Senate, the administration faced a divided Congress before the session began. The President's achievements in 1939 were negligible; the domestic New Deal, for all intents and purposes, made no more striking gains.

These external events, however, were not the only causes of Roosevelt's difficulties, nor should the President receive all the blame for the change. Two other developments—the changing nature of the liberal coalition and improved economic conditions—also contributed materially to the growth of congressional conservatism after 1936.

Roosevelt's liberal coalition had changed dramatically from the largely southern-western alliance of 1932 to a congeries of politically conscious pressure groups. Composed of labor unions, underprivileged ethnic groups, Negroes, and relief recipients, this aggregation was essentially northern-urban in character. Enormously encouraged by the 1936 election, these groups pressed relentlessly for their objectives in ensuing sessions, often without Roosevelt's approval. The sit-downs, for instance, were not Roosevelt's idea, and he refused to take sides in the matter. Similarly, relief workers and Democratic mayors badgered the President for higher relief expenditures than he was willing to seek. The fair labor standards bill, criticized by conservative southerners, faced even more serious opposition from AFL spokesmen fearful of government interference with collective bargaining. The President did not press either for housing or antilynching legislation, but liberal congressmen insisted upon introducing them, and bitter struggles ensued. Except for the court plan, unquestionably a major presidential blunder, Roosevelt made few tactically serious errors after 1936. But the well organized elements of his predominantly northern-urban coalition were demanding more aid at the same time that many other congressmen, not so dependent upon these elements for political survival, were convinced of the need for retrenchment. And many rural congressmen, while friendly to much of the New Deal, believed these urban elements were preempting funds or favors which might otherwise have benefited rural areas. The result was a largely urban-rural split within the unwieldy coalition which was the Democratic party.* No amount of presidential flattery could have prevented it.†

It is also worth noting that the changed emphasis of the New Deal in 1935—such as it was—was not nearly so distrubing to many congressmen as the pressure generated by urban elements in 1937. Southerners, Harrison and Byrnes for instance, had in 1935 approved social security, banking reform, and moderate tax reform. And men like Cox, hostile to abuses by private utilities, had even found it possible to vote for the death sentence clause of the utility bill. But none of these men favored the more urban liberalism espoused by liberal congressmen in 1937–1939. Prior to 1936 the economic emergency, together with the administration's emphasis upon measures benefiting all areas of the nation, had temporarily obscured the urban-rural fissures to apparent in the Democratic party in the 1920's. But when the urban wing of the party, awakened and dominant, sought to gain beneficial

---

*It was also true that rural overrepresentation in both houses aided the conservative cause. Yet since this overrepresentation also existed before 1936, emphasis here is placed upon other factors.

†James M. Burns, *Roosevelt*, 347–349, 375–380, suggests that if Roosevelt had committed himself earlier to developing a strong progressive element in Congress, he would have escaped many of his congressional dilemmas after 1936. Such an effort, however, would have required far too much time even to consider during the emergency years of the early New Deal. Moreover, Burns presents insufficient evidence to show that such an effort could have succeeded in overcoming entrenched party organizations in the states. Roosevelt, in working with rather than against the pressure groups from 1933 through 1936, was pursuing the only sensible course possible.

legislation in 1937–1939, the split reappeared to plague the New Deal and subsequent liberal administrations.

Improved economic conditions were of great significance to this split, for if one examines executive-congressional relations in the twentieth century, he finds that congressmen were never so tractable as in the desperate years from 1933 through 1935. Without detracting from Roosevelt's able congressional leadership in these years, it is certain that the emergency provided ideal conditions for the success of his program in Congress. Practically every congressman, besieged for relief by his constituents, responded with alacrity to the President's activist leadership. By 1937 this sense of crisis had diminished. Thus many of the same moderate congressmen who had so gratefully supported the administration through 1935 became unreliable two and three years later. And the recession of 1937–1938, far from reviving this sense of crisis, served instead to suggest that Roosevelt was not the magician he had previously seemed to be. Indeed, to many hostile congressmen the period was the "Roosevelt recession." In a sense, the economic state of the nation was the President's greatest ally before 1936, his greatest adversary thereafter.

The sit-down strikes, the defeat of the court plan and the purge, and the recession gave considerable confidence to many inherently conservative congressmen who had already been uneasy or restive with the New Deal in 1935–1936. The beginning of effective conservative opposition in Congress, accordingly, can be set in 1937. But the roots stemmed at least to 1935, and in retrospect it seems that the court plan merely hastened the development of an inevitable division among the disparate elements of the dominant Democratic party.

One major problem remains: how did the conservative bloc function as a group? Was it a well organized conspiracy, or was it simply a loose combination of the moment?

At a glance, the coalition appears to have been well organized. In the Senate fight against the court plan, Burton K. Wheeler of Montana led a bipartisan team against the President. Senators from both parties not only cooperated but met from time to time in private homes to plan joint strategy. And Republicans agreed to keep quiet lest their partisan charges antagonize moderate Democrats. As Vandenberg admitted later, there was a "bipartisan high command. . . . Only a coalition could succeed—a preponderantly Democratic coalition. This was frankly recognized. There was no secret about it. . . . Republicans voluntarily subordinated themselves and withdrew to the reserve lines. . . ."

Many of the senators who opposed the court plan remained at odds with the administration in the 1938 and 1939 sessions, and Wheeler led quite similar blocs against executive reorganization. And in the House, 1937 was the year when the conservative bloc in the Rules Committee first began to operate against the administration, refusing three times

between August 1937 and May 1938 to report out the fair labor standards bill. Unquestionably, conservatives in both houses developed net-
works of personal communications across party lines in 1937 and 1938.
On crucial roll call votes it was safe to predict that an all but unanimous
group of Republicans in both houses would be joined by at least 20
Democrats in the Senate and from 40 to 110 in the House.

Such evidence, however, does not prove the existence of a coordi-
nated group functioning as a team on all—or even most—issues. Wheeler, for example, was not so reactionary as liberals insisted, and he
continued after 1937 to back many administration relief, labor, and
farm bills. Conversely, Harrison and Byrnes remained loyal to the
administration during both the court and reorganization battles, while
stridently opposing the fair labor standards bill, increased spending for
relief, and the undistributed profits tax. And foreign policy questions
created completely different alignments.

That the type of issue determined the composition of the conservative bloc was especially clear in the 1939 session. In the Senate, conservative alliances defeated the administration in struggles over relief
spending in January and temporarily over reorganization in March.
The crucial votes were 47–46 and 45–44 respectively. On both occasions Republicans voted solidly against the administration; of the 23 in
the Senate, 20 voted against relief and 22 against reorganization. Of
the 69 Democrats, 26 opposed relief and 21 reorganization. But the
bloc was not monolithic. Eleven of the 26 Democrats against the relief
bill supported the President on reorganization; 7 Democrats who had
backed the President on relief deserted him on reorganization. A conservative nucleus of 20 Republicans and 15 Democrats opposed the
administration on both bills. The others shifted in and out at will. For
partisan reasons Republicans were remarkably united, but conservative
Democrats were seldom able to work together in either house.

Furthermore, even the predictable core of very conservative Democrats ordinarily voted with Republicans because there was a meeting of
the minds, not because they had conferred secretly with them in advance of crucial votes. The fate which befell the one serious effort in the
direction of long-range conservative planning revealed the insuperable
problems involved in developing such bipartisan agreement. This
effort occurred in the fall of 1937.

After the Supreme Court's "switch in time that saved nine" in the
spring of 1937, Bailey realized that the Senate must replace the court as
the bulwark of conservative strength in the country, and he became
anxious to form a more cohesive bloc against the New Deal. "What we
have to do," he wrote Byrd in September, "is to preserve, if we can, the
Democratic Party against his [Roosevelt's] efforts to make it the
Roosevelt Party. But above this we must place the preservation of Constitutional Representative Government. We must frame a policy and

maintain it—and this must be done in the next Congress. We must ascertain on whom we may rely—get them together and make our battle, win or lose."

When Bailey and his fellow conservatives returned for a special session in November they determined to put their coalition into effect. On December 2 ten conservative Democrats and two Republicans feasted on quail in a Senate dining room and laid plans for the future. As Vandenberg, one of the participants, put it privately, the group "informally resolved upon attempting a coalition statement to the country." For the next ten days this group, led by Vandenberg, Bailey, and Gerry, worked diligently at consulting conservative colleagues and trying to draft a statement of principles. They sought to present Roosevelt with a show of bipartisan strength and to persuade him to adopt a program more conciliatory to business. But their plan was also "replete with the possibility of open coalition upon the floor of the Senate." Senators who subscribed to the principles enunciated in the statement—broad phrases covering tax, spending, and labor policy— were expected to vote accordingly when these issues arose in subsequent congressional sessions.

Bailey's effort failed dismally. To begin with, moderately conservative Democrats like Harrison and Byrnes refused to participate. As southerners they did not relish formal associations with Republicans, nor did they wish to antagonize the President for no good purpose. Others naturally preferred to maintain their freedom of action in the future. And still others feared that such a challenge would drive Roosevelt, then pursuing an uncertain course in dealing with the recession, into the hands of the spenders. Before Bailey and his cohorts had time to circulate the finished document, McNary secured a copy and gave it to the press, which published it without delay on December 16. The surprised conservatives fumed silently. "Premature publicity— *thanks to treachery*—ended the episode," Vandenberg noted in his scrapbook. "The next time we want to plan a patriotically dramatic contribution to the welfare of the country, we shall let no one in who is not *tried and true*." Bailey added that the "premature publicity was brought about wholly because this man [McNary] and some of his associates took a partisan view that the declaration of principles would help the Democratic cause and hurt the Republican cause." As both men realized, McNary's action ended the frail hopes for a resounding, well-timed demonstration of conservative strength.

McNary's thinking was indeed party partisan. At that time he was conferring with Alfred M. Landon, Frank Knox, and other Republican leaders in the Capitol. Encouraged by Roosevelt's declining prestige, these men believed that Republicans could survive without seeking coalitions with conservative Democrats. The idea of a bipartisan statement of conservatism seemed to them considerably less attractive than it did to Vandenberg. Yet McNary's chief motivation was ideological; like other progressive Republicans, he frankly disagreed with the views of the conservatives involved. If Republicans associated with men like Bailey, he believed, they would give the GOP an even more reactionary coloring than it already wore. McNary's "treachery" was evidence both of the power of partisanship and of the divisions within his party.

Neither Bailey nor his fellow conservatives again pressed seriously for the plan. Republicans became increasingly partisan, driving Democrats of all persuasions into uneasy unity for the coming campaign. Despite the attempted purges which followed, both Republicans and Democrats in the ensuing primaries acted along partisan rather than conservative-liberal lines, and the flimsy chances for bipartisan conservative cooperation in the Senate faded quickly. Conservatives continued to vote together in 1938 and 1939 if there was a meeting of the minds; otherwise, as Bailey had feared, they voted apart. As a newsman close to the scene explained at the close of the 1939 session,

> in both houses, when a pro- and anti-New Deal issue is squarely presented, a shifting population of conservative Democrats can be counted upon to join the Republicans to vote against the President. The arrangement is not formal. There is nothing calculated about it, except the Republican strategy originated . . . by McNary of refraining from arousing the Democrats' partisan feelings by inflammatory oratory.

A conservative bipartisan bloc was often able by 1939 to block major legislative extensions of the New Deal. But it was not united, and it followed no blueprint. Conservative congressmen, representing widely differing states and districts, faced widely differing political exigencies. They refused to be chained to a "conspiracy." More important, most congressmen were first of all partisans. For all but a few the party organizations of their constituencies were the chief facts of their political careers, and few of these organizations, in 1937 or at any time, wished bipartisanship to operate for long.

11 A Case Study: The Negro and the New Deal

LESLIE H. FISHEL, JR.

Few early twentieth-century progressives had much interest in the problems of blacks; in fact, many were frankly racist in their attitudes. By the late 1960's, however, the aspirations of blacks had become the central concern of American liberalism. This growing attachment to the cause of racial equality unquestionably has been the most important change in the twentieth-century American reform tradition. As Leslie H. Fishel, Jr., president–emeritus of Heidelberg College, demonstrates in this selection, the New Deal played an important transitional role in this development.

Blacks found President Roosevelt personally inspiring, and many of FDR's lieutenants were strongly committed to the cause of civil rights. Many New Deal programs, moreover, provided much-needed economic benefits to a black population that had suffered terribly from the depression. Yet, as Fishel observes, "Roosevelt's actual commitments to the American Negro were slim." There was no significant New Deal program to meet the special problems of blacks; FDR was preoccupied with the depression and the need to obtain southern votes in Congress for New Deal economic reforms. Many of the New Deal agencies actually practiced racial discrimination of one type or another. Even in 1941, when Roosevelt under great black pressure established a Fair Employment Practices Commission, he refused to integrate the armed forces.

For blacks, then, the New Deal was a period of progress, but its

From "The Negro in the New Deal Era" by Leslie H. Fishel, Jr., *Wisconsin Magazine of History*, XLVIII (Winter, 1964–1965), 111–117, 120–123; reprinted in abridged form in *The Negro American: A Documentary History* by Leslie H. Fishel, Jr., and Benjamin Quarles. Copyright © 1967 by Scott, Foresman and Company.

mixed record was acceptable only because of the barrenness of the past. It moved well beyond the reformism of the progressive era, yet did little more than lay the groundwork for the increasingly frank and thoroughgoing approach to civil rights that has characterized the liberalism of the post–World War II era. Several factors have contributed to this new liberal concern: the growing sophistication and militance of black leadership; the national commitment against fascism during the World War II years; and, after the war, a prosperity that made it possible for white liberals to turn their attention to civil rights. But who can say that the new liberalism would have developed as it did had the New Deal not haltingly shown the way?

* * *

His voice exuded warmth and a personal inflection which brought him close to his listeners. His own physical affliction and the way he bore it earned him deserved admiration and gave encouragement to those who had afflictions of their own, even a darker skin. John Gunther testified to Roosevelt's attraction for people as "concrete and intimate. . . . He set up goals in human terms that the average man could grasp for." The general public responded to his magnetism; one of his secretaries selected a list of salutations which were used on letters addressed to him, and they ran the gamut from "Dear humanitarian friend of the people" to "My Pal!" and "Dear Buddy." Almost all of his callers remarked on his personal charm and persuasiveness.

These characteristics of FDR the man, taken with his consummate ability to personalize his understanding of human exploitation and underprivilege, made him the most attractive President, for Negro citizens, since the Civil War. Robert Vann, publisher of the Negro weekly Pittsburgh *Courier,* who was brought into the 1932 campaign by some of Roosevelt's lieutenants, advised his race to "go home and turn Lincoln's picture to the wall. The debt has been paid in full." Yet, like Lincoln, Roosevelt's actual commitments to the American Negro were slim. He was more a symbol than an activist in his own right. His compassion, though real, was tempered by his own background, by the enormity of the decisions which came up to him, and by political considerations. An enthusiastic politician, he used political weights and measures on a political scale to judge the evidence, and the Negro was often found wanting. When Walter White, the executive secretary of the NAACP, obtained an audience through the good graces of Mrs. Eleanor Roosevelt to plead for the President's public support of the antilynching bill, FDR demurred because he needed Southern votes in Congress on other matters.

Nevertheless, the FDR image eventually became a favorable one; his picture hung in living rooms and infant sons carried his name. At first, though, Negroes waited to be shown. Their publications granted him

the benefit of doubt when he spoke about justice and equality, in the
hope that he was talking, too, to Negroes. He called lynching murder,
remarked W. E. B. DuBois, and "these things give us hope." His ac-
knowledgement, through his Secretary of Labor, of the National Urban
League's survey of economic conditions among Negroes was, in the
words of an *Opportunity* editorial, "an evidence of his deep interest in
the Negroes' welfare." By midway through his first term, FDR had
captured the admiration and affection of the Negro people and, with
that, their votes. During the campaign of 1936, Negroes were outspoken in their support of the Democratic national ticket. Sixteen
thousand Harlem residents traveled to Madison Square Garden in
September of that year to attend a political rally, and sixty other cities
held similar and simultaneous rallies. The New Yorkers mixed a rich
fare of music and entertainment with leading New Dealers talking
politics, but it was an African Methodist Episcopal Bishop, the Rev-
erend C. Ransome, who symbolized the affair and its meaning by
reading a "New Emancipation Proclamation." The vote in November
was anticlimatic; the second Roosevelt had weaned the Negro away
from the Republican party.

Roosevelt did not publicly associate himself with Negro projects or
Negro leaders before 1935, but his programs and some of his associates
were more aggressive. Early in 1933, he approved of a suggestion that
someone in his administration assume the responsibility for fair treatment of the Negroes, and he asked Harold Ickes to make the appointment. A young white Georgian, Clark Foreman, came to Washington at
Ickes' request to handle the task, and brought in as his assistant an even
younger Negro of great promise, Robert C. Weaver. Foreman successfully made his way through the burgeoning maze of new agencies which
were springing up and did a respectable job of calling to the attention
of agency heads and their assistants an awareness of the special problems of Negroes. Along with Ickes, Daniel Roper, the Secretary of
Commerce; Harry Hopkins, FDR's relief administrator; and Aubrey
Williams, a Hopkins deputy, were sympathetic to committing the New
Deal to work more generously with and for Negroes.

From the first, the various New Deal agencies carried the major
burden of this emphasis, since they translated words into bread and
butter, shelter and schooling. For the Negro, the most significant were
the Federal Employment Relief Administration (FERA), the National
Recovery Administration (NRA), the Works Progress Administration,
later called the Work Projects Administration (WPA), the Agricultural
Adjustment Administration (AAA), the Tennessee Valley Authority
(TVA), the National Youth Administration (NYA), the Civilian Conservation Corps (CCC), and the public housing efforts of several agencies. There were others in the alphabetical jungle which assisted Ne-

groes, as whites, in more specialized ways, such as the Federal Writers'
Project and the Office of Education studies. The very number of agencies added credence to the emergent fact that, for the first time, the
federal government had engaged and was grappling with some of the
fundamental barriers to race progress.

It was one thing to engage and grapple with a problem at the federal
level, and another thing to implement it at lower levels. Most of the
New Deal agency programs ran afoul of local laws and customs and
most of them capitulated on very practical grounds. As a consequence,
Negroes vigorously attacked the inequities, even while they appreciated the limited benefits. FERA, the first New Deal agency to work
directly to alleviate the plight of the destitute, tried by locally administered dole and work-projects to pump more money into circulation.
Until the end of 1935, when it was abolished, it administered most of
the direct relief and work relief programs which the New Dealers
initiated, distributing about $4 billion. Its progress was dogged by ra-
cial discrimination, since the design of projects and allocation of funds
remained in local hands. Jacksonville, Florida, Negro families on relief
outnumbered white families three to one, but the money was divided
according to proportions of the total city population. Thus 15,000
Negro families received 45 percent of the funds and 5,000 white families got 55 percent. Along the Mississippi River, from Natchez to New
Orleans, Negroes were passed over for skilled jobs and frequently
received less than the stipulated minimum wage. When the state of
Georgia squeezed out of the FERA administrator the right to fix hourly
wages for Negroes below thirty cents an hour, *Opportunity* mournfully
questioned, "Does this presage the end of that heralded concern for
the Forgotten Man?"

If the relief program raised questions of discrimination, the NRA
brought howls of indignation. In the words of a Negro labor specialist,
the NRA administrator, General Hugh A. Johnson, was "a complete
failure" for not properly recognizing the Negro. The industrial codes
established under NRA deferred to geographic wage and employment
consideration so that the Negro worker generally earned less money
for equal time and was frozen out of skilled jobs. A young Negro
lawyer, John P. Davis, organized the Joint Committee on National
Recovery in the fall of 1933 to persuade federal authorities to rectify
these policies. "It has filed briefs, made appearances at public hearings," he wrote, and "buttonholed administrative officers relative to the
elimination of unfair clauses in the codes," but to little avail. In self-
defense, NRA officials explained the difficulty in bucking local customs, pointing out also that the NRA was responsible only for industrial workers. Agricultural laborers, domestic servants, and the service
trades were not included, and most of the unskilled workers were
exempted by statute from wage and hour minimums. "It is not fair,"

wrote an NRA administrator in a Negro journal, "to blame the NRA for not curing all these ills, if such they be, within a year." Until the Supreme Court decreed its demise in the spring of 1935, the NRA was a favored whipping boy for Negroes, as well as for others. "The Blue Eagle," a Virginia newspaper observed, "may be [for Negroes] a predatory bird instead of a feathered messenger of happiness."

The TVA and the AAA came under fire in the early years of the New Deal for similar reasons. Negro critics raged at the all-white model towns, such as Norris, Tennessee, which were established in conjunction with TVA. Homes for white workers on the project were substantial, while Negro workers lived in substandard temporary barracks. Skilled jobs went first to whites and most labor crews were segregated. TVA, it appeared to two observers in 1934, "aims to maintain the *status quo.*" A year later, the situation seemed little better. In one sample two-week period, Negroes were 11 percent of the working force, receiving only 9.5 percent of the payroll. Under AAA, Negro tenant farmers and sharecroppers, as the most dispensable laborers, suffered first from the crop-reduction policy and found themselves without employment. Concerned about the evolving discriminatory pattern, the NAACP in 1934 devoted a major share of its energy to trying to prevent white landlords from illegally depriving their Negro tenants of crop-reduction bonuses.

Two New Deal programs for young people operated with a minimum of discrimination: the CCC and the NYA. The CCC established segregated camps in the South and in some parts of the North; the great bulk of the integrated camps were in New England. By 1935, its peak year, CCC had over a half million boys in camp. In general, Negroes stayed in CCC camps longer than whites, were not moved up to administrative posts in camps as readily as whites, and were restricted to less than 10 percent of the total enrollment. Since the proportion of young Negro men in need was substantively higher than this, the quota system was actually inequitable. The NYA, which Mary McLeod Bethune served as administrator of Negro affairs, was shaped to help young men and women in school and with schooling. It grew out of the university and college student relief program established under FERA, and by the end of its first six months, in late 1935, had distributed more than $40 million. Conforming to existing state and regional patterns, the NYA still managed to help a critical age group among Negroes.

The debit side of the New Deal's efforts to assist Negroes fell far short of its material and psychological credits. Never before had Negro leaders participated in government affairs as freely and as frequently. The Department of Commerce had E. K. Jones, on leave from the National Urban League; the NYA had Mrs. Bethune; Interior had

William H. Hastie and Weaver; the Social Security Board had Ira DeA.
Reid; Labor had Lawrence W. Oxley; the Office of Education had
Ambrose Caliver, to mention a few. Never before had there been so
great a stress on improving the education of Negroes. Many relief programs included elementary education and training classes as part of the
regimen. Negro colleges and universities received funds for buildings.
The Office of Education, along with other agencies, began an important study of the status of Negro education.

Professional opportunities opened up in government, although not
at the rate at which Negroes were graduating from college. For the first
time, Negroes were employed as architects, lawyers, engineers, economists, statisticians, interviewers, office managers, case aids, and
librarians. Nonprofessional white-collar jobs, which had rarely been
within reach of the race, now became available to trained stenog-
raphers, clerks, and secretaries. While many of these jobs centered
around programs for Negroes within the government, such as Negro
slum clearance projects, Negro NYA offices, and the like, they broke
the dam which had hitherto kept Negroes out of these kinds of positions.

Harold Ickes, a former president of the Chicago chapter of the
NAACP, was the first New Dealer to be recognized as a tried friend. He
quickly ended discrimination in his department and set the example by
placing professionally trained Negroes in responsible positions. He
first drew FDR's attention to Hastie as a candidate for the federal judge
vacancy in the Virgin Islands, and Roosevelt made the appointment in
1937. Ickes appeared at predominantly Negro functions and in 1936,
on the occasion of an address at Howard University, even went so far as
to wear a University of Alabama hood with his cap and gown because
"it seemed to have the best color effect. . . ." While Ickes could not
breach established segregation patterns in housing, one-eighth of the
federal housing projects planned before the end of 1935 were in mixed
neighborhoods. Approximately one-half of them were in Negro slum
areas and, thanks to the negotiating skill of Ickes' assistant, Robert C.
Weaver, the contracts for a substantial portion of these called for the
employment of both skilled and unskilled Negro workers.

Eleanor Roosevelt, the New Deal's conscience, made it her business
to reaffirm by word and deed her faith in the equality of opportunity
for all. She included Negro and mixed organizations on her itineraries,
welcomed mixed groups of adults and children to the White House,
and spoke up for the race at critical times. In 1936, as part of a long
memo on political strategy in the presidential campaign, she urged
party leaders to ask respected Negroes like Mrs. Bethune to participate
among Negro groups. The penalty for her unflagging advocacy of the
Negro's cause was abuse or occasionally embarrassing questions. As the
European war spread after 1939, she confronted questions about the

Negro's loyalty. "Rarely," she told a group of New Jersey college women in 1940, "do you come across a case where a Negro has failed to measure up to the standard of loyalty and devotion to his country."

Eleanor Roosevelt was more than a symbol of the New Deal's conscience; she was a vehicle for approaching and influencing the President. She performed this service for Walter White when the antilynching bill was before Congress. When the DAR refused to allow Marian Anderson to sing in Constitution Hall, Mrs. Roosevelt was the intermediary who secured permission to use the Lincoln Memorial for the concert. It was useful for the President to have his wife serve in these varying capacities, absorbing some of the criticism, supplying him with information he could get from no other source, and sparking his conscience, when that was needed. This relieved the President from having to punctuate his speeches and press conferences with references to the Negro. Before 1935, these were almost nonexistent; after 1935, they increased in frequence and directness, but Roosevelt did not directly commit himself, as his wife did, until his famous Executive Order 8802 of June 1941 established a Fair Employment Practice Committee to supervise all defense-contract industries.

In many ways, 1935 seemed to be a pivotal year for the President's public statements to and about the Negro. His annual message to Congress in January asserted that "in spite of our efforts and in spite of our talk, we have not weeded out the overprivileged and we have not effectively lifted up the underprivileged." Uplift and underprivilege were two words which Negroes understood, two words which footnoted their history; yet Roosevelt did not mention the Negro specifically. Shortly after that, he told WPA state administrators that "we cannot discriminate in any of the work we are conducting either because of race or religion or politics," and although he went on to speak of political pressures, the word "race" was there for Negroes to see. In two other public statements later in the year, FDR paid lip service to the accomplishments of the race and by 1936, an election year, he proclaimed his policy that "among American citizens there should be no forgotten men and no forgotten races." The transformation was more one of degree than of conviction; Roosevelt was beginning to speak to the Negro, however rarely, rather than to lump him without identification into massive generalizations. But his eye was ever on the balance of political forces and he never voluntarily came out foursquare for the Negro.

In perspective, Roosevelt's circumspection on some domestic issues was less significant than his New Deal legislative program. Labor unions received substantial encouragement from Section 7a of NRA and from the Wagner Act, although the White House maintained an equivocal position toward both labor and management. The jump in union memberships and the rise of the Committee on Industrial Organization, first within the AF of L and later as the independent Congress of Industrial Organizations (CIO), gained impetus from the newly established right to strike and the newly created federal board to mediate labor disputes. A strengthened labor movement confronted, as one of its problems, the question of Negro members. Older unions such as the United Mine Workers and the International Ladies Garment Workers Union welcomed Negroes without distinction. When the CIO broke from the AF of L, its nucleus of unions including the new and somewhat fragile organizations in the automobile, rubber, and steel industries accepted Negroes on an equal basis, except in those localities where race friction was high. The United Textile Workers attempted to do the same, but the existence of textile plants in southern states made this task more onerous. It was not enough for a union to resolve, as the CIO did, to accept members without regard to race, creed, or color, or even, as the UAW and the organizing committees of the steelworkers did, to offer Negro workers a chance to join up. Negroes still hung back, alternately tempted and frightened by management's offers and threats. The wave of the future was with the industrial unions, and *Opportunity's* declaration to Negro steelworkers that it would be "the apotheosis of stupidity" for them to stay out of the union battling for recognizance in 1937, was prophetic. The success of the Brotherhood of Sleeping Car Porters, under the leadership of A. Philip Randolph, in gaining recognition as the bargaining agent with the Pullman Company after a twelve-year struggle, marked the beginning of the race's influence in national labor circles and on national labor policy. After his union was recognized, Randolph prodded the AF of L to grant it an international charter, making it an equal with other member unions, and he never eased up his fight to liberalize the AF of L's racial policies. Even through he was not persuasive enough to break down these craft and railway-union prejudices, Randolph emerged before World War II as a dominant voice in Negro circles and a power to be reckoned with in American unionism.

When Harlem rioted in 1935, *The Crisis* explained that only the patience of the Negro had delayed it that long. Patience was not enough to counter the "sneers, impertinence, and personal opinions of smart-aleck investigators, supervisors and personnel directors." Unemployment, rent gouging, and the belief that Harlem had not received its share of relief money snapped the uneasy calm; the riot erupted with a frenzied attack on whites and the purposeful looting of food and clothing stores. The prompt on-the-scene appearance of New York City's popular mayor, Fiorello H. La Guardia, helped restore rationality. When the United States entered World War II, Harlem still seethed from overcrowding, white insolence, and price gouging, and again rioting broke out, followed by riots in other cities, most notably Detroit.

The hands of the clock had swung half circle and the Negro had learned from the white how to use violence and lawlessness when order and the law were not sufficient.

Toward the end of the 1930's the federal government turned more and more of its attention to the European conflict, the economy flourished as the industrial bastion of the embattled Allies, and the Negro had committed himself to the New Deal and to President Roosevelt. Polls in 1940 showed that Negro voters overwhelmingly supported Roosevelt for a third term, and the polls were right. The reason for this support was not difficult to surmise. Outside of what the Democratic administration had tried to do directly and indirectly, the decade itself was marked with identifiable milestones of progress. In athletics, Jesse Owens, was an Olympic champion, and Negro football players starred on many of the major college teams. Professional baseball still resisted, but its time was not far off. In interracial activities, conferences on a variety of subjects began to meet with overbearing regularity and, though self-consciously interracial, the pattern developed almost irrevocably. College students and adults met to talk about education, religion, economic matters, and, of course, civil rights. Even in the South, the indomitable Mrs. Bethune organized an interracial conference at the college she founded, and the white University of Florida tentatively sent delegates. In the deep South, interracial conferences were held on a segregated basis; Eleanor Roosevelt told of attending one in Birmingham and inadvertently sitting in the colored section. "At once the police appeared to remind us of the rules and regulations on segregation. . . . Rather than give in I asked that chairs be placed for us with the speakers facing the whole group." White Southerners began to speak up for the Negro. They were still a small minority, but the mere fact that a white state supervisor of schools in Georgia would admit to the inequalities of segregated schools, or a white North Carolina legislator would question a decreased appropriation for the Negro college, was a sign of chance. The rise of Huey Long in Louisiana brought a different attitude, one of ignoring race differences without changing race relationships. The all-white Mississippi Education Association established a committee in 1938 to recommend ways in which students might study Negro life, and several Northern newspapers in 1940 editorially acknowledged the importance of Negro History Week. The tide had turned, and Negroes credited the turning to the New Deal.

The sudden shock of the surprise attack which drew the United States into World War II served more to expose sore spots than to blanket them in loyalty. In the First World War, the protests against unequal treatment were slow to develop and not widely heard, but the Second World War was different. Even before Pearl Harbor, clamors arose from the South warning that the Negro was not going to "come out of this war on top of the heap as he did in the last one." However distorted the comparison, the attitude was clear, and it influenced the government's decision to extend pre–Pearl Harbor patterns into the war period.

The Negro soldier remained separate in the armed services, and not always welcome. Judge William L. Hastie resigned as civilian aide to the Secretary of War in protest against the dissembling tactics of the Army Air Corps to keep the Negro on the ground. *The Crisis,* returning to a World War I cry, criticized the appointment of Southern white officers for Negro troops and the explanation that they could handle them better. When FDR queried Walter White about the carelessness of the Negro press and the consistency of its attack on the war effort, White replied that better treatment for Negroes in the armed services and the invitation of Negro editors to presidential press conferences and top briefings would clear up the problem.

White became an important man in the war effort and was finally sent overseas as a war correspondent in early 1944. He toured every major front in Europe and the Pacific and his reports did not make soothing reading. Wherever he went, he later wrote, "there was a minority of bigots who were more determined to force their bigotry on others than they were to win the war." This was particularly true of officers, both Northern and Southern. Separation, he found, bred this spirit, especially when key officers were "prejudiced or weak, or both." When Negroes and whites actually fought together, as they did during the Battle of the Bulge in December of 1944, attitudes changed, according to polls among white officers and men. "After the first day," a white South Carolinian admitted, "when we saw how they fought, I changed my mind." The top combat brass, such as General Dwight Eisenhower and Admiral Chester Nimitz, were willing to co-operate, but they were hemmed in by Washington orders and junior officer reluctance.

At home, the intense feelings bared by war boiled up with wearying constancy. In the spring of 1941, A. Philip Randolph organized the March on Washington movement which threatened to march if the White House did not declare for fair employment practices in defense industries. President Roosevelt issued his famous Executive Order 8802 in June, establishing the FEPC and the principle of government concern with employment discrimination. Randolph continued the movement during the war, but it lapsed as the older organizations themselves became more militant.

The prosperity of war industry and the proscriptive Southern mores once again attracted thousands of Negroes to Northern cities. The consequent overcrowding and war tension heated racism to the boiling point, as the riots in New York, Detroit, and Los Angeles demonstrated. For the Negro, racism was the same wherever it appeared. In Roy Wilkins' words, "it sounds pretty foolish to be *against* park benches marked 'Jude' in Berlin, but to be *for* park benches marked 'Colored' in Tallahassee, Florida." Negroes could not understand why whites drew distinctions between the Nazi ideology of Aryan supremacy and the American ideology of white supremacy. Even back in 1933, *The Crisis* expressed its "unholy glee" at Hitler's attack on the Jews: "Now that the damned include the owner of the [New York] *Times,* moral indignation is perking up." The paradox which Wilkins illustrated could only be resolved by a change of face on the part of white America.

The war itself, by drawing thousands of men and women into a collaborative effort with whites, made such a change possible. Negroes served in the armed services in all ratings and at all ranks, though segregated. War industries hired skilled Negro men and women at supervisory and managerial levels. Government used colored workers in great numbers and in more sensitive positions than ever before. The Negro's political power was organized in an unprecedented manner during the wartime presidential election. The younger generation of Negro men and women who had grown up in prosperity and matured in depression were awakened to the infinite possibilities of an assimilated society, and from them came the trained leadership to plan the campaign.

The death of Roosevelt and the end of the war in 1945 terminated an era. The office of the Presidency now symbolized a concern for justice and equality for all Americans, including Negroes. The White House had taken a stand in favor of the principle of equal rights, although the practice had lagged. The new President, Harry S. Truman, a man of lesser parts, was to take the next practical step and declare in specifics his belief in the equality of men of whatever race under the law. Where Roosevelt concealed the particular in the general principle, Truman spoke out without check. Where Roosevelt used the excuse of war to delay integration, Truman used the excuse of peace to accelerate it. Where Roosevelt used the federal government to increase economic opportunities for all, Truman used the federal government to increase economic opportunities for Negroes. While the Truman Fair Deal never approximated the energy and the excitement of the Roosevelt New Deal, it was the former which capitalized on the Negro's readiness to take an equal place in American democracy.

V | Wider Perspectives

12 The New Deal and the Progressive Tradition

OTIS L. GRAHAM, JR.

Otis L. Graham, Jr., a professor of history at the University of California–Santa Barbara, is the author of *Encore for Reform*, the most thorough study yet undertaken of the relationship between early twentieth-century progressivism and the New Deal. Surveying the attitudes of 105 progressives who survived through Franklin D. Roosevelt's first term, he found that only 5 were consistently more radical than the New Deal, that another 40 generally supported it, and that 60 generally opposed it. The dominant outlook of the older reformers, he concludes, was fundamentally at variance with that of the New Deal.

The pro–New Dealers, he observes, tended to be from what historians customarily call the advanced wing of the progressive movement. They were reformers to whom the struggle against urban poverty had been most central: social workers, social gospelers, intellectuals. Having long advocated social welfare legislation, tending toward pragmatism in their approach to social problems, they embraced the New Deal with little regard to its methods or general outlook.

The anti–New Dealers, conversely, tended to be Jeffersonian individualists. As progressives, they were more likely to have been identified with good government crusades and moral reform causes. They were more receptive to business values. They often conceived of reform itself as primarily an educational process. Repelled by the collectivist, bureaucratic techniques of the New Deal and by its tenor of class conflict, they saw the Roosevelt leadership as one that rejected cherished old values while failing to offer new absolutes to replace them. It

191

is this group, Graham is convinced, that spoke the most authentic progressive voice.

One may question this last judgment. Graham's sample, although based on prodigious research, may not be as representative as he believes. It is so small, moreover, that the divisions within it may not be a reliable guide to the attitudes of the larger progressive population. One may say with some certainty that Graham is quite successful in demonstrating that different types of progressives approached public issues with divergent assumptions. His evidence implies that a considerable number of them, whether a majority or not, found in the New Deal the realization of many of their hopes, and indeed that they had helped lay the groundwork for it.

* * *

"They have been mad, confusing, discouraging years," said William E. Borah of the years 1912–37. He spoke for most of those who, thinking of themselves as associated with the reform hopes of the Roosevelt–Wilson era, survived to ponder the effects of their uprising and the prospects of the hopes they shared as young men. It had been their aim to arouse the People, to employ public indignation, the vengeance of the ballot, and wherever necessary the coercive power of a responsible government, all in an effort to set America back on the old paths. Could they take satisfaction in the condition of affairs at the end of the reforms of yet another Roosevelt? Was the promise of American life closer than when they began, or drifting farther out of reach?

The progressive remnant gave no single answer to these questions. Whatever our hopes for finding an uncomplicated realtionship between progressivism and the New Deal, we must be very careful in tracing the ideas and people bridging the two eras. Progressivism flowed in several channels after the war put an end to the exhilarating days when all reformers felt a part of a common effort. Each branch, each cause, had a different development in the interwar period, some gaining strength, some dying, all undergoing change. The sense of unity, joining them for one last brief time in the spring and summer of 1933, was never to be fully recovered. We have seen that most progressives who survived decided, after that initial enthusiasm, that the New Deal was destructive of their political and social hopes for America; that a smaller but still considerable number professed to see in it the culmination of a lifetime of effort; and that, for a very few, it was not nearly radical enough. By an uncanny coincidence, Ohio's three "Boy Mayors" who launched reform movements simultaneously in Cleveland, Cincinnati and Toledo at the height of Ohio progressivism wound up in the 1930's at three of the major terminals of the progressive experience. The better known of them, Newton Baker of Cleveland, opposed the New Deal; Henry T. Hunt of Cincinnati worked for the NRA, and Brand Whitlock of Toledo secluded himself at Cannes with his books, his memories, and his disillusionment. Whitlock, who had given up on reform early in the war years, disliked the New Deal intensely, when he allowed himself to think about politics at all.

II

The New Deal drew strength from several sectors of the original movement. Chief among them was the profession of social work, particularly those among the early social and settlement workers who shared an interest in the preventive possibilities of social action. Their aid to the New Deal has been noted earlier. Joanna Colcord has detailed the contributions of individual social workers and voluntary associations in the field of social service to the early stages of the adventures in Federal relief. The role of those whom Brandeis tartly called "the social work–progressive crowd" in the drafting and legislative support of the Social Security Act of 1935 and the Wages and Hours Act of 1938 may be followed in Robert Bremner's *From the Depths,* or in the recently published account of the writing of the Social Security Act by Edwin E. Witte. The pressure they brought to bear on the New Deal had its clear beginnings in the stirrings of the middle class conscience, i.e., among progressives, in the early years of this century.

The study of survivors has indicated other groups and areas of pronounced affinity for the New Deal. Many members of the academic community, men like E. A. Ross or Dean William Draper Lewis of Pennsylvania or John R. Commons, men Joseph Dorfman called the "Elders," thought Roosevelt's use of government was closely in line with ideas they had advanced for years. The clergy were conspicuous among those hailing the Roosevelt years; notably, Charles Stelzle, Stephen S. Wise, Herbert Seely Bigelow, Bishop McConnell, and, always seeking more for the poor, John Haynes Holmes. And if a small sample gives any ground for generalizing, women progressives almost invariably followed their progressivism straight into the arms of the New Deal—notably Lillian Wald, Mary Simkhovitch, Mary Wooley, and probably Frances Kellor, Irene Osgood Andrews, and Mary White Ovington. One can then say of the New Deal progressive that he or she was likely to be a person who lived in one of the larger cities and whose work was of the social work, social settlement, religious, or voluntary association variety, rather than a part-time involvement in political or moral "clean-ups" undertaken from a professional base such as law or politics (and, by the 1930's, long since over). An astonishing number of friends of the New Deal, progressive and otherwise, were recruited in New York City.

Because the New Deal found strong support among progressives associated with urban social problems, it was natural that a part of its program and of its characteristic spirit reflected their own approach to American issues. When the administration secured Federal programs in old age and job security, Federal underpinnings to relief of poverty, Federal limitations on hour and wage standards and the employment of children, it was but implementing programs that had been largely the custody of one group of progressives, the professional altruists of the social work fraternity. The expansion of government into these areas had never seemed to them unwise or unconstitutional. "If we turn to government with confidence, and act with vigor," Homer Folks said in his seventieth year, "we will not be disappointed." And they shared with the New Dealers, those men and women of the social service field and their allies from clerical and academic professions, an urgent concern for the pragmatic result, without deliberation about the possible violation of constitutional or other metaphysical limits. The social worker, Folks said in 1923, "looks only to results; he is not made afraid by any labels or precedents, or any device or plan which, to the satisfaction of all reasonable tests, contributes to human well-being."

Along with specific and time-ripened proposals in the field of social welfare, and an attitude hostile to abstractions which might impede the immediate realization of relief and support for society's lesser members, they brought that irreducible optimism which is the *sine qua non* of any social experimentation. Florence Kelley, Felix Frankfurter remembered, always referred to herself as "the most unwearied hoper"; that same untiring optimism sustained Jane Addams, Homer Folks, Lillian Wald, Graham Taylor, and others, long after events seemed to some to have made their persistence ridiculous. The New Deal borrowed heavily from that same "anything can be done" spirit.

III

Because of these close affinities between the two reform eras, reducible always to the use of government to achieve both economic and humanitarian ends not served by the processes of the market place, a good many old progressives found it possible to participate in or support popular movements in both periods. They should be regarded, however, as the exception to the rule, outnumbered by those who saw in Roosevelt's work those same fatal tendencies they had long contested against. Even some of those who finally voted for Roosevelt in 1936 were less than enthusiastic. When Harlan Fiske Stone said, "I suppose no intelligent person likes very well the way the New Deal does things," he alluded to that combination of haphazard methods, contradictory and pyramiding agencies, and collective solutions to hitherto individual problems, which seemed almost more than some old reformers, basically inclined to wish the New Deal well, could take. Ray Stannard Baker was a loyal Democrat, as behooved the biographer and admirer of Wilson, and was a humane and open-minded man with a long and honorable record in the service of reform. He finally voted for Roosevelt in 1936, but his support was grudging: "I am going up soon to vote for FDR, not because I think him a Savior, . . . but because that between the two the country will be safer with Roosevelt. But it will not be safe. . . . Our government has ceased to be a duty, to be sacrificed for, and become a privilege somehow to be used for ministering to our needs and our greeds."

Even Herbert Seely Bigelow, who voted and talked as a New Deal enthusiast during his two terms in Congress (1934–38), admitted at the end that "I did not [when I voted for the New Deal measures] believe in regimentation. . . . I believed that with a new money system and a more rational tax system we could raise wages naturally and restore prosperity and get away from all this government planning of private industry and go back to Jeffersonian democracy." He repeated these complaints on the floor of the Congress a year later: "We are getting all bogged down with political machinery. . . . Is it possible that with different treatment we might dispense with this mushroom growth of bureaus and political managers and return to the Jeffersonian idea that the government is best which governs least? As a member of the Seventy-fifth Congress I have voted for this New Deal legislation, but never with complete confidence. It does seem to me that there is a better way."

IV

If even these friends had doubts and objections about the New Deal, it was no surprise that more progressives could see no progress in it at all, and stood over against it in such numbers as to constitute a sort of progressive referendum against the reforms of the 1930's.

As with the others, they generally came from predictable areas within the broad spectrum of progressivism. The reformer who became a politician, and especially one who adjusted easily to political life and held elective office for many years, usually found the New Deal indulging in too many constitutional innovations and trying to apply Federal solutions with alarming frequency. If he had been a journalist, the odds were heavy that he would sympathize more with the leaders of business than with the young professors and idea men of the new era, and that he would pen some mild or not so mild condemnation of the New Deal—or, failing to penetrate its mysteries as readily as he had the mayoral campaigns or stock swindles of an earlier day, he might retreat to a condemnatory silence. Politicians and writers, along with many lawyers and businessmen who had devoted part of their time to citizens' better government groups, produced most of the progressive criticism of the reformer in the White House after 1933.

Herbert Croly had very early dismissed most of progressivism as "a species of higher conservatism," and without accepting all that he meant by that judgment, we can agree that, more often than not, those progressives who survived until the New Deal era were basically conservative. They should have recognized that the part of the progressive legacy they drew upon to oppose the New Deal closely resembled the arguments used against progressivism itself by their old enemies, the corporation counsels and standpat politicians of the days of George Baer. Class unity, progress through public education rather than extensive institutional alteration, a Jeffersonian distrust of the state, a deep-set fear of collective action involving (as it nearly always did) some reduction of individual liberty, and the determination to put to any proposed change the requirement that it leave America as little changed as possible—these principles were not new to progressivism, but were moved to the foreground by the actions of Franklin Roosevelt.

When the New Deal recognized and dealt with particular classes and social groups, it undid the work of years of progressive effort, for it divided rather than united the American people. The original progressive intention had been to fight the growing gap between those with something and those with nothing to lose. This could be done by filling that gap with one's physical self, as the settlement people had done (Graham Taylor liked to call it "standing in the breach"), or by exhorting all within range to talk, not of the material issues that divided, but of higher (meaning "spiritual") matters that united us.*

They detected the New Deal's redistributionist tone and intent even if they overestimated its success, and they complained that Roosevelt could not seem to resist the political power produced by the agitation of material issues. In this he did not adhere to the progressive design. "What a sordid decade is passing," William Allen White wrote in 1940. "The spirit of our democracy has turned away from the things of the spirit. . . . What a joy it would be to get out and raise the flaming banner of righteousness."

Righteousness, here, should be read "non-economic issues," and White was expressing the same preference for a healing national self-denying fervor that caused Carl Vrooman to remember the war-bond

---

*While they placed chief reliance, in this matter of the prevention of class animosities, upon the avoidance of the wrong sort of talk, a good number believed to greater or less extent in the sort of actual redistribution of wealth which they provided for in the Sixteenth Amendment, and which they advocated and occasionally secured through higher inheritance taxes.

drives of World War I as the high point of the progressive movement. Arthur Koestler once wrote that political and social change, in symbolic terms, must come by way either of the Yogi or the Commissar. The Yogi places his hope in internal change, in the gradual elevation of the mind and spirit of individuals, while the Commissar, impatient, turns to radical and even violent changes in institutions. The progressives, by an overwhelming margin, preferred the way of the Yogi, which is to say that they relied upon education rather than coercion whenver possible. When the New Dealers seemed to be abandoning the ideal of educating the electorate as a whole, they had provided, as Rush Welter writes, "the bridge by which former progressives might cross over to the conservative position." Welter adds: "So many made the journey that at times they seemed to be the leading figures in the opposition."

A final vital principle with them, an individualism so stubborn that very few forms of collective action were really acceptable, had once been a revolutionary principle, in the days of the young Republic. This individualism had been the heart of nineteenth-century liberalism, the faith of their Mugwump fathers, and they had not rejected it as decisively as their resort to government might lead us to believe. Their advocacy of increased governmental activity was closely hedged about by the requirements that the right man be entrusted with power, that reformers display the right spirit of deliberation and caution, that they move according to a clear plan. Only under these conditions, progressives were willing to enlarge the state.

Still they were individualists at heart—the word "individualism" appears hundreds of times in their literature—and they typically practiced an individualistic politics. The early progressives in the Congress were dubbed "Insurgents" to denote that ungovernable, kick-over-the-traces attitude that made it so difficult for them to unite in substantial numbers behind any one leader, subscribe to any one program toward any one end. William E. Borah exemplifies this innate maverick quality to a well-publicized perfection, but many progressives, especially those who were visible in politics or muckraking, were similarly unsuited by temperament to enduring the very collective controls the progressive movement is historically credited with advancing.

Some would submit to the yoke of party (they were usually Southerners), but little else could bind most progressives to a belief or policy determined by remote authority. Hutchins Hapgood, although an extreme case of this unruly individualism, confessed to it in the following words: "I attack the powerful and prevailing thing in art, industry, in all fields, just because it is prevailing, irrespective of the merits of the case." Few of Hapgood's contemporaries in the reform era were as irreverent as he, but they were perhaps more amply endowed than the average American of that era with a stiff-backed individualism that resisted most forms of coercion. They had revolted in the first place when they discovered that the trusts were plotting to fasten control over them. At that, their revolt was characterized more by energy than by co-ordination, for the average progressive did not take easily to direction or to the subordination of his own pet theories to some organizational doctrine. Without that individualistic temperament, of course, there would have been no citizens' uprising at all, and the progressive movement offered many outlets for a man who was ready to fight to give the individual more responsibility and more freedom from restraint. But it could have been predicted that men of that temperament would probably not approve of the reform cause in this country if it shifted its primary goals from freedom to security, and if it came to rely more on compulsion than on exposure and enlightenment. They wanted to do good, but they wanted to do it at the demand of their own conscience—else there would be no pleasure or credit in doing it at all. They were less than enthusiastic over doing the right thing as part of some obedient mass and at the demand of some bureaucrat. Understandably, many of them found the "conservative" side, the side of individualism and liberty, congenial in the 1930's.

Felix Frankfurter was perhaps too harsh on one of them, Ellery Sedgwick, when he said of him that "he wanted to be on the side of the angels. He wanted to be for decency, he wanted to be for 'liberalism'—provided it didn't cost him too much with what he regarded as the 'right people.'" But when progressives battled against Franklin Roosevelt, a fellow progressive from the group that supported him could be even harsher. In the constitutional crisis of 1937, with Roosevelt's Court Plan being defeated by a widespread defection among "liberals," the progressive Madison (Wisconsin) newspaper editor William T. Evjue wrote to Oswald Garrison Villard: "The President is licked because some of the so-called liberals who have been deprecating the trend toward a judicial oligarchy failed to stand back of him. It is the same old story—the President didn't do it the right way. Mr. Villard wants it done this way. Mr. Shipstead wants it done another way . . . and other weak-kneed progressives who talked about these issues abstractly were afraid to meet the issue when the actual test came."

To find this preponderance of progressive sentiment against the New Deal is to become conscious of considerable differences between the two reform movements of the first half of this century. This does not mean that the New Deal was as revolutionary as so many progressives feared; on the contrary, they misread its intentions and exaggerated its extent as badly as did the business classes. But the strong dissimilarities are there, and we may speak of them without forgetting that the New Deal nonetheless little merited the fears of its progressive opponents and the uneasiness of so many of its progressive friends. The response of surviving progressives reminds us that important intellectual sources of the New Deal were more recent than progressivism. One of the preoccupations of the progressives who were unhappy with the New Deal was to cite new figures with new ideas, men who had come from nowhere and who were going too far. They overworked the names of Tugwell and Berle and Corcoran, perhaps, but some of them were aware of Stuart Chase, John A. Ryan, Foster and Catchings, Eccles and Keynes, Lewis Mumford and Frederic Delano—and, of course, Coughlin, Townsend, and Long.

But a part of the responsibility for the generation of such ideas, for the sudden importance of such men, and for the incorporation of their schemes in Federal legislation, rested with the progressives themselves. There is, of course, the delicate question of the culpability of the progressives for the breakdown of a system they had so recently improved. We may, however, seek a less speculative level. Walter Lippmann, in an article in 1934, pointed out that there was no body of progressive economic thought which could be made available to an administration in desperate need of an understanding of the business cycle and anti-depression economics. The work of a few well-known progressives, such as that of Taussig in international trade and tariffs, or of Edwin Seligman in taxation and public finance, was of little importance in the present emergency. Most progressives either accepted the impassioned economics of Henry George, or resigned themselves to knowing little about that opaque subject. As George Record told Amos Pinchot, a few months before he died, "we have got to learn more about this money question. We are not up to date."

In line with that advice, Pinchot joined the Sound Money League and began to study monetary theory, but he was never sure of himself in economic matters. In that he was typical, for a great many of the old reformers found the depression baffling. A few were willing to admit the irrelevance of their own experience and accumulated expertise to the crisis of the early and middle 1930's. Ray Stannard Baker wrote in his Notebook toward the end of 1936: "Of this I am sure. I cannot settle . . . the tremendous problems now plaguing the world. Most often I cannot fully understand. The factors are too complex." Ernest Poole, an associate in the muckraker movement in New York, complained in his autobiography that he found it hard in the 1930's to write as he had written earlier, about reformers and the urban poor, because he found at the center of things the "brilliant young men" of the New Deal who offered only "plans and figures that gave no chance whatever to my humble writer's pen. I've always liked more human stuff." Poole added: "As the New Deal rushed on its way, it grew more complicated and bewildering all the time."

Another old muckraker, Wallace Irwin, was even more candid: "It is difficult for an old man, who has gone through three wars and had so little to do in any of them, to confess anything more than the philosophy of Confusion. I call this book 'I Look at Me,' yet today whenever I gaze into my shaving mirror, I see no more than the baffled face of a worn human who in youth took sides ardently, cheerfully, and in age finds himself a-straddle of the fence."

It was precisely at this point, where the New Deal became so heavily engaged in economic matters, that New Deal liberalism began to disengage itself from the earlier reform tradition. While it resumed certain old progressive tasks—conservation, the regulation of sectors of the business community, and toward the end some trust-busting—the New Deal ignored most of the agenda the progressives had been working on when they were interrupted. Clarke Chambers has remarked how the New Deal actually collided head-on with at least two important progressive aspirations and the organizations formed to realize them—the "dry" forces and the many groups, usually composed of women, formed to advance world peace. Progressivism, in its larger aspect individualistic and oriented toward freedom from both the conditions and the sensation of restraint, was not to be fulfilled in a movement that increased the power of the meddling state. Focusing always on what was morally right, and finding that invariably in a state of mind that looked beyond self and class, the progressives felt defeated by any "reform" that accepted special claims and honored them. Aimed at unifying the American people, progressivism would produce few men who, even after the social education acquired during lenthy careers in public affairs, could accept frank class legislation.

With such goals as they had, in fact, they could hardly have met with any substantial success. Centralization was the forecast for America, in industry, in government, in demography. Only those progressives who limited their hopes to a more humane treatment of the poor were able to find satisfaction in the achievement of Roosevelt's general welfare state. A short time before he died in 1933, George Record, speaking for those progressives whose original and sustaining impulse had been to restore the small-town synthesis their fathers had presumably enjoyed, was able to sum up their efforts in a sentence: "I think if you are going to write the history of that movement you ought to write it from the standpoint that it was a failure."

V

The student of history sees in a longer perspective what any American observes in his lifetime, the inexorable democratization of our common life—the enlargement of political rights, material security, meaningful freedom. Liberalism is the name of the movement that, through ideas and political action, has sought to hasten this process. In an era when institutions and social patterns are transformed every generation, it is not just the ordinary, conservative citizen who finds himself and his standards outmoded by the arrival of the next generation with its new problems and its inevitable irreverence. Such is the pace of change that the greatest losses of liberalism are by defection. There are men whose function it is at one phase of history to announce new social imperatives to a reluctant community and to demolish the resisting barriers of habit and self-interest; but who, lingering too long, cannot find it in themselves to abandon the issues and techniques of their great campaigns, and all too often become gradually identified with views and social classes which are either irrelevant or reactionary. This was in fact the fate of a great number of the progressives.

Innumerable careers illustrate this mismatch between human flexibility and the pace of change. William E. Borah remained in the Senate until 1940, keeping alive and undiluted a widely shared brand of progressivism. Many were disappointed that his career was so unproductive, that he squandered the last decades of his life in windy senatorial speeches which were invariably negative. In the forefront of reform in Wilson's day, Borah was to take almost no constructive part in any social advance for the rest of his career. During two decades when some men grieved for lynched Negroes, German Jews, or the peddlers of Dedham, Borah grieved for the Constitution. He was never again near the front lines of liberal reform.

The explanation is uncomplicated; it rests in the consistency of his life and outlook. When as a young man he had asserted that government might not be used by selfish interests, he was a reformer; it came out only later that he, and many progressives with him, took their Jefferson undiluted, without Croly's Hamiltonian admixture. Borah's constitutional views were those of Justice Stephen J. Field, but Borah was consistent. Freedom was threatened by collective power, economic or political. The plutocracy at the turn of the century had captured both kinds, and reform meant not recapturing that power but shrinking the institutions through which it operated. Progressivism meant that no one was to be allowed special advantages through combination. Left alone, the citizens would resume as individuals the national march toward greatness.

It was pure Jefferson, and while these views were suited to the disestablishment of the special interests that were reaching for unlimited power as the twentieth century began, they prevented any national solutions to a host of national problems when antitrust failed to set the nation right. Borah, like most progressives, would never become a tory. Throughout the interwar years he spoke for the "rights" of labor, criticized the standpatters in his own party, and quietly voted for more New Deal measures than his oratory seemed to allow. But that powerful, famous voice was to be raised time after time against the New Deal. Borah, and progressives of his ideology like Edgar Lee Masters, William Randolph Hearst, Albert S. Burleson, A. Mitchell Palmer, James

A. Reed, and all of those who stood in the Jeffersonian tradition, held to their distrust of the state with the tenacity of men who were not sufficiently adroit intellectually to admit how varied were the prerequisites of true freedom, and who could not learn to balance their distrust of power against the necessary use of it. But if Borah could not see his way to a new conception of freedom, he could at least follow with stubborn courage and unflinching consistency the only political economy he knew.

The same difficulties with Federal power eventually brought a more intelligent and resourceful reformer, Oswald Garrison Villard, to the same unproductive end. Heir to a magnificent reform tradition reaching back to abolitionism and the revolution of 1848 in Prussia, it was natural that Villard would be prominent in the progressive era agitation. No one could question his radicalism; although a reformer of average zeal during the Wilson reforms, he foreshadowed his capacity for growth by taking up the cause of the Negro as one of the founders of the NAACP. He took over as editor of *The Nation* in 1918, and that sedate journal, mired for decades in the now conservative mugwump attitudes of Godkin and Schurz, became in the postwar years a leading advocate of social reform and civil liberties. Villard's *Nation* was always to the Left of the winning presidential candidate, and when the New Deal came, Villard in its early years spoke in a clear voice for "planning" and a "new era."

Yet when Villard saw what Roosevelt's New Era was like, he could not endorse it. At times he wrote as if Roosevelt had not done enough for the poor, and while he could never bring himself to embrace socialism, he voted for Norman Thomas in 1936. But the close observer could tell that what Villard wanted was all of the goals of the New Deal *without a welfare state.* The more he saw of the state, with its military potential and its inclination to trample the rights of dissenters, the less he could feel at ease with domestic advances reached through government. Granted, as Michael Wreszin argues, his pacifism soured him on Roosevelt, but it is also true that he came out against the Court Plan, criticized the labor militancy of 1937, and even regretted the "tremendous power" the NAACP had become by the end of the war and registered his continuing faith in the Booker T. Washington philosophy. He relinquished the editorship of *The Nation* in 1933, and after the election of 1936 felt that the journal was becoming too radical. In 1940, the year he voted for Wilkie (he had not backed a winner since 1912, and approved of no President after Grover Cleveland), he gave up his column amid a gathering flurry of critical letters. "I feel that I have been left high and dry by a backwash," he wrote John Haynes Holmes, "and I wonder if you and I, and other steadfast liberals, are not merely back numbers left stranded because of the alarming clash between radical and fascist forces." And to William Allen White in

1939: "I feel as though I had lived too long. I had hoped for another kind of world which I hoped we would reach through another corridor. . . ."

Of course it was war that most depressed him, war in the main that had set him against two Democratic reformers, Wilson and Roosevelt. But pacifism does not explain his uneasiness with the New Deal, whether he appeared to criticize from Left or Right. He shared with Borah that final inability to expect progress from collective solutions, from the raw power of majorities who were unwilling to wait for the awakening of individual virtue. He sent this poem to his son, one month before Pearl Harbor:

> He grew old in an age he condemned,
> Felt the dissolving throes
> Of a social order he loved
> And like the Theban Seer
> Died in his enemies' day.

Most progressives fell somewhere between Borah's moderate progressivism, with antimonopoly its main hope, and Villard's more headlong indignation at social injustice. And just as were Borah and Villard, most of them were troubled by the interventionist state of the 1930's, and went reluctantly, often unwillingly, into a future where the state took on such powers, where the individual counted for so little. It may seem odd that they proved in the end to have such a distrust for a democratic government, since their generation is remembered chiefly for its use of national power. But only a gifted few progressives understood that they were helping to create a new political philosophy. It is easy for us now to see that their era was the crucible where, by the classic Hegelian process, a new political philosophy was in the making. From the time of the Founders there had been two attitudes toward the state: the Jeffersonian, relying upon a minimal state, decentralized institutions, and the good sense of the local yeomanry; and the Hamiltonian, at home with vigorous government and a national outlook, but interested before all else in the welfare of the managers and owners of the commercial, banking, and industrial enterprises of the country. By the beginning of this century there was emerging a third, the liberal-collectivist, sharing with the first its democratic sympathies and with the second its national and statist focus.

The progressives may have played an important part in this intellectual transition, but they did not do so consciously in most instances. They had not moved as far from the Founders' fear of political power as their practice suggested. With the example of Italy and Germany before them in the 1930's, they were not convinced that the confident democratic planners of the new school could avoid falling, along with their enlarged state, into the hands of the Hamiltonian plutocrats who knew a few tricks of their own about governing. The progressives were fated to life and act in the age when the tactics and political philosophy of democrats were being altered to take into account the fantastic private governments being erected all around them. They shared in that alteration, but they did not find it intellectually or emotionally easy. The New Deal in part actually mirrored their confusions, and the unreconciled state of American political ideas, but it was less concerned with polity than politics, afraid not of rash action but of not acting at all. It, therefore, despite its apparent good intentions (in which only a minority of them consistently believed), threatened rashly to deliver the hopes of liberalism into the hands of those who wished nothing more than to be handed the instruments of tyranny.

With the American future as the stakes, their crippling apprehensions and confusions are more readily forgivable. To accept what Roosevelt and the New Dealers had done and wished to do demanded more openness to experiment with political institutions, more trust in the tractability of the state to democratic purposes, more willingness to turn the cumulated rancor of the lower third against the upper, than most progressives could produce, although these had been the very qualities that had marked them as reformers, sometimes as radicals, in their own day.

The space that separated reform periods was less than twenty years. Yet, as Rex Tugwell once remarked, the 1920's were the longest decade in history, a time of vast and accelerating changes in morality, technology, and human density. Measured by mental and physical changes, the progressive era was thus farther back than the calendar admits, and to sense this is to bring into focus at once the dynamics of history and the revolutionary nature of our material life. The pace of that change in the twentieth century made it a near impossibility for men who had been born of fathers who fought for Lincoln, who lived from the world of the barge and the wagon to the world of the *Enola Gay* and through all the social revolution her cargo symbolized, to claim, at the end, a lifetime of reform.

13 The New Deal and American Federalism

JAMES T. PATTERSON

James T. Patterson occupies a unique position among historians of the New Deal—he is a leading authority not only on conservatism but also on a related, yet distinct, topic, the impact of the New Deal on state politics. In this article, drawn from the research for his book *The New Deal and the States: Federalism in Transition,* he finds that in general the New Deal failed to produce sustained reform drives on the state and local levels. Superficially, it is true, there seemed to be a resurgence of reform as numerous states adopted social legislation, spent more on relief for the needy, and undertook new programs for the public welfare. Yet most "little New Deals" were abortive efforts that lasted only a few years before tasting defeat at the hands of conservatives; and most new state spending was financed by regressive consumer taxes that bore most heavily on lower- and middle-income groups.

Professor Patterson discerns many reasons for this limited accomplishment, most of them inherent in the nature of federalism and the encouragement it tends to provide the forces of inertia. The role of the states had been in decline even before the New Deal; in the nineteenth century, the states had been innovators in economic development and social reform, but they were unprepared for the challenges of the 1930's. Part of the problem was the difficulty of raising revenue; the national government having largely preempted the income tax, the states simply did not enjoy Washington's financial flexibility. The mere six-year duration of the New Deal and the uncertain constitutionality of much of its legislation during five of those years also hampered the

From "The New Deal and the States" by James T. Patterson, *American Historical Review,* LXXIII (October 1967), 70–84. Copyright © by The American Historical Association. Reprinted by permission of the American Historical Association.

spread of reform. State courts and state constitutions frequently presented major institutional obstacles. State legislatures tended to be
dominated by rural conservatives, the chief beneficiaries of unfair
apportionment systems. The state Democratic parties, enjoying considerable autonomy from the national organization, were often faction-
ridden and resentful of a lack of consideration from the Roosevelt
administration. FDR and the national party leadership, conversely,
could not hope to muster the resources to control forty-eight different
state organizations. The unsuccessful "purge" of 1938 demonstrated
the hopelessness of such a task.

It would have been unwise, Patterson concludes, for Roosevelt to
have undertaken a greater effort to influence the state parties and
spread the New Deal to the state level in a more comprehensive
fashion. The federal system imposed too many inhibitions. FDR wisely
worked with established Democratic state leaders and machines and
concentrated on the more important priority, that of achieving national legislation. Implicity acknowledging that the center of political gravity in the American system already was in Washington, he assured that
it would remain there for generations to come.

*   *   *

While a rough consensus may be developing concerning the aims and
philosophy of the New Deal, only controversy surrounds the question
of its effect on the states. One group speaks of the "new federalism" of
Franklin D. Roosevelt—a potentially cooperative relationship enriched
by matching grants and mutual advantage. Conservatives, however,
have talked of a Leviathan state. "We are all beginning to look to Uncle
Sam to be Santa Claus," one Democratic governor complained in 1935.
"I think the toughest problem that we as Governors have is to stay away
from it if we can. . . ." And liberals, reflecting a third view, have maintained that the New Deal failed to pull the states out of an entrenched
and miasmatic conservatism. "Since 1930," a critic has remarked, "state
government has dismally failed to meet responsibilities and obligations
in every field. . . . The federal government has not encroached on state
government. State government has defaulted."

Although scholars are only beginning to test these viewpoints, a
wealth of evidence exists with which to attempt a synthesis. Two questions especially need more study. To what extent did state politics and
services change from 1933 to 1945? To what extent were these changes
or lack of changes the result of the New Deal?

In many ways state government appeared to change dramatically in
the 1930's. States seemed willing to spend more for positive purposes,
disbursing some $2 billion in 1927 and between $2.8 billion and $3.4
billion annually from 1932 through 1934. When economic conditions

improved after 1935, the rise in state spending was considerable—to $4.6 billion in 1938 and to $5.2 billion in 1940. State legislators, perhaps, were at last recognizing the need to provide costly services. Much of this increased spending was for relief, a trend that seemed to reflect the diversion of public funds toward "other Americans." Many states developed central welfare agencies by removing both the financial responsibility for and administration of poor relief from the archaic local units that had monopolized the field. State spending for welfare purposes rose from 35 cents per capita in 1922 to 77 cents per capita in 1932 and to $4 per capita in 1942.

Labor also seemed to benefit from state action in the 1930's. In 1933 alone fourteen states passed the child labor amendment, while only six had approved it between 1924 and 1932. Eight more did so from 1934 to 1938. By 1939 nineteen states had adopted laws modeled along lines of the Norris-La Guardia anti-injunction act of 1932, and twenty-five had enacted legislation providing for minimum wages for women and children. And five states passed so-called "Little Wagner Acts" in 1937. Compared to the inaction or hostility of legislatures in the 1920's and 1950's, this flurry of progressive labor law was remarkable.

Federal-state relations also appeared cooperative. Certainly, many federal officials sought to involve the states in New Deal programs. As one observer remarked in 1936, Washington agencies "are better organized, know better what they want, and are more insistent upon getting it than in any previous year. . . . The National Emergency Council employed officials to explain and report on federal efforts in the states and to coordinate the many new federal-state programs. Spurred by this activity, states passed an impressive amount of coordinating legislation. By 1937 forty-two states had facilitated administration of the Federal Housing Act, and thirty-two had acted to implement the lending activities of the Farm Credit Administration. In 1935 alone five hundred state laws cleared the path for Public Works Administration grants to localities. Every state had created state planning agencies by 1937 (only fourteen such agencies had existed in 1933), and all states had assisted the Social Security Act within three years of its passage.

A few states went beyond mere cooperation and enacted "Little New Deals." The 1937 legislative session in Georgia under Governor Eurith D. Rivers was, one observer said, the "bill passin'est session since Oglethorpe climbed out on Yamacraw Bluff." Legislation included welfare reorganization, free school textbooks, state support of public schools for seven months, and larger appropriations for public health. In Pennsylvania Governors Gifford Pinchot and George H. Earle transformed the Keystone State from one of the most reactionary into one of the most progressive. Earle followed national trends so closely that Pennsylvania legislation during his tenure appeared to pass "by ear." Rhode Island and New York under Governors Theodore F.

Green and Herbert H. Lehman were two other eastern states to enact sizable portions of New Deal legislation.

Liberal governors also appeared in other states. In Indiana Governor Paul V. McNutt anticipated much of the New Deal with a remarkable record in the legislative session of January 1933. Culbert L. Olson, governor of California from 1939 to 1943, fought valiantly if unsuccessfully for liberal legislation, as did Governor Frank Murphy of Michigan from 1937 to 1939. And Wisconsin under Philip La Follette and Minnesota under Floyd B. Olson tried to surpass the New Deal. The Wisconsin legislature, after some prodding, produced a "Little NRA," a state planning board, and a surtax on incomes, dividends, and utility companies in 1935; and a "Little TVA," a state reorganization act, and a "Little Wagner Act" in 1937. Despite conservative legislative opposition, Olson succeeded in achieving a progressive income tax, the abolition of yellow-dog contracts, an anti-injunction statute, and a maximum work week of fifty hours for women.

Given the activities of most states in the 1920's, these various developments were heartening to liberals. They suggested a resurgence of state progressivism, dormant for some years. It also seemed that the New Deal was partly responsible for this resurgence, that there was indeed a new federalism, and that henceforth the national government would serve as the model for states to emulate.

There was also a gloomier side. States in the 1930's witnessed conflict as well as cooperation, conservatism as well as progressivism, reaction as well as reform.

State spending was far from revolutionary when considered in long-range terms. While it increased some 90 percent from 1932 to 1942, it had increased some 100 percent from 1922 to 1932 and would increase some 300 percent from 1942 to 1952. Given the depressed conditions and the increased federal spending of the 1930's, the comparatively small increase in state expenditures is not surprising. It is nonetheless important to stress that insofar as spending is a guide, positive state government was not a product of the 1930's but a fluctuating movement since the late nineteenth century.

Trends in state taxation during this period were even more revealing. At a time when some New Dealers were demanding steeper taxes upon the wealthy, many states were seeking revenue through increased levies on consumers. The result was a powerful sales tax movement. The first modern retail sales taxes did not become effective until 1932, yet by 1938 thirty-four states were depending on them. By 1942 general sales taxes accounted for 11 percent of all state revenue from state sources, and gasoline taxes for 18 percent more. Individual and corporate income taxes brought in only 9 percent.

The remarkable aspect of these statistics is not that income taxes produced so little: many states looked hungrily in this direction, only to discover that the federal government had devoured this source of sustenance. Nor should it be surprising that states were seeking new revenue, for the desperate financial condition of local governments in the depression years forced states to finance formerly local functions. And it is not strange that states shied from deficit financing; so did most New Dealers. The total picture is nonetheless striking. While per capita state and local spending increased from $60 in 1927 to $69 in 1940, per capita state and local taxation rose considerably more—from $66 to $89. States and local subdivisions not only balanced their budgets; often they were able to retire past debts. Far from revolutionary in spending policy, states in the 1930's were more regressive than in the past in raising revenue.

States were also penurious in relief spending. New Deal field agents were alternately astounded and embittered by the conservative and sometimes corrupt policy of state officials. New Jersey's relief administration, one agent noted, "is not a question of mal-administration and it is not altogether inefficient administration. I should say it is inept." An Arkansas agent was more blunt. "We have got to bear down on these local units of administration," he wrote the Federal Emergency Relief Administration head, Harry L. Hopkins. "I am convinced there is an enormous amount of crookedness going on in them." Governor Charles Bryan of Nebraska, brother of the Peerless Leader, received the most unflattering portrait of all. "His idea of social work," the FERA man wrote, "is that performed in cleaning up a political situation, with possibly some value in work done by ladies of the WCTU or the Elks in distributing Christmas baskets."

If these agents were unhappy, Miss Lorena Hickok, Hopkins' perceptive roving observer, was dismayed. Denouncing Maine officials, she wrote that "to be a 'deserving case' in Maine, a family has got to measure up to the most rigid Nineteenth Century standards of cleanliness, physical and moral. . . . A woman who isn't a good housekeeper is apt to have a pretty rough time of it. And Heaven help the family in which there is any 'moral problem.'" The situation in Georgia was worse. "Oh, this IS the damnedest state!" she wrote. "I just itch to bring all the unemployed teachers and doctors and nurses and social workers in the North down here and put them to work! Which is, of course, no solution at all." By the time she reached Texas, she was approaching despair. Describing the factionalism that was impairing relief, she cried, "God help the unemployed." "If I were twenty years younger and weighed 75 pounds less," she added, "I think I'd start out to be the Joan of Arc of the Fascist movement in the United States." California was worst of all. "It's California politics, that's all, God damn it, and I think we ought to let Japan have this state. Maybe they could straighten it out."

Most of these complaints were justified. Under the FERA federal money accounted for 71 percent of all public relief spending in 1934 and 1935. Hopkins struggled constantly to persuade states to contribute their shares to the relief fund, but often only the threat of cutting off federal money coerced economy-conscious legislators. Hopkins had to federalize relief administration in six states rather than leave it in the hands of state and local officials, and had he not been anxious to avoid the appearance of federal dictation, he might have federalized many more.

When the national government abandoned the task of aiding unemployables in 1935, the result was often disastrous for the destitute. Twelve states spent less than 50 cents per month for each recipient of direct poor relief in 1939; thirteen more contributed nothing at all, leaving poor relief in the hands of inefficient local officials. The situation in too many states resembled that in Illinois in 1940 where "the administration of general assistance in Illinois, since the exit of the FERA, has been a retreat to the poor law." Although relief administration improved in some states, the picture was far from satisfactory and states continued to lag far behind the federal government in distributing relief.

Labor's gains on the state level were also more apparent than real. Because the Supreme Court did not rule in favor of the Wagner Act and minimum wages until 1937, many states considered it folly to enact complementary statues before that time. The sit-down strikes of 1937 then turned many moderates against organized labor. The conflict between the AFL and CIO was also harmful; in Minnesota the AFL, fearing that a state labor board would favor the CIO, helped defeat a "Little Wagner Act." Other states were reluctant to pass progressive labor laws that might hurt them in the competitive struggle to attract industry. Finally, state legislatures continued to be dominated by the same kinds of people who had ruled in more conservative times: lawyers, farmers, and businessmen. Few of these men encouraged unionism.

For these reasons organized labor made few gains in the states after 1937. As the assistant director of the Division of Labor Standards wrote ruefully in 1939, "the legislatures, in almost every instance, are dominated by farmers and big business. Very little labor legislation will be enacted." The Pennsylvania legislature amended its "Little Wagner Act" on behalf of business interests; Wisconsin legislators repealed theirs. Minimum-wage legislation received unsympathetic hearings, and only two new laws passed in 1939. A federal agent reported that the "outstanding feature" of labor legislation in 1939 was the "tendency in several states to enact measures seriously restricting the rights of labor to organize and to bargain collectively." Right-to-work laws in the early 1940's served to emphasize the accuracy of his remarks.

Federal-state relations were also far from smooth. Officials of the National Recovery Administration worked diligently to persuade states to create "Little NRA's" covering intrastate matters, but with disappointing results. One field agent wrote, "the hope we have is very slim. We find NRA and Codes decidedly unpopular in the rural regions and it is these regions that dominate our legislature. . . ." Another added, "there is a natural antagonism toward federal legislation in general and NRA in particular, existing in the minds of a great many legislators. . . . Too many requests for legislation are coming from the various branches of the Federal Government." By 1935 when the Supreme Court invalidated the NRA, few states had cooperated earnestly.

Many liberals were equally dismayed by the failure of the planning movement, encouraged by some New Dealers to induce states to consider long-range solutions for their problems. As long as states received federal money to finance planning (they obtained some $1.8 million in 1937), they were willing to cooperate superficially. They set up planning boards, conducted studies, and issued reports. But when the money declined, so did the boards. A careful survey in 1938 observed that "the boards have been groping, experimenting, feeling their way. . . . There exists confusion." Boards were "precarious" in one-third of the states and either "nonexistent or relatively inactive" in another one-third. Neither the depression nor the New Deal was able to persuade state legislators to indulge in the frills of long-range planning.

Federal-state conflicts were common in the 1930's. Such friction was partly the result of the emergency situation: the New Deal enacted so many new laws calling for state implementation that some confusion was inevitable. New Dealers, moreover, were too often unable to clarify their intentions for state officials. One competent observer saw little "formal organization for handling the federal-state legislative relationship." New Dealers, he continued, were "unaware of the part that state legislation plays in departmental activity." The National Emergency Council, supposedly the coordinator, was merely a group of people who "assisted the President in gauging political winds."

Hickok, surprised to find that many state officials had never heard of the NEC, was especially disillusioned. The NEC, she wrote, "hasn't even begun to live up to its possibilities. . . . And I think that one trouble is that the coordinating end of it has been 'nobody's baby.' Just a grand idea that nobody ever really did much about." State NEC agents, she advised, should have authority to "'crack down' on the heads of the other government agencies in the state, or to interfere with policies laid down by the heads of those agencies in Washington." Urging more frequent meetings between state and federal officials, she concluded wisely, "There's nothing else in the world quite so effective as personal contact—hours of conversation over a highball—to break down this kind of thing." The New Deal, far from autocratically imposing its programs upon the states, sometimes failed to impose them at all.

The fate of the "Little New Deals" also revealed the transitory nature of state progressivism in the 1930's. In Georgia, Rivers managed to win again in 1938, only to plunge into partisan warfare with conservative legislators. Soon the state had financial troubles, and Rivers' prestige disappeared. Of the three Democratic candidates in the 1940 gubernatorial primary, not one endorsed the New Deal, and former Governor Eugene Talmadge, a staunch foe of liberalism, swept to victory on an economy platform.

Other progressive administrations failed to survive the 1938 elections. Harold Stassen defeated the Farmer-Labor administration in Minnesota; a conservative Republican replaced La Follette in Wisconsin; the Republican victor in Pennsylvania set out to make good his pledge to burn all three thousand pages of liberal legislation signed by Pinchot and Earle; and Murphy was defeated in Michigan, to be replaced after the death of his opponent by an eighty-year-old lieutenant governor who bragged, "I have a pipe-line to God," and whose friends referred modestly to themselves as "just a couple of fellows hanging on the public tit." A few progressive governors remained after 1938, but none succeeded in enacting much of the New Deal, and in many states the liberal programs achieved in the mid-1930's remained on the defensive for the next two decades.

Various factors help explain the difficulties encountered by state progressivism in the 1930's. Perhaps the most obvious was the limited nature of positive state action prior to the depression. Scholars have rightly shown that states contributed materially to nineteenth-century economic development, that they preceded the national government in efforts to regulate corporations, and that they often served as laboratories of social reform. But neither the states nor the federal government prior to the depression had been forced to think seriously of costly welfare legislation, deficit spending, or legislation beneficial to organized labor. Since these were the staples of the new progressivism of the 1930's, it was not strange that state leaders, like many New Dealers, were slow to adopt them.

Lack of funds provided a second problem. Even before the depression, real-estate and personal property taxes—until then the chief sources of state and local revenue—had proved burdensome, and states, faced with the enormously expensive task of road building in the 1920's, had been forced to turn to bond issues. When the depression descended so sharply, it caught many states in an unsound financial position, which they tried to escape first through drastic economies and then through regressive taxation. Chastened by this experience, these states lacked faith in renewed deficit financing, and they therefore shunned costly progressive services.

Another difficulty was a peculiar one of timing. The reform impulse of the 1930's, unlike that of the progressive era, was federal in origin and limited in duration. Pressed for funds in the early years of the depression, states awaited federal action. But since many key New Deal laws affecting states—social security, the Wagner Act, and fair labor standards—were passed in or after 1935, and since the Supreme Court did not sustain them until 1937 or later, many states were reluctant to enact "Little New Deals" before 1937. Then the conservative reaction of 1937–1938 descended, and the main chance was gone. While several states managed to accomplish much in 1935 or 1937, the great majority needed more time.

Institutional factors presented a fourth hurdle. Just as courts thwarted the New Deal, so they interfered with progressive state legislation. State constitutions imposed unrealistic obstacles to financing new services, and state legislatures continued to be dominated by ill-trained, inexperienced, and poorly paid men, chosen according to systems of apportionment that were inequitable in forty-one state senates and thirty-six assemblies. In practically every case, this unfair apportionment favored rural areas; in such key urban states as Connecticut and Ohio this fact helped prevent comprehensive "Little New Deals."

A more serious institutional problem was the incorrigible factionalism of state Democratic parties. This factionalism was sometimes selfish, sometimes the result of new, liberal elements challenging an existing organization, but it almost always blocked cohesive party policy. When Democratic National Chairman James A. Farley asked state politicians to voice their complaints, he received innumerable protests against selfish factions that were damaging the President's program. "The Democratic organization has fallen down," a Montana Democrat wrote. "I never went to a single county that factions did not exist. . . . The party has simply got to be reorganized from the bottom." An Ohio Democrat added in 1938:

> Things are not as good in Ohio as they were two years ago. We have had too much discord among the leaders and the near-leaders in the party. We have been in office quite a while; we are well fed. This makes for unnecessary and unseemly ambition on the part of too many Democrats who are "hell-bent to be first in the kingdom."

Federal field agents concurred. One wrote to Hopkins: "Legislation would be much simpler in Iowa if there was one good political boss. There is no leadership. The legislature is divided into numerous factions . . . and these factions are not split along party lines." Hickok concluded:

In each of these states you have *one or more* of the boys trying to build up
Tammany organizations overnight, with plenty of opposition from other
Democrats, while the Republicans piously hold their noses! And the President, if he isn't actually dragged into it, is left without any organization, or
any spokesman.

Democratic politicians, moving ambitiously to majority status, gathered
like bees about the honey, and all too often the progressives fell to the
ground.

What could New Dealers have done to assure a deeper impact upon
the states? Little. The limited nature of predepression state progressivism was not the fault of the New Deal, nor was the financial chaos of
many states in the early 1930's. Indeed, federal aid to the states, which
increased from $217 million in 1932 to $2 billion in 1935, was indispensable in rehabilitating state finances. Problems presented by state
courts, unfair apportionment, and state constitutions were soluble by
state action alone.

Federal coercion was not the answer. Men such as Farley and Hopkins realized only too well that state officials were easily offended and
that to charge in, as Roosevelt did in the purge of 1938, was to invite
defeat. As Hopkins said of a factional struggle in Delaware, "I am not
disposed to do anything in this administrative jam. I think this is up to
Delaware. I am disposed to let them stew in their own juice." Farley was
equally cautious. California Democrats besieged him with pleas in 1934
to halt the factionalism surrounding Upton Sinclair's "End Poverty in
California" campaign. One correspondent complained: "The Democrats here are all fighting among themselves. . . . Frankly, you are the
only one who could save the situation. These Democratic factions
should unite and concentrate upon one good man, with your approval." Farley passed the letter to Louis McH. Howe, Roosevelt's friend
and political adviser. Howe was no help. "You are running California,"
he cracked. "What will I tell this man?" Farley was at a loss: "I don't
know what to say to you, Louis, except to pass the letter back to you and
write him and say you will call the matter to my attention. It is a terrible
mess but how we are going to be able to do anything, I don't know.

Patronage problems also revealed the dilemma faced by Roosevelt
and his advisers. To many Republicans it seemed that only Democrats
were receiving key administrative positions. As the decade advanced,
charges that relief spending was "Farleyized" were especially loud, cul-
minating in widespread attacks on the WPA in 1938.

In fact the opposite was often true, and Republicans managed to
secure important federal jobs in many states. Early in the New Deal
Farley approved a procedure whereby job seekers had to receive the
endorsement of county chairmen, congressmen, or senators. The

Democratic National Committee would then review the endorsements, filling jobs on the basis of ability and past support of Roosevelt. The system failed. For one thing, there were too many applicants—some 10 for each of the 150,000 jobs. Worse, it was easy to get endorsements from local politicians anxious to please hard-pressed constituents. "Endorsers," one observer commented, "are as undiscriminating as poppy girls at a Legion ball." Distribution of New Deal patronage was far from centralized, and many appointees proved unsympathetic with the programs they were supposed to administer.

As if this situation were not troublesome enough, some New Dealers, notably Hopkins and Interior Secretary Harold L. Ickes, refused to allow Farley to interfere with their staffing procedures. The result was incessant complaining from disgruntled Democrats. "I do not want you to understand that I am desirous of making a political football out of the WPA," an Illinois county chairman wrote, "but I certainly object to the WPA being operated to the disadvantage of the Democratic Party." A Michigan national committeeman added: "I would appreciate greatly anything you can do in Washington to encourage Harry Hopkins to go along with us in a [sic] effort to make this machinery balance up to the point of making it a nonpartisan picture. It is now and has been a 90% Republican picture." Another complainer was Senator Harry S Truman. Missouri, he told Farley, gave Roosevelt a large majority, but "when the patronage was handed out the people who control things in the party in this State were not recognized. . . . It is rather discouraging to say the least." Even Hickok, ordinarily contemptuous of politicians who tried to control relief administration, was concerned over the number of conservative Republican appointees. She complained to Hopkins, "I can't see that leaving it [relief] all in the hands of the gang that handled it under Hoover—and who are about as popular out here as grasshoppers—was exactly smart. It hasn't 'taken' well, I can assure you. Yours for a REAL DICTATORSHIP."

Far from being controlled for the benefit of the Democratic party, relief administration was remarkably nonpartisan in the 1930's and often hostile to the New Deal. But what were Hopkins and Ickes to do? Had they chosen to make relief and public works the province of machine Democrats, relief standards might have been no better, and the critics of "Farleyization" would have been all the more vociferous. Federal restraint was the wisest policy.

The politics of America is state politics. The effect of the New Deal thus depended on the creation and sustenance of forty-eight strong liberal Democratic machines, and this the New Deal failed to do. One critic perceived this failure as early as 1935:

> The Democratic machine of the early thirties is in no remarkable way distinguishable from the political machines, Republican or Democratic,

which have preceded it. It is not, that is to say, a device upon which the
United States Patent Office would look with interest. Aside from certain
improvements in the timing gears . . . it is a dead ringer for earlier and too
familiar models.

And a liberal columnist, commenting of Democratic defeats in 1938,
warned that the election should "persuade Roosevelt that the local
Democratic machines which have flourished under his Administration
are liabilities, and that the work of spreading the gospel is not a proper
mission for gorillas." It is undeniable that Roosevelt, working with
often unprogressive state and local Democratic parties, failed to con-
struct a liberal Democratic apparatus in many states.

But his alternatives were restricted. New Dealers, especially in the
busy first term, did not have much time to devote to political questions
in non-election years. It was simpler to work within the existing
machinery, much of which functioned in city halls rather than state-
houses, than to embark upon the difficult task of liberalizing state
parties. And given the autonomy of state political organizations, it is
doubtful that the strongest pressures would have succeeded. Had
Roosevelt systematically sought to purge Democratic organizations of
uncooperative elements at the height of his popularity in 1936, he
might have made a start. But it is not at all certain that he would have
succeeded, and politicians of all persuasions would have hotly resented
the attempt.

Few historians would maintain that the New Deal left the states un-
changed. States centralized services, applied new taxes, approved progressive labor laws, and increased relief spending. A host of ambitious
federal agencies prodded state departments into new services. Without
the depression and New Deal, the striking developments in state government of the 1940's and 1950's might not have come so quickly. The
over-all picture, however, reveals almost as much continuity as change
on the state level from the progressive period (excepting perhaps the
1920's) to the 1960's, and it suggests that historians would do well to
revise nationalistic interpretations of the New Deal. The New Deal
years witnessed neither federal dictation, a completely cooperative
federalism, nor a dramatically new state progressivism. Moreover,
many of the changes that did occur, notably in relief administration
and taxation, were forced upon the states by the depression and not by
the New Deal.

New Dealers must unquestionably accept some responsibility for this
limited effect on the states. Some federal officials neglected state
affairs; others appointed hostile personnel; still others were unneces-
sarily fearful of offending entrenched machines. The lack of coordination among various federal agencies was at times distressing. But the
most striking feature of federal-state relations during the 1930's was

not the failure of New Dealers but the limits in which they had to operate. Time was short, courts hostile, state institutions blocked change, and state parties were often divided, conservative, or concerned with patronage instead of policy. Roosevelt, by working with instead of against the *status quo* in the states, kept federal-state friction to a minimum and concentrated on achieving the national legislation that proved more important in assuring social change in twentieth-century America.

14

A Comparative Approach: The New Deal, National Socialism, and the Great Depression

JOHN A. GARRATY

The Great Depression was a worldwide phenomenon, yet few American historians have exhibited the industry and talent to move beyond the confines of national history in examining its impact and the efforts of statesmen to deal with it. John A. Garraty, a professor of history at Columbia University, has made what is to date the most impressive attempt. In this audacious and pathbreaking essay, he draws one parallel after another between the ways in which Roosevelt's New Deal and Hitler's National Socialism coped with the depression. For purposes of contrast, he provides brief vignettes of the seemingly ineffectual, but actually equally successful, struggles of British and French leaders.

Garraty carefully delineates the obvious contrast between Hitler's totalitarian fascism and Roosevelt's liberal democracy; it amounted, he reminds us, to a difference in kind, not in degree. Nevertheless, the similarities in technique and in political appeal were great. Both the New Deal and National Socialism resorted to large-scale public employment and relief programs. Both proceeded from inconsistent economic assumptions. Both experimented with "corporatist" state planning and organization. Both sought support from the working classes. Both engaged in similar programs to organize agriculture and protect farmers from price fluctuations; both tended to romanticize rural life. Roosevelt and Hitler themselves derived much of their political strength from an extraordinary personal appeal to their populations. Both men attempted to maximize their charisma through the use of the latest techniques of communication and persuasion. Both addressed

From "The New Deal, National Socialism, and the Great Depression" by John A. Garraty, *American Historical Review*, LXXVIII (October 1973), 907–944. Copyright by John A. Garraty. Reprinted by permission of the author.

the Great Depression as a crisis requiring extraordinary measures, not as a serious problem to be handled in a more routine fashion. Partly in consequence, both emphasized national recovery over international economic cooperation; and both represented themselves as social reformers attempting to overhaul societies in need of drastic change. All the same, neither regime was more successful than less spectacular governments in coping with the depression. Prosperity would come only through military spending and war.

*　*　*

The Great Depression of the 1930's was a unique phenomenon in that it happened simultaneously over almost the entire globe. It was experienced directly, not merely through its repercussions, by the people of nearly every nation and social class. Neither of the so-called world wars of this century was so pervasive, and while many distinct combinations of past events, such as the French Revolution, may be said to have had global results, these usually have been felt only over extended periods of time, long after the "event" itself has ended. The depression therefore presents a remarkable opportunity for historians interested in comparative study and analysis. It provides a kind of independent variable; when we look at how different nations or groups of people responded to the Great Depression, we can be sure, at least in a sense, that we are examining one single "thing," the existence of which was universally recognized at the time. Contemporaries disagreed among themselves about the causes of the depression (to say nothing of their disagreements about how it might be ended), but that there *was* a world-wide depression and that their own depression was related directly to those of their fellows, few denied.

In this article I shall compare the response to the depression in the United States and Germany during the period from 1933 to about 1936 or 1937—that is, during the early years of the regimes of Franklin Roosevelt and Adolf Hitler. The choice is neither capricious nor perverse. I hope to demonstrate that Nazi and New Deal antidepression policies displayed striking similarities. Since the two systems, seen in their totality, were fundamentally different, these similarities tell us a great deal about the depression and the way people reacted to it.

The differences between nazism and the New Deal scarcely need enumeration; within the context of Western industrial society two more antithetical systems would be hard to imagine. The Nazis destroyed democratic institutions. They imprisoned and murdered dissidents, even those, such as the Jews, who simply did not fit their image of a proper German. The New Dealers, whatever their limitations, threw no one in jail for his political beliefs and actually widened the influence of underprivileged elements in the society. Furthermore the historical experience, the traditions, and the social structure of the two nations could hardly have been more unlike. The Great War and its aftermath affected them in almost diametrically opposite ways. All the major economic groups in the two countries—farmers, industrialists, factory workers, and so on—confronted the problems of the depression with sets of expectations and values that differed greatly.

But these were the industrial nations most profoundly affected by the Great Depression, measured by such criteria as the percentage decline of output, or by the degree of unemployment. When Hitler and Roosevelt came to power both nations were in desperate straits; Hitler and Roosevelt followed leaders who had spectacularly failed to inspire public confidence in their policies. Both the severity of the depression and the sense of despair and crisis that existed in Germany and America in early 1933 set the stage for what followed.

I have focused on the early New Deal and Nazi years because at that time the new governments were primarily concerned with economic problems resulting from the depression. Hitler's expansionist ambitions no doubt existed from the beginning, but it was not until after the adoption of the Four Year plan in 1936 that he turned the German economy toward large-scale preparation for war. Similarly, although his motive was clearly defensive, after 1937 Roosevelt also began to be influenced by military considerations.

Needless to say, by considering the similarities in American and German experiences during the depression, I do not mean to suggest that the New Deal was a form of fascism or still less than nazism was anything but an unmitigated disaster. I slight the basic differences between the New Deal and Nazi experiments here partly because they are well known but also because the differences did not affect economic policy as much as might be expected. The worse horrors of nazism were unrelated to Nazi efforts to overcome the depression. Hitler's destruction of German democracy and his ruthless persecution of Jews had little impact on the economy as a whole. Discharging a Jew and giving his job to an "Aryan" did not reduce unemployment. The seizure of Jewish property merely transferred wealth within the country; it did not create new wealth. Moreover, actions undertaken by New Dealers and Nazis for different reasons often produced similar results. My argument concentrates on policies and their effects, not on the motives of the policy makers.

Finally, the fact that countless Germans were deluded by Nazi rhetoric (or that large but lesser numbers were repelled by the system) does not mean that nothing the Nazis did helped anyone but themselves and their sympathizers. Moral abhorrence should no more blind us to the success of some Nazi policies than should admiration of the objectives of the New Deal to its failures. As the English economic historian C. W. Guillebaud warned in *The Social Policy of Nazi Germany*, written in the midst of the Battle of Britain, "Modern Germany is a highly complex phenomenon, with much that is good and bad in it, and nothing is achieved except distortion and absence of reality by any attempt to reduce it to a simple picture of a vast population deluded and oppressed by a small number of brutal gangsters."

Consider first how the two governments dealt with poverty and mass unemployment. Both combined direct relief for the indigent with public-works programs to create jobs. The Americans stressed the former, the Germans the latter, with the result that while acute suffering was greatly reduced in both nations, unemployment declined much more rapidly in Germany. Congress appropriated $3.3 billion for public works in 1933, but Roosevelt, unconvinced that public works would stimulate the economy and fearful of waste and corruption, did not push the program. Briefly, during the winter of 1933–34, he allowed Harry Hopkins to develop his Civil Works Administration, which found jobs for over four million people, but in the spring the program was closed down to save money. Only in 1935 did federal public works become important. Then, under Hopkins's Works Progress Administration and Harold L. Ickes's Public Works Administration, countless roads, schools, bridges, dams, and public buildings were constructed. The Germans, on the other hand, immediately launched an all-out assault on unemployment. Expanding upon policies initiated under Franz von Papen and Kurt von Schleicher, they stimulated private industry through subsidies and tax rebates, encouraged consumer spending by such means as marriage loans, and plunged into the massive public-works program that produced the autobahns, and housing, railroad, and navigation projects. If some New Deal projects seemed to critics wasteful and unnecessary, so did the Nazi penchant for gigantic stadiums and other public buildings, as described in Albert Speer's memoirs. The American boondoggle had its parallel in what the Germans called *Pyramidenbau*, pyramid-building.

It is fashionable, and not of course inaccurate, to note the military aspect of German public-works policies, although in fact relatively little was spent on rearmament before 1935. It is less fashionable, but no less accurate, to point out that the aircraft carriers *Yorktown* and *Enterprise*, four cruisers, many lesser warships, as well as over one hundred army planes and some fifty military airports (including Scott Field in Illinois, the new Air Force headquarters) were built with Public Works Administration money—more than $824 million of it. There was, furthermore, little difference in appearance or intent between the Nazi work camps and those set up in America under the Civilian Conservation Corps. Unlike the public-works programs, these camps did not employ many industrial workers who had lost their jobs, nor were they expected to have much of a stimulating effect on private business. Both employed enrollees at forestry and similar projects to improve the countryside and were essentially designed to keep young men out of the labor market. Roosevelt described work camps as a means for getting youth "off the city street corners," Hitler as a way of keeping them from "rotting helplessly in the streets." In both countries much was made of the beneficial social results of mixing thousands of young people from different walks of life in the camps and of the generally enthusiastic response of youth to the camp experience.

Furthermore, both were organized on semimilitary lines with the subsidiary purposes of improving the physical fitness of potential soldiers and stimulating public commitment to national service in the emergency. Putting the army in control of hundreds of thousands of young civilians roused considerable concern in the United States. This concern proved to be unfounded; indeed, the army undertook the task with great reluctance and performed it with admirable restraint. It is also difficult to imagine how so large a program could have been inaugurated in so short a time in any other way. The CCC program nevertheless served paramilitary and patriotic functions not essential to its announced purpose. Corpsmen were required to stand "in a position of alertness" while speaking to superiors and to address them as "Sir." Camp commanders possessed mild but distinctly military powers to discipline their men, including the right to issue dishonorable discharges. Morning and evening flag-raising ceremonies were held as "a mark," the civilian director of the CCC, Robert Fechner, explained, "of patriotism, of good citizenship and of appreciation by these young men of the thoughtful care being given them by their government." Army authorities soon concluded that six months' CCC service was worth a year's conventional military training, and Secretary of War George Dern claimed that running the camps provided the army with the best practical experience in handling men it had ever had. Summing up the military contribution of the CCC, John A. Salmond, the most sympathetic historian of the agency, wrote:

> To a country engaged in a bloody war, it had provided the sinews of a military force. It had given young officers valuable training in command techniques, and the nearly three million young men who had passed through the camps had received experience of military life upon which the Army was well able to build.

New Deal and Nazi attempts to stimulate industrial recovery also resembled each other in a number of ways. There was at the start much jockeying for position between small producers and large, between manufacturers and merchants, between inflationists and deflationists, between planners, free enterprisers, and advocates of regulated competition. In Germany the great financiers and the leaders of the cartelized industries, most of them bitterly opposed to democratic institutions, demanded an authoritarian solution that would eliminate the influence of organized labor and increase their own control over the economy, whereas small operators, shopkeepers, and craftsmen wanted to reduce the power of bankers and to destroy not only the unions but also the industrial monopolies and chain stores. The former sought to manipulate the Nazis, the latter comprised, in the main, the Nazis' enthusiastic supporters, but Hitler and the party felt and responded to pressures from both camps. In the United States most big business interests had no open quarrel with the existing order, but by 1933 many were calling for suspension of the antitrust laws in order to end the erosion of profits by competitive price cutting. Other interests wanted to strengthen the antitrust laws, still others favored various inflationary schemes, still others some attempt at national economic planning. All clamored for the attention of the new administration.

The ideas of these groups were contradictory, and neither Roosevelt nor Hitler tried very hard to resolve the differences. Roosevelt's method was to suggest that the contestants lock themselves in a room until they could work out a compromise. But Hitler, who freely admitted to being an economic naïf, was no more forceful. "I had to let the Party experiment," he later recalled in discussing the evolution of his industrial recovery program. "I had to give the people something to do. They all wanted to help. . . . Well, let them have a crack at it."

Out of the resulting confusion emerged two varieties of corporatism, a conservative, essentially archaic concept of social and economic organization that was supposed to steer a course between socialism and capitalist plutocracy. Corporatist theory argued that capitalists and workers (organized in industry-wide units) should join together to bring order and profit to each industry by eliminating competition and wasteful squabbling between labor and management. These associations should be supervised by the government in order to protect the public against monopolistic exploitation. In 1933 corporatism was already being experimented with by the Portuguese dictator Antonio de Oliveira Salazar and more tentatively by Benito Mussolini. It also had roots in American and German experience. The American trade association movement of the 1920's reflected basic corporatist ideas (with the important exception that industralists were opposed to government representation in their councils). When the depression undermined the capacity of these "voluntary" associations to force individual companies to honor the associations' decisions, some trade association leaders became willing to accept government policing as a necessary evil. Among others, Gerard Swope of the General Electric Company attracted considerable attention in 1931 with his Swope Plan for a nationwide network of compulsory trade associations supervised by the Federal Trade Commission. President Herbert Hoover, who had been among the most ardent supporters of trade associations, denounced the Swope Plan as both a threat to industrial efficiency and "the most gigantic proposal of monopoly ever made." He considered all such compulsory schemes fascistic. But a number of early New Dealers— Hugh Johnson, Donald Richberg, and Lewis Douglas among others— found corporatism appealing. In Germany the concept of government-sponsored cartels that regulated output and prices had a long tradition, but the existence of powerful trade unions precluded the possibility of a truly corporative organization before 1933. Hitler's success changed that swiftly. Nazi ideologues such as Gottfried Feder combined with big industrialists like Fritz Thyssen and leaders of small business interests like Dr. Heinrich Meusch to push the corporative approach. The works of one of the leading theorists of corporatism, Professor Othmar Spann of the University of Vienna, were widely discussed in Germany in 1933, and the Nazis established a complex system of "estates" governing all branches of industry.

In America the process went not nearly so far, but the system of self-governing industrial codes established under the National Recovery Administration was obviously in the same pattern. Production controls, limitation of entry, and price and wage manipulation were common characteristics of government policy in both countries. So were the two governments' justifications of drastic and possibly illegal or unconstitutional changes in the way the economy functioned on the ground that a "national emergency" existed, and the enormous propaganda campaigns they mounted to win public support.

The drafters of the National Industrial Recovery Act were not deliberately imitating fascist corporatism (although Hugh Johnson, a key figure among them, was an admirer of Mussolini). *Fortune*, which devoted an entire issue in 1934 to an analysis of the Italian system, was scarcely exaggerating when it stated that corporatism was "probably less well known in America than the geography of Tibet." As Gilbert H. Montague, a lawyer who had played a small role in the design of the code system, later wrote, the NRA was only "unconsciously" fascistic. It would be hard to find a better illustration of the common impact of the depression on two industrial nations committed to the preservation of capitalism.

During the early stages big business interests dominated the new organizations and succeeded in imposing their views on government. In Germany the radical Nazi artisan socialists who wanted to smash the cartels and nationalize the banks, led by Gregor Strasser and Gottfried Feder, lost out to the powerful bankers and industrialists, represented by Hjalmar Schacht. In the United States victory went to the large corporations in each industry, which dominated the new code authorities.

But bewildering crosscurrents of interest and faction hampered the functioning of corporatism. In theory the system promised harmony and efficiency within industries, but in practice it seldom provided either. It did not even pretend to solve interindustry conflicts, yet these were often more disturbing to government authorities. Under corporatism workers were supposed to share fairly in decision making and in the rewards resulting from the elimination of conflict and competition; in both countries industrialists resisted allowing them to do so, with the consequence that the governments found themselves being pushed to enforce compliance. In America workingmen were a potent political force and a vital element in the New Deal coalition. German workers did not count as voters after 1933, but their cooperation and support remained essential to Nazi ambitions. Small businessmen also maintained a steady drum-fire of complaint, and both New Dealers and Nazis were sensitive to their pressure. Even the great industrialists were sometimes at odds with the system. Many German tycoons objected to sharing authority with labor and small producers, others to particular decisions imposed on the new estates by the government. German steel and chemical manufacturers like the Krupps and the I. G. Farben interests benefited from Hitler's emphasis on building up war-oriented industry and backed him enthusiastically, but producers dependent upon foreign raw materials or primarily concerned with the manufacture of consumer goods suffered from Nazi trade and monetary policies and held back. And as for the American industrialists, however much they profited under NRA codes, most of them came increasingly to resent the regimentation that codes entailed and to fear the growing interference in their affairs by bureaucrats.

To the Nazis corporatism seemed at first compatible with the political process called *Gleichschaltung,* or coordination, a process by which nearly every aspect of life in their totalitarian state was brought under the control of Hitler and the party. It quickly became apparent, however, that the autonomous character of any corporatist organization made direct control from above difficult. America, fortunately, was never *gleichgeschaltet.* But, in any case, by 1935 and 1936 the Roosevelt and Hitler governments were abandoning corporatism and taking a more anti-big-business stance. In America this meant, aside from the demise of the NRA, more support for industrial labor, stricter regulation of public utilities, higher taxes on the rich and on corporations, rhetorical attacks on "economic royalists," and—by 1938—revived enforcement of the antitrust laws. In Germany, although the traditional cartel structure was retained, it involved limitations on corporate dividends; forced reductions in the interest rates paid on government bonds; government construction and operation of steel, automobile, and certain other facilities in competition with private enterprise; and higher taxes on private incomes and on corporate profits. As in the United States, but to a much greater degree, freedom of managerial decision making was sharply curtailed.

The success or failure of American and German efforts to stimulate industrial recovery is a separate question not central to my argument here. What is central to the argument is this: both were marked by vacillation, confusion, and contradictions, by infighting within the administering bureaucracies, by an absence of any consistently held theory about either the causes of the depression or how to end it. Both also subordinated economic to political goals. The "primacy of politics" in Nazi Germany is a commonplace, its most glaring expression occurring in 1936 when shortages of raw materials and foreign exchange led Hitler to choose between guns and butter. He chose, of course, guns. The problem could be solved by an act of will, he insisted; it was the task of the economy to supply the military needs of the state—so be it! When Schacht, his chief economic adviser, urged a more balanced use of available resources, the Führer fired him. Such ruthless subordination of economic interests to the state did not occur in the United States, although when military considerations began to dominate American policy after 1939 Roosevelt was also prepared to substitute guns for butter. I need only mention his famous announcement that he was replacing "Dr. New Deal" with "Dr. Win the War" as his prime consultant.

But conventional "politics"—the accommodation of political leaders to the pressures of interest groups—affected economic policy in both nations. Beset by business interests seeking aid, by trust busters eager to break up the corporate giants, by planners brimming with schemes to rationalize the economy, the Roosevelt administration survived in a state of constant flux, making concessions to all views, acting in contradictory and at times self-defeating ways. "The New Dealers," writes Ellis W. Hawley, "failed to arrive at any real consensus about the origins and nature of economic concentration." Nor did they follow any consistent policy in the fight against the industrial depression. And Roosevelt's inconsistency, as Hawley also notes, "was the safest method of retaining political power, . . . a political asset rather than a liability." The Nazis, as I have shown, also permitted pressures from various economic interests to influence policy. They did so partly because even a totalitarian dictatorship could profit from the active cooperation of powerful economic groups and partly because the Nazi party had no fixed economic beliefs. Roosevelt responded to pressure groups, Hitler for a time suffered them to exist—a most vital distinction—but the practical result was the same. Put differently, Hitler had a clear political objective—it was actually an obsession—but he was almost as flexible about specific economic policies as Roosevelt. "As regards economic questions," he boasted in 1936, "our theory is very simple. We have no theory at all."

New Deal and Nazi labor policies were also shaped by the Great Depression in related ways. On the surface this statement may appear not simply incorrect but perverse, but only because of our tendency to identify labor with unionization. It is true that Hitler totally destroyed the German unions and that Roosevelt, in part unwittingly and surely with some reluctance, enabled American unions to increase their membership and influence enormously. But New Deal and Nazi policies toward unions had little to do directly with the depression and throw little light on the national policies toward workingmen. Hitler would no doubt have destroyed the Weimar unions as autonomous organizations in any case—he destroyed all autonomous organizations in Germany. But it was because they were anti-Nazi that he smashed the unions so quickly. Roosevelt was at first indifferent to organized labor; he encouraged the American unions in order to gain labor's support, not to speed economic recovery. In each instance the decision was essentially political.

It is not difficult to demonstrate Nazi concern for industrial workers. The "battle against unemployment" had first priority in 1933, and it was won remarkably swiftly; by 1936 something approaching full employment existed in Germany and soon thereafter an acute shortage of labor developed. Of course the military draft siphoned thousands of men out of the German labor market, contributing to the shortage, but this was also true in the United States after 1940. Certainly full employment was never approached in America until the economy was shifted to all-out war production.

Moreover, Nazi ideology (and Hitler's prejudices) inclined the regime to favor the ordinary German over any elite group. Workers—as distinct from "Marxist" members of unions—had an honored place in the system. To the extent that the Nazis imposed restrictions on labor, they did so for the benefit of the state, not of employers. In a sense the Nazi Courts of Social Honor may even be compared with the New Deal National Labor Relations Board. These courts did not alter power relationships between capital and labor as the NLRB did; they represented the interests of the Nazi party rather than those of labor. But they did adjudicate disputes between workers and bosses, and there is considerable evidence that the Courts of Social Honor tended more often than not to favor workingmen in these disputes. Furthermore the very existence of these courts put considerable psychological pressure on employers to treat labor well.

It is beyond argument that the Nazis encouraged working-class social and economic mobility. They made entry into the skilled trades easier by reducing the educational requirements for many jobs and by expanding vocational training. They offered large rewards and further advancement to efficient workers, and, in the Strength Through Joy movement, they provided extensive fringe benefits, such as subsidized housing, low-cost excursions, sports programs, and more pleasant factory facilities. Eventually the Nazi stress on preparation for war meant harder work, a decline in both the quantity and quality of consumer goods, and the loss of freedom of movement for German workers, but the hierarchy imposed these restrictions and hardships belatedly and very reluctantly because of its desire to win and hold the loyalty of labor. If the question is: "Did the Nazi system give workers more power?" the answer of course is that it did not. But that question, albeit important, has little to do with the actual economic position of workingmen or with the effectiveness of the Nazi system in ending the depression.

New Deal and Nazi methods of dealing with the agricultural depression also had much in common. Both sought to organize commercial agriculture in order to increase farm income, under the New Deal Agricultural Adjustment Act through supposedly democratic county committees to control production, in Germany through the centralized Estate for Agriculture. The purpose was to raise agricultural prices and thus farm income through a system of subsidies, paid for in each instance by processing taxes that fell ultimately on consumers. Both governments also made agricultural credit cheaper and more readily available and protected farmers against loss of their land through foreclosures.

These similarities are not remarkable; nearly every nation sought, more or less in these ways, to bolster agricultural prices and protect its farmers. What is interesting, given the profound differences between American and German agriculture, is the attitudes of the two governments toward the place of farmers in the society and toward rural life. Although there was no American counterpart to Hitler's racist, anti-intellectual glorification of the German peasantry, Nazi thinking was at least superficially similar to that of generations of American farm radicals. (David Schoenbaum has aptly called Gottfried Feder "a kind of Central European William Jennings Bryan.") The typical American farmer was no more like a German peasant than the owner of a Southern plantation was like a Junker, but under the impact of the depression farmers large and small in both countries were expressing the same resentments and demands, and these affected Nazi and New Deal policies in related ways. Furthermore, the ideas of Roosevelt and Hitler about farmers were quite alike. Both tended to romanticize rural life and the virtues of an agricultural existence. They hoped to check the trend of population movement to the cities and to disperse urban-centered industries. Roosevelt spoke feelingly of the value of close contact with nature and of the "restful privilege of getting away from pavements and from noise." Only in the country, he believed, did a family have a decent chance "to establish a real home in the traditional American sense." He did not deny the attractions of city life, but he argued that electricity, the automobile, and other modern conveniences made it possible for rural people to enjoy these attractions without abandoning the farm. While governor of New York he set up a program for subsidizing unemployed city families on farms so that "they may secure through the good earth the permanent jobs they have lost in over-crowded cities and towns."

Hitler called the German peasantry "the foundation and life source" of the state, "the counterbalance to communist madness," and "the source of national fertility." The superiority of rural over urban life was a Nazi dogma—especially the life of the self-sufficient small farmer, free from the dependency and corruption of a market economy. "The fact that a people is in a position to nourish itself from its own land and through that to lead its own life independent of foreign nations has always in history been significant," a Nazi agricultural expert wrote in 1935. "Families on the land also have the biological strength to maintain themselves and to compensate for population losses resulting from migration to cities and from war." Nazi leaders referred to Berlin as "Moloch Berlin" and deplored the influx of Germans from the east into the capital. The Nazis' housing policy sought to stimulate suburban development in order to bring industrial workers closer to the land and to reduce urban crowding. They placed all construction under government control, made funds available for low-interest, state-guaranteed mortgage loans, and provided tax relief to builders of small apartments and private homes.

The Tennessee Valley Authority and the rural electrification program made important progress toward improving farm life, but efforts to reverse the population trend yielded very limited results. As president, Roosevelt dreamed of decentralizing industry and of relocating a million families on small farms, but during the whole of the New Deal his Resettlement Administration placed fewer than 11,000 families on the land; even the best-known of the settlements, Arthurdale in West Virginia, which benefited from the particular interest and financial support of Eleanor Roosevelt, never became a viable community until the outbreak of the war. That the Resettlement Administration was run by Rexford Tugwell, who considered the back-to-the-land movement impracticable, contributed to the ineffectiveness of this program, but the agency's greenbelt town program of planned suburban development, which Tugwell did think practicable, also produced miniscule results—only three of the sixty originally planned greenbelt towns were built.

Although Nazi ideologues hoped to reverse Germany's urban-rural ratio, which was 70 percent urban in 1933, their rural resettlement and "rurban" programs proved equally disappointing. Between 1933 and 1938 the Nazis resettled about 20,000 families, but this was scarcely more than half the number the Weimar government had managed to relocate between 1927 and 1932. Nor did the German "rurban" development program ever get very far off the ground. In both the American and German cases efforts to check the movement of population to the cities foundered on the opposition of real-estate and construction interests and still more on the conflicting objectives of government policy makers and their unwillingness to allocate sufficient funds to enable much progress to be made. In 1937 Roosevelt established the Farm Security Administration to coordinate the various New Deal rural rehabilitation programs, but again relatively little was accomplished. Large sums were made available to help tenants buy their own farms, but local agents, concerned for the sake of their own records with making sure that the money was repaid, tended to make loans to tenants who were better off rather than to the most poverty stricken. While many families benefited, the overall impact upon American agriculture was negligible. The sums spent were measured in the millions, whereas, as one critic put it, only if billions had been appropriated could "the drift into tenancy and degradation be stopped and reversed." In Germany the very success of the Nazis in ending unemployment and their post-1936 drive to build their war machine created a shortage of industrial labor that made a meaningful back-to-the-soil movement impossible.

There were significant differences between the objectives of American and National Socialist agricultural policies, the former, for example, seeking to limit output, the latter to increase it. All in all, the New Deal was the more successful in solving farm problems; far less was accomplished in Germany toward modernizing and mechanizing agriculture during the thirties. On the other hand, Nazi efforts in behalf of farm laborers were more effective than those of the New Deal; the AAA programs actually hurt many American agricultural laborers and also tenants and sharecroppers. In both nations agricultural relief brought far more benefits to large landowners than to small.

The complications of German and American monetary and fiscal policies during the depression and of questions relating to foreign trade preclude their detailed discussion here. I shall only mention a few common themes. Both nations increased government control of the banking system but did not nationalize the banks. Both, following the precepts of economic nationalism, sought to improve the competitive position of their export industries, the Americans by devaluing the dollar, the Germans by subsidies, both by sequestering the national gold supplies and prohibiting the export of gold. Both paid most of the costs of their recovery programs by deficit financing. However, both also ignored the newly developing Keynesian economics and remained inordinately fearful of inflation.

Nazi and New Deal policies were not essentially different from those of other industrial nations in these respects. However, they adopted them sooner and pursued them more vigorously than, for example, the

British or the French. Thus when Roosevelt decided against international stabilization of foreign exchange rates and thus "torpedoed" the London Economic Conference, the British and French were bitterly disappointed but the Germans were delighted. Roosevelt's opinion, expressed in his "bombshell" message, that "the sound internal economic situation of a nation is a greater factor in its well-being than the price of its currency," was Nazi orthodoxy. In a radio message beamed to the United States the German foreign minister, Konstantin von Neurath, praised Roosevelt's "fearlessness" and spoke of the "heroic effort of the American people . . . to overcome the crisis and win a new prosperity." Reichsbank president Hjalmar Schacht told a *Völkischer Beobachter* reporter that FDR had adopted the philosophy of Hitler and Mussolini: "Take your economic fate in your own hand and you will help not only yourself but the whole world."

In the early months of the New Deal Roosevelt toyed with the idea of stimulating exports by means of subsidized dumping and by barter agreements, trade tactics that the Nazis adopted wholeheartedly. A mighty behind-the-scenes battle was fought within the administration in 1933 and 1934 between supporters of this approach and those who believed in lowering tariff barriers by making reciprocal trade agreements based on the unconditional most-favored-nation principle. Rexford Tugwell, Raymond Moley, and George W. Peek argued the former psoition; the secretary of state, Cordell Hull, and the secretary of agriculture, Henry Wallace, the latter; and the president—after one of his typical attempts to get the protagonists to reconcile the irreconcilable—finally sided with Hull and Wallace. Roosevelt nevertheless continued for some time to flirt with the idea of bilateral agreements, especially one suggested by Schacht involving 800,000 bales of American cotton. The rejection of this and similar proposals resulted more from Roosevelt's growing political and moral distaste for Hitlerism than from economic considerations. But despite Roosevelt's antifascism and the internationalist, free-trade rhetoric of the reciprocal trade program, it seems clear that New Deal foreign policy was as concerned with advancing national economic interests as was German policy. State Department alarm at Nazi "penetration" of Latin America, publicly expressed in strategic and moral terms, had a solid base in lost and threatened markets for American exports.*

There remains the question of leadership, that is, of the personal roles of Roosevelt and Hitler in their nations' campaigns against the

---

*The reciprocal trade program, despite the high hopes of its supporters, had little effect upon American trade or the world economy. Furthermore the argument of Secretary Hull and others that the "non-discriminatory" reciprocal trade policy was particularly high-minded and that bilateralism and barter agreements were per se destructive of the interests of underdeveloped nations makes little sense.

Great Depression. To overemphasize Roosevelt and Hitler as individuals would be to approach the problem simplistically, but certain parallels merit examination. It cannot be proved that neither would have achieved national leadership without the depression, but the depression surely contributed to the success of each. Yet on the surface they seem most improbable leaders of the two countries at that particular time. In an economic crisis of unprecedented severity, neither had a well-thought-out plan. Both lacked deep knowledge of or even much interest in economics.*

It is no less than paradoxical that the American electorate, provincial in outlook, admiring of self-made men and physical prowess, and scornful of "aristocrats," should, at a time when millions were existing on the edge of starvation, choose for president a man who lived on inherited wealth, who came from the top of the upper crust, who had been educated in the swankest private schools, who had a broad cosmopolitan outlook, and (to descend to a lesser but not politically unimportant level) who was a cripple. But no more a paradox than a country whose citizens were supposed to have an exaggerated respect for hard work, for education and high culture and family lineage, and who had a reputation for orderliness and social discipline should follow the lead of a high-school dropout, a lazy ne'er-do-well, a low-born Austrian who could not even speak good German, the head of a rowdy movement openly committed to disorder and violence. Equally strange, Roosevelt and Hitler appealed most strongly to their social and economic opposites: Roosevelt to industrial workers, to farmers, to the unemployed and the rejected; Hitler to hard-working shopkeepers and peasants, and, eventually, to industrialists, great landowners, and the military.

It may of course be true that these seeming contradictions are of no significance. Probably any Democrat would have defeated Hoover in 1932, and although Hitler became chancellor in a technically legal way, his subsequent seizure of total power was accomplished without the consent, if not necessarily without the approval, of a majority of the German people. Yet the personal impact of Roosevelt and Hitler on the two societies in the depths of the Great Depression was very large. Their policies aside, both exerted enormous psychological influence upon the citizenry. Roosevelt's patrician concern for mass suffering, his

---

*Even Fusfeld, who argues that Roosevelt "had a well-developed economic philosophy," admits that it was not derived from the writings of economists or other thinkers. Roosevelt's own opinion is perhaps revealed in a remark he made to Marriner Eccles after listening to a debate between Eccles and a conservative senator: "You made the problem so simple that even I was able to understand it." John D. Heyl argues that "Hitler's economic ideas are worth considering," but in essence claims little more than that "Hitler acquired a certain familiarity with economic issues." And he quotes Hitler as saying in 1934: "Don't allow yourself to be deceived by cut-and-dried [economic] theories. Certainly I know less today about these matters than I thought I knew a few years ago."

charm, his calm confidence, his gaiety, even his cavalier approach to
the grave problems of the day had, according to countless witnesses, an
immediate and lasting effect upon the American people. Hitler's resentment of the rich and well born, however psychotic in origin,
appealed powerfully to millions of Germans. His ruthless, terrifying
determination, always teetering on the edge of hysteria, combined with
the aura of encapsulated remoteness that he projected to paralyze those
who opposed him, to reduce most of his close associates to sycophancy,
and to inspire awe among masses of ordinary Germans. Both the
euphoria of the Hundred Days and the nationalistic fervor that swept
Germany in the early months of 1933 made millions almost incapable
of thought, let alone of judgment. Bills swept through Congress ill
drafted and scarcely debated, basic rights were abolished in Germany
without even an attempt at resistance, and both were possible largely
because of the personalities of the two leaders.

Much of this was probably spontaneous, but not all. Roosevelt and
Hitler employed the latest technologies to dramatize themselves and to
influence public opinion. Roosevelt's flight to Chicago to accept the
Democratic nomination and Hitler's whirlwind tours testify to their
swift grasp of the psychological as well as the practical value of air
travel to politicians. And no greater masters of the radio ever lived—
Roosevelt with his low-keyed, fatherly, intimate fireside chats, Hitler
with his shrill harangues beneath the massed swastikas at Nuremberg.
Both were terrible administrators in the formal sense but virtuosos at
handling subordinates. Their governments were marked by confusion,
overlapping jurisdictions, and factional conflicts, yet somehow they
transformed these inadequacies into political assets—symbols not of
weakness or inefficiency but of energy and zeal in a time of grave
emergency.*

---

*Judgments of Roosevelt's and Hitler's abilities as administrators are of course highly
subjective. Furthermore the internal workings of any government seem confused when
examined in detail. It is clear nevertheless that both Roosevelt and Hitler were exceptionally prone to set up confused lines of responsibility among their subordinates and to tolerate
and at times encourage interdepartmental and intradepartmental rivalries. Waste and
ineffectiveness frequently resulted. Thus, Burns writes: "Again and again Roosevelt
flouted the central rule of administration that the boss must co-ordinate the men and
agencies under him. . . . [He] put into the same office or job men who differed with each
other in temperament and viewpoint." Bracher concludes that "friction, waste, duplication" were deliberate Hitlerian techniques, whereas Fischer argues that when Hitler
"made at least two and most often many more boards, agencies, and men responsible for
each assignment" he was merely revealing the senselessness and lack of guiding principles
of his system, but they (and other scholars) agree as to the facts. Burns considers Roosevelt
"an artist in government," master of the technique of divide and rule, whose "first concern
was power," the subjection of the bureaucracy to executive control. Bracher writes that
Hitler displayed "matchless virtuosity" in making others dependent upon him. "The
Leader was the sole figure standing above the confusion of jurisdictions and command
chains."

Both also made brilliant use of the crisis psychology of 1933, emphasizing the suffering of the times rather than attempting to disguise or minimize it. "The misery of our people is horrible," Hitler said in his first radio address after becoming chancellor. "To the hungry unemployed millions of industrial workers is added the impoverishment of the whole middle class and the artisans. If this decay also finally finishes off the German farmers we will face a catastrophe of incalculable size." Roosevelt's personal style was more reassuring than alarmist, but he also stressed the seriousness of the situation and the urgent need for decisive action: "Action, and action now," as he put it in his inaugural.

Both the Roosevelt and Hitler governments tried to influence public opinion in new and forceful ways. Roosevelt did not create a propaganda machine even remotely comparable to Goebbels's, but under the New Deal the government undertook efforts unprecedented in peacetime to sell its policies to the public. The NRA slogan "We Do Our Part" served the same function as the Nazis' incessantly repeated *Gemeinnutz geht vor Eigennutz*. With Roosevelt's approval, General Hugh Johnson, head of the NRA and designer of its Blue Eagle symbol, organized a massive campaign to rally support for the NRA. "Those who are not with us are against us," Johnson orated, "and the way to show that you are a part of this great army of the New Deal is to insist on this symbol of solidarity." Johnson denounced "chiselers" and "slackers"; his office plastered the land with billboard displays; distributed posters, lapel buttons, and stickers; dispatched volunteer speakers across the country; and published *Helpful Hints* and *Pointed Paragraphs* to provide them with The Word. Roosevelt himself, in a fireside chat, compared the Blue Eagle to a "bright badge" worn by soldiers in night attacks to help separate friend from foe. Placed beside the awesome Nazi displays at Nuremberg, even the 10-hour, 250,000-person NRA parade up Fifth Avenue in September 1933 may seem insignificant, but it and other NRA parades and hoopla were designed to serve the same functions: rousing patriotic feelings and creating in the public mind the impression of so extensive a support for government policies as to make disagreement appear close to treason. As Johnson himself explained, the purpose was to "put the enforcement of this law into the hands of the *whole* people."

Another example of New Deal propaganda is provided by the efforts of the Resettlement Administration and the Farm Security Administration under Rexford Tugwell. Because Pare Lorenz's government-sponsored films, *The Plow That Broke the Plains* (1936) and *The River* (1938), and the still photographs of Dorothea Lange, Walker Evans, Margaret Bourke-White, Gordon Parks, and others were esthetic achievements of the highest order, we tend to forget that they were a form of official advertising designed to explain and defend the New Deal approach to rural social and economic problems. They differed from Leni Riefenstahl's *Triumph of the Will* (also a cinematic master-piece) and the annual volumes of photographs celebrating National Socialism chiefly in style—"soft" rather than "hard" sell—and point of view.

The New Deal efforts at mass persuasion were unparalleled among democracies in peacetime—nothing comparable was attempted in France or Great Britain before the outbreak of war in 1939.* They reflect the attitude of the Roosevelt government, shared by Hitler's, that the economic emergency demanded a common effort above and beyond politics. The crisis justified the casting aside of precedent, the nationalistic mobilization of society, and the removal of traditional re-straints on the power of the state, as in war, and it required personal leadership more forceful than that necessary in normal times. That all these attitudes were typical of Hitler goes without saying, but Roosevelt held them too. Consider this passage in his first inaugural:

> I assume unhesitatingly the leadership of this great army of our people. . . . Our true destiny is not to be administered unto but to minister to ourselves. . . . In the event that Congress shall fail . . . I shall ask the Congress for the one remaining instrument to meet the crisis—broad ex-ecutive power to wage a war against the emergency, as great as the power that would be given to me if we were in fact invaded by a foreign foe.†

Roosevelt was neither a totalitarian nor a dictator, real or potential, but his tactics and his rhetoric made it possible for anti-New Dealers and outright fascists to argue that he was both. Many of the accusations of conservatives and Communists in the United States were politically motivated, as were, of course, Nazi comments on the president. But during the first years of the New Deal the German press praised him and the New Deal to the skies. Before Hitler came to power he was, although impressed by Henry Ford's automobiles and the racially oriented American immigration laws, basically contemptuous of the United States, which he considered an overly materialistic nation dominated by Jews, "millionaires, beauty queens, stupid [phonograph]

---

*As early as 1908 the Department of Agriculture was producing short educational and instructional movies, and the Department of the Interior and other government agencies also made such films in considerable numbers beginning in 1911. These were not, however, designed for general distribution, as both *The Plow* and *The River* clearly were. During the 1920s and early 1930s the British Empire Marketing Board and later the British Post Office produced films advertising their activities, but not for commercial distribution.

†This last sentence evoked the loudest cheering Roosevelt's speech produced. Eleanor Roosevelt found the response "a little terrifying." Commenting on it later, she said: "You felt they would do *anything*—if only someone would tell them *what* to do." Leuchtenburg writes: "Roosevelt personified the state as protector."

records, and Hollywood." Nevertheless, he and his party were impressed by New Deal depression policies. "Mr. Roosevelt . . . marches straight to his objectives over Congress, lobbies, and the bureaucracy," Hitler told Anne O'Hare McCormick of the New York *Times* in July 1933. In July 1934 the *Völkischer Beobachter* described Roosevelt as "absolute lord and master" of the nation, his position "not entirely dissimilar" to a dictator's. Roosevelt's books, *Looking Forward* (1933) and *On Our Way* (1934) were translated into German and enthusiastically reviewed, the critics being quick to draw attention to parallels in New Deal and National Socialist experiences.*

A friendly German biography, *Roosevelt: A Revolutionary with Common Sense*, by Helmut Magers, appeared in 1934. Magers described the New Deal as "an authoritarian revolution," a revolution "from above," and pointed up what he called the "surprising similarities" it bore to the Nazi revolution. That there appeared to be some basis for this view at the time is suggested by the fact that Ambassador William E. Dodd wrote a foreword to Magers's book in which he praised the author's "outstanding success" in describing both conditions in the United States and the nation's "unique [*einzigartig*] leader" and spoke of the "heroic efforts being made in Germany and the United States to solve the basic problem of social balance."

Dodd was vehemently anti-Nazi, but he hoped that German moderates like Schacht and Neurath would be able to overthrow Hitler or at least restrain him. He considered the Magers volume an "excellent, friendly, unpartisan book . . . without a sentence that could have been quoted to our disadvantage" and allowed his foreword to be published despite State Department objections. The Germans, for their part, went out of their way to welcome Dodd. A throng of reporters and Foreign Office officials greeted him when he arrived in Berlin. He was put up in the six-room royal suite of the Hotel Esplanade and charged only ten dollars a day. He was invited to lecture at the University of Munich. Hitler assured him that Germany had no warlike intentions. When he criticized authoritarian rule and economic nationalism in a speech, the German press reported his remarks fairly and accurately.

At the end of Roosevelt's first year in office Hitler sent him a message through diplomatic channels offering sincere congratulations for "his heroic efforts in the interests of the American people. The President's successful battle against economic distress is being followed by the entire German people with interest and admiration," Hitler

---

*Mussolini wrote a widely publicized review of *Looking Forward* in which he noted a number of similarities between Roosevelt's thinking on economic policy and his own. He concluded, however, that while Roosevelt's ideas were superficially related to "fascist Corporatism . . . it would be an exaggeration to say anything more."

announced. In November 1934 the *Völkischer Beobachter* characterized Democratic gains in the Congressional elections as an "exceptionally personal success" for Roosevelt. The tone of this article was almost worshipful, the rhetoric hyperbolic. The president (a man of "irreproachable, extremely responsible character and immovable will" [*tadelsfreie verantwortungsvolle Gesinnung und . . . unverrückbarer Wille*]) had shown himself to be a "warmhearted leader of the people with a profound understanding of social needs" as well as an energetic politician. This attitude ended in 1936, although even after Roosevelt's "quarantine" speech the Nazi propaganda machine refrained for tactical reasons from attacking him personally. It is clear, however, that early New Deal depression policies seemed to the Nazis essentially like their own and the role of Roosevelt not very different from the Führer's.*

The importance of these leaders in the fight against the depression lies less in what they did to revive the economy than in the shift in public mood they triggered. In early 1933 that mood was profoundly pessimistic. For four years business conditions had been growing almost steaily worse. The promises and optimistic predictions of innumerable political and business leaders that the tide would turn had all proved illusory. Millions had lost not merely their jobs and savings, but hope itself. It was the duration more than the depth of the decline that was truly depressing.

The Great Depression was totally unlike any earlier economic slump. Men had noted as early as the eighteenth century that economic activity tended to rise and fall in recurrent patterns, and during the nineteenth century the concept of the business cycle was firmly established. Cycles were variously explained, and the terminology was not precise, but it was accepted that the world economy moved in an irregular but unending path through periods of expansion, crisis or panic, recession or depression, and then returned to expansion. Before the collapse of the 1930's a cycle was usually identified by its most dramatic phase, the crisis or panic: witness the American "panics" of 1819, 1837, 1857, 1873, 1893, and 1907. The business slump that followed panics was characteristically precipitous but mercifully brief. In his classic study of *Business Cycles* (1913), Wesley Clair Mitchell wrote: "The lowest ebb of the physical volume of industrial production usually comes in either

---

*In May 1940 *Das Reich* published an article comparing Nazi and New Deal policies to combat the depression: "Hitler and Roosevelt: A German Success—An American Attempt." The anonymous author blamed what he called the weaknesses of the New Deal not on Roosevelt but on the "sacrosanct Constitution" of the United States and on the "parliamentary-democratic system" that forced Roosevelt to cater to conflicting interests. "We began with an idea and carried out the practical measures without regard for consequences. America began with many practical measures that without inner coherence covered over each wound with a special bandage."

the first or the second year after a severe crisis."* The German and French words *die Krise* and *la crise* reflect this same focus on the panic aspect of the "normal" business cycle. However, the recession that came after the "panic of 1929" did not follow the expected pattern. Interminably, or so it seemed, it continued. By the end of 1932 industrial production in both the United States and Germany was scarcely more than half of what it had been in 1929.

By the early 1930's professional economists were beginning to realize that the character of business cycles was changing. The first edition of the *Encyclopedia of the Social Sciences*, published between 1930 and 1935, contains an article on *crises* by Jean Lescure, a French expert on business cycles. "A crisis," Lescure wrote, "may be defined as a grave and sudden disturbance of economic equilibrium." Lescure went on to discuss the nature and history of crises, paying special attention to the impact of industrialization and of the growth of cartels and trusts, which he believed had reduced the acuteness of crises but also delayed the process of recovery. "It would seem," he concluded, "that for the term crisis one may henceforth substitute that of depression; it is reasonable to speak today of a world depression rather than of a world crisis."

Lescure's emphasis on the word "depression" highlights the psychological impact of the long economic decline, the pessimism, the sense of hopelessness that had little to do with the size of an individual's pocketbook. A constricting pall appeared to have descended upon the world. Among economists, stagnation theorists flourished and learned authorities spoke of a "mature" economy and the end of the era of economic growth spawned by the Industrial Revolution. Many recommended what the French called a "Malthusian" approach, the reduction of output to the current level of consumption rather than the attempt to increase consumption. Governments, faced with the most extended fall in prices since the 1890's, responded not with inflationary measures but by adopting deflationary monetary policies and by slashing already shrunken budgets.† Businessmen feared to make new

---

*The general acceptance of this theory helps to explain President Hoover's often-derided optimistic prognostications in 1930 and 1931. Businessmen, according to Joseph Schumpeter, were "by no means overpessimistic" even in late 1930. The collapse of the American banking system in early 1933, Schumpeter claimed, finally destroyed hope. "The psychic framework of society, which till then had borne up well, was at last giving way."

†"The deflationary spiral was, in most countries, accentuated by orthodox Government financial policy as then conceived. The automatic effect of a depression was to reduce tax revenue and increase expenditure for the relief of the unemployed, and hence to produce a budgetary deficit. Orthodox finance demanded that the budget should be balanced annually, by rigid economies in expenditure and the imposition of additional taxes." H. W. Arndt, *The Economic Lessons of the Nineteen-Thirties* (Oxford, 1944), 254.

investments. Trade languished. Unions dealt with mounting unemployment by urging that youths be kept longer in school, that working women return to the home, that older men retire early. The mood of unemployed workers, some 20 million in the United States and Germany alone by early 1933, was more apathetic than rebellious. It was this general pall of despair and listlessness that the New Deal and the Nazi revolution, personified by Roosevelt and Hitler, dispelled. Long before their economic policies had much effect on the stalled business cycle, they had revitalized the two societies.

Comparison with Great Britain and France is suggestive. Economic historians disagree about the character of Britain's economic recovery in the 1930's, but the argument concerns the growth *rate* and its causes, not the fact of expansion. By 1937 industrial output was over 30 percent larger than in 1933, and unemployment had been almost halved. Even allowing for the facts that the British economy had been sluggish in the 1920's, unemployment extremely high, and, therefore, that the world depression seemed a less dramatic collapse in Britain than it did in the United States or Germany, the improvement between 1933 and 1937 marked a very substantial change.

Furthermore, during these years the British government made many efforts to improve conditions. To aid industry it adopted tactics strikingly similar to those of the NRA. It allowed coal operators to limit and allocate output, fix prices, and amalgamate companies; it encouraged cotton textile manufacturers to scrap inefficient machinery, and the steel industry to cartelize its operations. Both the ailing shipbuilding industry and the healthy automobile industry received government subsidies. Electric utility companies were assisted in consolidating their activities by the Central Electricity Board. The remarkable British housing boom, it is true, was largely the work of private enterprise, but government construction was significant—and focused where it was most needed, on slum clearance and homes for the poor. Agriculture was also assisted through a complex mixture of import quotas, tariffs, subsidies, and marketing schemes.

The government also acted to help British labor. Unemployment insurance and relief services were well established long before 1933, but beginning with the Unemployment Act of 1934 the system was considerably improved. Insurance was put on a sounder financial basis, and an Unemployment Assistance Board was set up to administer the relief program. In 1936 half a million agricultural wage earners were brought into the insurance system. Other laws sought to encourage the movement of labor from the economically stagnant north and west to the more prosperous southeast, and manufacturers willing to build factories in the depressed areas received subsidies. Economic recovery was thus accompanied by considerable social reform; by 1937 the combination of a progressive tax structure and extended social services was transferring 5 or 6 percent of the national income from rich to poor, raising the real income of the working classes by some 8 to 14 percent. In the United States, by way of contrast, New Deal legislation had almost no measurable effect on income distribution.

Yet the people of Great Britain had no sense of experiencing a new era. It seems clear (although such things are difficult to measure) that the national mood remained depressed, despite economic progress. No political leader was able to generate a sense of common commitment to the battle against the depression. When David Lloyd George announced a plan for a "New Deal for Britain" in 1935—it was little more than a rehash of proposals he had made repeatedly in the 1920's—Ramsay MacDonald's cabinet was thrown almost into a panic and gave serious consideration to inviting both Lloyd George and Winston Churchill to join the government, but it did not do so. Chancellor of the Exchequer Neville Chamberlain wrote in his diary at this time: "The P.M. [MacDonald] is ill and tired, S[tanley] B[aldwin] is tired and won't apply his mind to problems." (Contrast this state of mind with the mood in government circles in Washington and Berlin.) "It is certainly time there was a change," Chamberlain also wrote, having himself in mind as the person to institute it. But after Chamberlain became prime minister in 1937, the national mood was no different. Chamberlain was a conservative of the finest type, hard working and public spirited; no one in Great Britain contributed more to social reform in the interwar years. But he was by this time also aging and ailing—unable to inspire public enthusiasm. As he said of himself, he could not "unbutton."

Thus the 1930's passed into memory in Great Britain as a time of inactivity and decline—the Great Slump. "The man in the street's view of Britain's experience . . . is that activity was stagnant and very depressed," the economic historian Harry W. Richardson writes—this even though "any glance at the evidence shows it to be a misconception." Surely this helps to explain why fascism became a more formidable force in Britain than in the United States, despite economic recovery and the far more serious and immediate threat that the Nazis posed to the British.

The French experience provides another opportunity to study this aspect of the depression. Its full force struck France late, but by 1935 conditions were very bad. Farm prices had collapsed. Industrial output was down sharply. French workers were probably worse off than those of any other industrial nation: wage rates as low as eighty centimes an hour (the franc was worth about five cents) were not unknown; employers were autocratic, superfically well organized, and adamantly opposed to collective bargaining; unemployment was increasing rapidly and was far greater than French statistics indicated. Over 503,000 persons were receiving relief payments in February 1935, an increase of more than 150,000 in one year, and many of the unemployed were unable to meet all the eight "general conditions" required to qualify for aid. Furthermore, in counting the unemployed the French government made no allowance for those who had given up looking for work, for individuals who had lost their jobs and returned to family farms, or for unemployed foreigners who had no work permits. The Ministry of Labor, which compiled the unemployment statistics, itself confessed that the number of *employed* Frenchmen had declined by 1,880,000 since 1930, and this estimate was probably too low.

Moreover, French governments, aside from the fact that no party or coalition was capable of staying in power for more than a few months, were not merely ineffective but complacent in dealing with the problems of the depression. In 1935, when organized business sought a law (*le projet Marchandeau*) much like the NRA codes enforcing restrictive trade agreements, the bill was defeated. The official position of the Ministry of Labor on unemployment, repeatedly enunciated in its annual reports, ran as follows: "The state cannot pretend to be able to eliminate or diminish unemployment since its activities do not get at the causes of the evil." The minister's report of June 22, 1936, praised local relief officers for their "very important" services in "not allowing unemployed workers to get aid unless they met all the requirements." Thus "public funds have been safeguarded."

Then quite suddenly in the spring of 1936 the electoral victory of the Popular Front unleashed a spontaneous, grass-roots outburst of protest, signalized by a wave of sit-down strikes that brought the economy to a standstill. Thoroughly alarmed, the leaders of industry swiftly capitulated, throwing themselves on the mercy of the new Socialist premier, Léon Blum. Within a matter of days a new system of labor-management relations, buttressed by a host of laws similar to those of the New Deal, was hammered out by representatives of big business and the unions and pushed through parliament by the Blum government: state-supervised collective bargaining, large wage increases, a forty-hour week, and paid vacations, along with banking reform and a program to support agricultural prices were all instituted in one hectic burst of activity.

This transformation was, of course, shortlived; by 1939 France was more divided and lacking in any sense of commitment to common national purposes than in 1935. To what extent a lack of leadership and particularly Léon Blum's personal inadequacies caused this reversal is a very difficult question. Blum's performance can be criticized from two perspectives. First of all, should he, as a lifelong socialist, have attempted to use the crisis to change France more radically? In a brilliant article, "*Tout est possible*," the left-wing socialist Marceau Pivert urged him to try. "The masses are much more advanced than we imagine," Pivert insisted. They are ready not merely for "an insipid cup

of medicinal tea," but for "drastic surgery," including the nationaliza-
tion of banks, utility companies, and "trusts," and the confiscation of
the wealth of "deserters of the franc." Blum rejected these proposals,
being backed by most of the Socialists and also by the Communists, the
union leaders, and the Radicals who made up his coalition. He did so
on the reasonable, indeed honorable ground that the Popular Front
parties, having campaigned on a platform of moderate reform within
the capitalist system, had no mandate for revolutionary change. "Our
duty," he later said, "was . . . to show ourselves scrupulously faithful to
the program." He felt that he must "keep loyally, publicly, the promise
that I had made." But it can be argued that the upheavals of 1936 *were*
revolutionary, even that (as Pierre Mendès France said many years
later) the election of 1936 was not a plebiscite for any particular reform
but "an affirmation of a popular desire to see the country break out of
its deflationary rut and conservative structures." Socialist critics, re-
reading some of Blum's modest and diffident comments about the
responsibilities of his high office, have been impressed by a "crushing
masochism" in his character, a defeatist attitude, an exaggerated concern for punctilio. Blum was too much the "grand bourgeois," Pivert
recollected, "too subtle, too refined to be a revolutionary leader."
Georges Lefranc, both a participant in and one of the leading historians of the events of 1936, put the question this way: perhaps everything was not possible, "but can one say that everything that was possible was tried?"

One can reject this line of argument, but it remains true that Blum
failed not merely to build upon the reforms of 1936 but even to protect
them adequately against counterattack. He of course faced staggering
difficulties: the antediluvian mentality of French industrialists, the doctrinaire rigidity of union leaders, the slavish commitment of the Communists to the policies of the Soviet Union, the tragic divisions resulting
from the Spanish Civil War, the noisy rightist "patriotic" groups, the
perverse individualism of nearly every Frenchman. Probably no political leader could have overcome the shortsighted selfishness and inertia
or resisted the splintering factionalism that plagued French society in
the late thirties.

Yet Blum's efforts were pitifully inadequate, no better or worse than
those of the uninspired premiers who preceded and followed him.
Long years of balancing his socialist principles against his political
ambitions and responsibilities had made him, in Joel Colton's words, a
"tightrope-walker." Before the formation of the Popular Front he had,
when forced to make a choice, always put his socialism above political
accommodation. After he finally made the other choice in 1936, he
became too much the politician, telling workers, despite the still-
lagging French economy, that it was time for a "pause," that they must
exercise "moderation and patience." It was not of central importance

that, as the historian Alfred Sauvy has said, Blum's ignorance of economics was matched only by his sincerity. He could muster neither the flexibility of Roosevelt (whom he greatly admired) nor the ruthlessness of Hitler (whom he dested).

During Blum's brief second term as premier, he revised his economic thinking. Aided by Georges Boris, author of an admiring study of the New Deal, *La Révolution Roosevelt* (1934), and one of the few Frenchmen familiar with the new Keynesian economics, Blum drafted a comprehensive program involving tax relief and government credits for defense industries, tax relief for the construction industry and small business, suspension of redemptions of the national debt, a special capital levy on the rich, a more progressive income tax, and rudimentary exchange controls. A massive common effort was necessary, he said, in order to build up French defenses, expand production, and maintain "social solidarity." The Assembly supported Blum's plan, but when the Senate voted it down he meekly resigned without even demanding the vote of confidence that might have compelled the Senate to yield. "To make the project succeed," Sauvy writes, "would have required a resounding appeal to all the forces of a country threatened with collapse. Unfortunately, Blum was not capable of such an effort."

What he lacked was not courage but firmness, and the daring to step beyond the comfortable security of conventional political procedures. After the fall of his second government he confessed: "Perhaps, if I committed errors it was because of not having been enough of a leader." None of this proves that a Blum like Roosevelt or—God forbid— Hitler could have provided France with the kind of *élan* that developed in the United States and Germany. It does, however, point up the psychological importance of Roosevelt and Hitler in their own countries.

These parallels suggest a number of generalizations about how the Great Depression influenced the United States and Germany. They do not, as I said at the start, indicate that the New Deal was a variant of fascism. The extraordinary expansion of the role of the federal government that took place in America cannot be equated with the Nazi totalitarian system, nor Hitler's despotism with the new executive power that Roosevelt exercised. The differences are qualitative not merely quantitative. But both governments experienced the depression as a tremendous crisis, and this fact shaped their responses in related ways. Furthermore the two regimes suffered from common intellectual, emotional, and organizational limitations that also led to analogous reactions to the depression.

Before Hitler and Roosevelt achieved power, more rigid and conservative leaders had tended to see the depression as a world-wide disease that would yield to international rather than national cures and indeed as one that governmental medicines could not alone eradicate. Hoover, despite his belief that European selfishness and shortsightedness had caused the depression, proposed his moratorium of 1931 "to give the forthcoming year to the economic recovery of the world," and Heinrich Brüning defended what he himself called his "draconian" emergency decrees as necessary to enable Germany "to meet its international obligations" and "conquer the economic crisis." Brüning, like Hoover, also believed that governmental policies of any kind could influence the economy relatively little. After the disastrous German elections of 1930, which made the Nazis a formidable political force, Brüning informed Hitler complacently: "According to our estimation, the crisis will last about four or five years more." And in a message on New Year's Day, 1931, he told the nation: "I am anxious to stress the limitations of any policy so that you will not indulge in any illusions."

Nazis and New Dealers adopted more parochial but also more intense tactics, placing the economic well-being of their own societies ahead of world recovery and taking a far more optimistic view of what government could accomplish. While assuming the continuance of capitalism and in many ways adding to the wealth of private business groups, each nation sharply restricted the individual's freedom to pursue his economic interests and construed the power of government, and of executive power within the political system, in very broad terms. In addition, New Dealers and Nazis insisted that economic recovery could not be achieved without a certain amount of social restructuring and, furthermore, that society could be changed without exacerbating class conflicts. Indeed in both cases social reform was supposed to moderate such conflicts. But in both Roosevelt's America and Hitler's Germany economic and social objectives were subordinated whenver necessary to political aims.

That other nations adopted many of the tactics employed by New Dealers and Nazis scarcely needs demonstration. Depression policies everywhere were certainly based on national self-interest narrowly conceived, despite the obvious fact that the same plague was ravaging all. The tendency of governments to extend their sway in economic affairs and of leaders to be heavily influenced by political considerations was virtually universal. Whether conservative, moderate, or radical, few if any of the statesmen of the thirties remained indifferent to the suffering of their constituents or unwilling to sanction changes designed to alleviate it. The difference between the American and German depression experiences and those of other nations was in large measure psychological, resulting from Roosevelt's and Hitler's personal qualities of leadership and from their responses to the particular conditions in the two countries.

Again the comparison with Hoover and Brüning is at least suggestive: both lacked political tact and the ability to project an impression of warmth, sympathy, and self-assurance. In 1931 Walter Lippmann described Hoover as "indecisive and hesitant in dealing with political issues," and Arthur Krock commented on his "awkwardness of manner and speech and lack of mass magnetism." A recent student of the Hoover administration, Albert U. Romasco, remarks on his "inability to master the political techniques of leadership." As for Brüning, the historian Theodor Eschenburg, who knew him personally and considered him a "statesman of the highest intellectual gifts," admits that he had neither "the psychological talent" to win public backing nor "the tactical ability" to manage politicians. "He thought in terms of policy, not of human beings." And Andreas Dorpalen, another historian who lived through the Brüning period as a student in Germany, describes him as a "shy, withdrawn man [who] was unable to arouse the nation," a person lacking in warmth and imagination. Dorpalen's statement that the German public "mistook the chancellor's sober factualness for cynical coldness" could as well be applied to Hoover.

So far as the depression is concerned, Roosevelt and Hitler, the one essentially benign, the other malevolent, justified far-reaching constitutional changes as being necessary to the improvement of economic conditions in a grave emergency but used change also as a device for mobilizing the psychic energies of the people. Yet both their administrations were plagued by infighting and confusion, partly because of genuine conflicts of interest and philosophy within the two diverse societies, but partly because of ignorance. No one really knew how to end the depression or even how best to serve the different interests the governments presumed to represent. Time after time major American and German policies produced results neither anticipated nor desired, some of them—the effect of New Deal farm policy on share croppers and of its public housing policy on racial segregation, and that of Nazi rearmament on urban concentration, for example—directly contrary to the leaders' intentions.

Hitler papered over confusion, doubts, and rivalries with the *Führerprinzip*, unquestioning obedience to the leader, who was presumed to know what was best. Roosevelt, on the other hand, made a virtue of flexibility and experimentation. Both, however, masterfully disguised the inadequacies and internal disagreements in their entourages and to a remarkable extent succeeded in convincing ordinary citizens of their own personal wisdom and dedication.

The differences in the degree and intensity with which psychological pressures were applied by Nazis and New Dealers were so great as to become differences in kind—leaving aside the brute Nazi suppression not merely of those who resisted or disagreed, but of all who did not fit the insane Hitlerian conception of the proper order of things. The two movements nevertheless reacted to the Great Depression in similar ways, distinct from those of other industrial nations. Of the two the

Nazis were the more successful in curing the economic ills of the 1930's. They reduced unemployment and stimulated industrial production faster than the Americans did and, considering their resources, handled their monetary and trade problems more successfully, certainly more imaginatively. This was partly because the Nazis employed deficit financing on a larger scale and partly because their totalitarian system better lent itself to the mobilization of society, both by force and by persuasion. By 1936 the depression was substantially over in Germany, far from finished in the United States. However, neither regime solved the problem of maintaining prosperity without war. The German leaders wanted war and used the economy to make war possible. One result was "prosperity": full employment, increased output, hectic economic expansion. The Americans lacked this motivation, but when war was forced upon them they took the same approach and achieved the same result.

Selected
Bibliography

The most important and monumental study of the New Deal is Arthur M. Schlesinger, Jr., *The Age of Roosevelt* (Boston: Houghton Mifflin, 1957–1960); three volumes have been completed: *The Crisis of the Old Order* (1957), *The Coming of the New Deal* (1959), and *The Politics of Upheaval* (1960). The best one-volume survey is William E. Leuchtenburg, *Franklin D. Roosevelt and the New Deal* (New York: Harper & Row, 1963). George Wolfskill, *Happy Days Are Here Again!* (Hinsdale, Ill.: Dryden, 1974), is a brief, perceptive interpretation. Basil Rauch, *The History of the New Deal* (New York: Creative Age Press, 1944), was an important pioneering effort. Paul K. Conkin, *The New Deal* (2nd ed.; Arlington Heights, Ill.: AHM Publishing, 1975), is an influential critique from the Left, as is Barton J. Bernstein's essay in Bernstein, ed., *Towards a New Past* (New York: Pantheon, 1968). John Braeman *et al.*, eds., *The New Deal: The National Level* (Columbus: Ohio State University Press, 1975), is a collection of original essays by important New Deal historians. On the depression itself, see Dixon Wechter, *The Age of the Great Depression* (New York: Macmillan, 1948); Broadus Mitchell, *Depression Decade* (New York: Rinehart, 1947); and Lester V. Chandler, *America's Greatest Depression, 1929–1941* (New York: Harper & Row, 1970).

The best collection of documentary material is Howard Zinn, ed., *New Deal Thought* (Indianapolis: Bobbs-Merrill, 1966), useful also for the editor's provocative New Left introduction. See also Frank Freidel, ed., *The New Deal and the American People* (Englewood Cliffs, N.J.: Prentice-Hall, 1964), and William E. Leuchtenburg, ed., *The New Deal: A Documentary History* (Columbia: University of South Carolina Press, 1968). Among the most important published primary sources are Samuel I. Rosenman, ed., *The Public Papers and Addresses of Franklin D. Roosevelt* (13 vols.; New York: Random House, 1938–1950); Elliott Roosevelt, *F.D.R.: His Personal Letters* (4 vols.; New York: Duell, Sloan and Pearce, 1947–1950); Max Freedman, ed., *Roosevelt and Frankfurter: Their Correspondence, 1928–1945* (Boston: Little, Brown, 1967); John M. Blum, ed., *From the Morgenthau Diaries* (3 vols.; Boston: Houghton Mifflin, 1959–1967); Harold Ickes, *The Secret Diary of Harold L. Ickes* (3 vols.; New York: Simon & Schuster, 1953–1954); and Edgar B. Nixon, ed., *Franklin D. Roosevelt and Conservation, 1911–1945* (Washington, D.C.: U.S. Government Printing Office, 1957).

Frank Freidel has published four volumes of his *Franklin D. Roosevelt* (Boston: Little, Brown, 1952–1973): *The Apprenticeship* (1952), *The Ordeal* (1954), *The Triumph* (1956), and *Launching the New Deal* (1973). The first three volumes are a nearly definitive account of Roosevelt's pre-presidential career; the last an extensive survey of the first year of his Presidency. See also Freidel, *F.D.R. and the South* (Baton Rouge: Louisiana State University Press, 1965). Kenneth S. Davis, *FDR: The Beckoning of Destiny, 1882–1928* (New York: Putnam, 1972), is a first-rate popular biography. Joseph P. Lash, *Eleanor and Franklin* (New York: Norton, 1971), sensitively examines a fascinating relationship. James MacGregor Burns, *Roosevelt: The Lion and the Fox* (New York: Harcourt Brace Jovanovich, 1956), remains the most important and persuasive critique of its subject. Edgar Eugene Robinson, *The Roosevelt Leadership* (Philadelphia: Lippincott, 1955), goes after FDR from the opposite direction. Other significant studies are Bernard Bellush, *Franklin D. Roosevelt as Governor of New York* (New York: Columbia University Press, 1952); Daniel R. Fusfeld, *The Economic Thought of Franklin D. Roosevelt and the Origins of the New Deal* (New York: Columbia University Press, 1956); and Alfred Rollins, Jr., *Roosevelt and Howe* (New York: Knopf, 1962).

No old New Dealer has written more extensively about FDR and the experience of the 1930's than has Rexford G. Tugwell; perhaps the most significant of his several books are *The Democratic Roosevelt* (Garden City, N.Y.: Harper & Row, 1957); *The Brains Trust* (New York: Viking, 1968); and *In Search of Roosevelt* (Cambridge, Mass.: Harvard University Press, 1972). Other important memoirs are Raymond Moley, *The First New Deal* (New York: Harcourt Brace Jovanovich, 1967); Frances Perkins, *The Roosevelt I Knew* (New York: Viking, 1946); Samuel I. Rosenman, *Working for Roosevelt* (New York: Harper & Row, 1952); and Marriner Eccles, *Beckoning Frontiers* (New York: Knopf, 1951).

On New Deal politics, see especially John M. Allswang, *The New Deal and American Politics: A Study in Political Change* (New York: Wiley, 1978), and James T. Patterson, *Congressional Conservatism and the New Deal* (Lexington: University Press of Kentucky, 1967). Samuel Lubell, *The Future of American Politics* (3rd ed.; New York: Harper & Row, 1965), remains a seminal work, although its primary concern is the fate of the New Deal coalition after FDR's death. Elliot A. Rosen, *Hoover,*

Roosevelt, and the Brains Trust (New York: Columbia University Press, 1977), is a valuable study of the New Deal's political origins. Bernard Donahoe, *Private Plans and Public Dangers: The Story of FDR's Third Nomination* (Notre Dame, Ind.: University of Notre Dame Press, 1965); Herbert Parmet and Marie Hecht, *Never Again: A President Runs for a Third Term* (New York: Macmillan, 1968); and Warren Moscow, *Roosevelt and Willkie* (Englewood Cliffs, N.J.: Prentice-Hall, 1968) all examine the 1940 campaign and election. Congressional politics during the New Deal's final years are covered in two books by David L. Porter: *Congress and the Waning of the New Deal* (Port Washington, N.Y.: Kennikat 1979), and *The Seventy-sixth Congress and World War II, 1939–1940* (Columbia: University of Missouri Press, 1979). Prominent congressmen are portrayed in J. Joseph Huthmacher, *Senator Robert F. Wagner and the Rise of Urban Liberalism* (New York: Atheneum, 1968); Richard Lowitt, *George W. Norris: The Triumph of a Progressive* (Urbana: University of Illinois Press, 1978); and Martha H. Swain, *Pat Harrison: The New Deal Years* (Jackson: University of Mississippi Press, 1978).

Harvard Sitkoff, *A New Deal for Blacks* (New York: Oxford University Press, 1978), and John B. Kirby, *Black Americans in the Roosevelt Era: Liberalism and Race* (Knoxville: University of Tennessee Press, 1980), are two major surveys of a very important topic. Donald L. Parman, *The Navajos and the New Deal* (New Haven: Yale University Press, 1975), covers a less visible minority group. For the political and intellectual reactions of the nation's largest religious minority, see two books by George Q. Flynn: *American Catholics and the Roosevelt Presidency, 1932–1936* (Lexington: University Press of Kentucky, 1967), and *Roosevelt and Romanism: Catholics and American Diplomacy, 1937–1945* (Westport, Conn.: Greenwood Press, 1976); consult also David J. O'Brien's important *American Catholics and Social Reform: The New Deal Years* (New York: Oxford University Press, 1968).

Any student of the New Deal's impact at the state and local levels must begin with James T. Patterson, *The New Deal and the States: Federalism in Transition* (Princeton: Princeton University Press, 1969); Bernard Sternsher, ed., *Hitting Home: The Great Depression in Town and Country* (New York: Quadrangle, 1970); John Braeman et al., *The New Deal: The State and Local Levels* (Columbus: Ohio State University Press, 1975); and Lyle W. Dorsett, *Franklin D. Roosevelt and the City Bosses* (Port Washington, N.Y.: Kennikat, 1977). Studies of specific leaders and movements include Robert E. Burke, *Olson's New Deal for California* (Berkeley: University of California Press, 1953); George H. Mayer, *The Political Career of Floyd B. Olson* (Minneapolis: University of Minnesota Press, 1951); Robert P. Ingalls, *Herbert H. Lehman and New York's Little New Deal* (New York: New York University Press, 1975); Elmer L. Puryear, *Democratic Party Dissention in North Carolina, 1928–1936* (Chapel Hill: University of North Carolina Press, 1962); Francis W.

Schruben, *Kansas in Turmoil, 1930–1936* (Columbia: University of Missouri Press, 1969); Michael P. Malone, *C. Ben Ross and the New Deal in Idaho* (Seattle: University of Washington Press, 1970); Michael S. Holmes, *The New Deal in Georgia: An Administrative History* (Westport, Conn.: Greenwood, 1974); Richard D. Lunt, *The High Ministry of Government: The Political Career of Frank Murphy* (Detroit: Wayne State University Press, 1965); Sidney Fine, *Frank Murphy: The Detroit Years* (Ann Arbor: University of Michigan Press, 1975), and *Frank Murphy: The New Deal Years* (Chicago: University of Chicago Press, 1979); Patrick J. Maney, *"Young Bob" La Follette* (Columbia: University of Missouri Press, 1978); Bruce M. Stave, *The New Deal and the Last Hurrah: Pittsburgh Machine Politics* (Pittsburgh: University of Pittsburgh Press, 1977); Charles H. Trout, *Boston, the Great Depression, and the New Deal* (New York: Oxford University Press, 1977); Ronald H. Bayor, *Neighbors in Conflict: The Irish, Germans, Jews, and Italians of New York City, 1929–1941* (Baltimore: Johns Hopkins University Press, 1978).

Various types of political opposition to the New Deal receive coverage in Donald McCoy, *Landon of Kansas* (Lincoln: University of Nebraska Press, 1967); James T. Patterson, *Mr. Republican: A Biography of Robert A. Taft* (Boston: Houghton Mifflin, 1972); George Wolfskill, *The Revolt of the Conservatives: A History of the American Liberty League, 1934–1940* (Boston: Houghton Mifflin, 1962), and *All But the People: Franklin D. Roosevelt and His Critics, 1933–1939* (New York: Macmillan, 1969); David H. Bennett, *Demagogues in the Depression* (New Brunswick: Rutgers University Press, 1969); T. Harry Williams, *Huey Long* (New York: Knopf, 1969); Charles J. Tull, *Father Coughlin and the New Deal* (Syracuse: Syracuse University Press, 1965); Sheldon Marcus, *Father Coughlin* (Boston: Little, Brown, 1973); Abraham Holtzman, *The Townsend Movement* (New York: Bookman Associates, 1963); Edward Blackorby, *Prairie Rabel: The Public Life of William Lemke* (Lincoln: University of Nebraska Press, 1963); and Ellsworth Barnard, *Wendell Willkie: . . . Fighter for Freedom* (Marquette: Northern Michigan University Press, 1966).

The political and intellectual history of the Left in the 1930's has attracted many historians, most of whom treat it as a central organizing principle for the cultural history of the decade. See, e.g., Arthur A. Ekirch, Jr., *Ideologies and Utopias* (Chicago: Quadrangle, 1971), and Richard H. Pells, *Radical Visions and American Dreams* (New York: Harper & Row, 1977), the more successful of the two volumes. Charles C. Alexander, *Nationalism in American Thought, 1930–1945* (Chicago: Rand McNally, 1969), is built around a broader integrating theme. William Stott, *Documentary Expression in Thirties America* (New York: Oxford University Press, 1973), is important. James B. Gilbert, *Writers and Partisans* (New York: Wiley, 1968); surveys the literary scene around the *Partisan Review*; Daniel Aaron, *Writers on the Left: Episodes in American Literary*

Communism (New York: Harcourt Brace Jovanovich, 1961), remains a standard account. Frank A. Warren has written two important volumes: *Liberals and Communism: The "Red Decade" Revisited* (Bloomington: Indiana University Press, 1966), and *An Alternative Vision: The Socialist Party in the 1930s* (Bloomington: Indiana University Press, 1976). Donald McCoy, *Angry Voices: Left-of-Center Politics in the New Deal Era* (Lawrence: University of Kansas Press, 1958), is still useful. More recent approaches to the same topic include R. Alan Lawson, *The Failure of Independent Liberalism, 1930–1941* (New York: Putnam, 1971), an award-winning study; and Donald L. Miller, *The New American Radicalism: Alfred M. Bingham and Non-Marxian Insurgency in the New Deal Era* (Port Washington, N.Y.: Kennikat, 1979).

Bernard Sternsher, *Rexford Tugwell and the New Deal* (New Brunswick, N.J.: Rutgers University Press, 1964), discusses an increasingly disenchanted New Dealer. Theodore Rosenof, *Dogma, Depression, and the New Deal: The Debate of Political Leaders Over Economic Recovery* (Port Washington, N.Y.: Kennikat, 1975), is a useful survey. Otis L. Graham, Jr., *Toward a Planned Society: From Roosevelt to Nixon* (New York: Oxford University Press, 1976), begins with a long chapter on "Franklin D. Roosevelt and the Planning Idea."

Graham's *Encore for Reform: The Old Progressives and the New Deal* (New York: Oxford University Press, 1967), remains the most ambitious treatment of its subject. Graham's work builds upon two suggestive essays by one of his teachers, Richard Hofstadter, in Hofstadter, *The Age of Reform* (New York: Knopf, 1955), and to a lesser degree upon Carl Degler's interpretation of the New Deal in Degler, *Out of Our Past* (New York: Harper & Row, 1959). Richard S. Kirkendall's essay, "The Great Depression: Another Watershed in American History?" in John Braeman *et al., Change and Continuity in Twentieth-Century America* (Columbus: Ohio State University Press, 1964), takes issue with Hofstadter and Degler. The debate remains unresolved and, one senses, of declining interest to historians; the question is so protean that there has been little agreement on the terms of the argument, and the sides frequently have talked past each other rather than directly to each other's points.

New Deal agricultural policy has attracted an extraordinary amount of attention, yet no scholar has produced a comprehensive treatment. Edward L. and Frederick H. Schapsmeier, *Henry A. Wallace of Iowa: The Agrarian Years, 1910–1940* (Ames: Iowa State University Press, 1968), surveys the career of Roosevelt's first Secretary of Agriculture, and Dean Albertson, *Roosevelt's Farmer: Claude R. Wickard in the New Deal* (New York: Columbia University Press, 1961), covers his successor. Perhaps the two closest approaches to an overall account are Christiana MacFadyen Campbell, *The Farm Bureau and the New Deal* (Urbana: University of Illinois Press, 1962), and Richard S. Kirkendall, *Social Scien-*

tists and Farm Politics in the Age of Roosevelt (Columbia: University of Missouri Press, 1966). Van L. Perkins, *Crisis in Agriculture: The Agricultural Adjustment Administration and the New Deal, 1933* (Berkeley: University of California Press, 1969), thoroughly examines its topic. For other aspects of the agricultural scene in the 1930's, see John L. Shover, *Cornbelt Rebellion: The Farmers' Holiday Association* (Urbana: University of Illinois Press, 1965); David E. Conrad, *The Forgotten Farmers: The Story of Sharecroppers in the New Deal* (Urbana: University of Illinois Press, 1965); Donald H. Grubbs, *Cry From the Cotton: The Southern Tenant Farmers Union and the New Deal* (Chapel Hill: University of North Carolina Press, 1971); Sidney Baldwin, *Poverty and Politics: The Rise and Decline of the Farm Security Administration* (Chapel Hill: University of North Carolina Press, 1967); Paul K. Conkin, *Tomorrow a New World: The New Deal Community Program* (Ithaca: Cornell University Press, 1959); and Donald Holley, *Uncle Sam's Farmers: The New Deal Communities in the Lower Mississippi Valley* (Urbana: University of Illinois Press, 1975).

The major work on labor and the New Deal is Irving Bernstein, *Turbulent Years* (Boston: Houghton Mifflin, 1969), a monumental study that will long stand as the nearly definitive word on the subject; Bernstein, *The New Deal Collective Bargaining Policy* (Berkeley: University of California Press, 1950), traces the development of the Wagner Act. George Martin, *Madame Secretary: Francis Perkins* (Boston: Houghton Mifflin, 1976), covers the career of the Secretary of Labor; Melvyn Dubofsky and Warren Van Tine, *John L. Lewis* (New York: Quadrangle, 1977), is the latest and best biography of the period's most dynamic union leader. See also Jerold S. Auerbach, *Labor and Liberty: The La Follette Committee and the New Deal* (Indianapolis: Bobbs-Merrill, 1966); Milton Derber and Edwin Young, eds., *Labor and the New Deal* (Madison: University of Wisconsin Press, 1957); Walter Galenson, *The CIO Challenge to the AFL* (Cambridge, Mass.: Harvard University Press, 1960); and James O. Morris, *Conflict within the AFL* (Ithaca: Cornell University Press, 1958). Sidney Fine, *Sit-Down: The General Motors Strike of 1936–1937* (Ann Arbor: University of Michigan Press, 1969), covers an important episode.

Ellis W. Hawley, *The New Deal and the Problem of Monopoly* (Princeton: Princeton University Press, 1966), remains the most important study of New Deal policy toward business; see also Wallace E. Davies and William Goetzmann, eds., *The New Deal and Business Recovery* (New York: Holt, Rinehart, 1960). On the NRA, consult Robert F. Himmelburg, *The Origins of the National Recovery Administration* (New York: Fordham University Press, 1976); Bernard Bellush, *The Failure of the NRA* (New York: Norton, 1975); and Sidney Fine, *The Automobile under the Blue Eagle* (Ann Arbor: University of Michigan Press, 1963). Specific problems receive attention in Susan E. Kennedy, *The Banking Crisis of 1933* (Lexington: University Press of Kentucky, 1973); Helen M. Burns, *The American Banking Community and the New Deal Banking Reforms, 1933– 1938* (Westport, Conn.: Greenwood, 1974); Ralph F. De Bedts, *The New Deal's SEC: The Formative Years* (New York: Columbia University Press, 1964); Michael E. Parrish, *Securities Regulation and the New Deal* (New Haven: Yale University Press, 1970); and Charles O. Jackson, *Food and Drug Legislation in the New Deal* (Princeton: Princeton University Press, 1970).

New Deal relief and social welfare programs are studied in Searle F. Charles, *Minister of Relief: Harry Hopkins and the Depression* (Syracuse: Syracuse University Press, 1963); Paul Kurzman, *Harry Hopkins and the New Deal* (New York: Burdick, 1974); John A. Salmond, *The Civilian Conservation Corps* (Durham: Duke University Press, 1967); Paul E. Mertz, *New Deal Policy and Southern Rural Poverty* (Baton Rouge: Louisiana State University Press, 1978); Roy Lubove, *The Struggle for Social Security, 1900–1935* (Cambridge, Mass.: Harvard University Press, 1968); Arthur E. Altmeyer, *The Formative Years of Social Security* (Madison: University of Wisconsin Press, 1966); Edwin E. Witte, *Development of the Social Security Act* (Madison: University of Wisconsin Press, 1962); Timothy McDonnell, *The Wagner Housing Act* (Chicago: Loyola University Press, 1957); and Joseph L. Arnold, *The New Deal in the Suburbs: A History of the Greenbelt Town Program, 1935–1954* (Columbus: Ohio State University Press, 1971). The New Deal's concern for creative intellectuals is treated in Jane De Hart Matthews, *The Federal Theater, 1935–1939* (Princeton: Princeton University Press, 1967); Jerre Mangione, *The Dream and the Deal: The Federal Writers' Project, 1935–1943* (Boston: Little, Brown, 1972); Richard D. McKinzie, *The New Deal for Artists* (Princeton: Princeton University Press, 1973); and Monte N. Penkower, *The Federal Writers' Project* (Urbana: University of Illinois Press, 1977).

Other important topics are covered in Philip J. Funigiello, *Toward a National Power Policy: The New Deal and the Electric Utility Industry* (Pittsburgh: University of Pittsburgh Press, 1973); Thomas K. McCraw, *Morgan vs. Lilienthal: The Feud within the TVA* (Chicago: Loyola University Press, 1970), and *TVA and the Power Fight* (Philadelphia: Lippincott, 1971); Wilmon Droze, *High Dams and Slack Waters: TVA Rebuilds a River* (Baton Rouge: Louisiana State University Press, 1965); Barry Dean Karl, *Executive Reorganization and Reform in the New Deal* (Cambridge, Mass.: Harvard University Press, 1963); and Richard Polenberg, *Reorganizing Roosevelt's Government* (Cambridge, Mass.: Harvard University Press, 1966). There is no adequate scholarly volume on the Court-packing controversy, but William E. Leuchtenburg has produced several articles on the topic, including "Franklin D. Roosevelt's

Supreme Court 'Packing' Plan," in Harold Hollingsworth and William Holmes, eds., *Essays on the New Deal* (Austin: University of Texas Press, 1969). Two other very important articles are Leuchtenburg, "The New Deal and the Analogue of War," in John Braeman *et al.*, *Change and Continuity in Twentieth-Century America*, cited above, and Richard S. Kirkendall, "Franklin D. Roosevelt and the Service Intellectual," *Mississippi Valley Historical Review*, XLIX (December 1962), 456–471.

The impact of World War II on the New Deal has received increasing attention. Within the past several years, four significant studies of the war's imprint upon American society have appeared: Richard Lingeman, *Don't You Know There's a War On?* (New York: Putnam, 1971); Richard Polenberg, *War and Society* (Philadelphia: Lippincott, 1972); Geoffrey Perrett, *Days of Sadness, Years of Triumph* (New York: Coward, McCann, 1973); and John M. Blum, *V Was for Victory* (New York: Harcourt Brace Jovanovich, 1977). James MacGregor Burns, *Roosevelt: The Soldier of Freedom* (New York: Harcourt Brace Jovanovich, 1970), devotes the bulk of its attention to foreign policy. Henry A. Wallace, the leading spokesman of the New Deal tradition, is the subject of Edward L. and Frederick H. Schapsmeier, *Prophet in Politics* (Ames: Iowa State University Press, 1970); Norman D. Markowitz, *The Rise and Fall of the People's Century* (New York: Free Press, 1973); and John M. Blum, ed., *The Price of Vision: The Diary of Henry A. Wallace, 1942–1946* (Boston: Houghton Mifflin, 1973). Alonzo L. Hamby examines the ways in which the New Deal tradition was affected by the war in "Sixty Million Jobs and the People's Revolution: The Liberals, the New Deal, and World War II," *The Historian*, XXX (August 1968), 578–598. Several authors have written on aspects of wartime black history. See especially Neil A. Wynn, *The Afro-American and the Second World War* (New York: Holmes & Meier, 1976); Richard M. Dalfiume, *Desegregation of the U.S. Armed Forces* (Columbia: University of Missouri Press, 1969); and Louis Ruchames, *Race, Jobs, and Politics* (New York: Columbia University Press, 1953). Roland Young, *Congressional Politics in the Second World War* (New York: Columbia University Press, 1956), is less than satisfactory. Newer and more useful accounts of political topics are Philip J. Funigiello, *The Challenge to Urban Liberalism: Federal-City Relations during World War II* (Knoxville: University of Tennessee Press, 1978); John W. Jefferies, *Testing the Roosevelt Coalition: Connecticut Society and Politics in the Era of World War II* (Knoxville: University of Tennessee Press, 1979); and James C. Foster, *The Union Politic: The CIO Political Action Committee* (Columbia: University of Missouri Press, 1975).

An extremely useful guide to much of the hard-to-find academic literature is William J. Stewart, compiler, *The Era of Franklin D. Roosevelt: A Selected Bibliography of Periodical, Essay, and Dissertation Liter-*

ature, 1945–1971 (Hyde Park: Franklin D. Roosevelt Library, 1974). Richard S. Kirkendall, "The New Deal as Watershed: The Recent Literature," *Journal of American History,* LIV (March 1968), 839–852, evaluates the contributions of the mid-1960's in detail.